bra

The Idea and Practice of
World Government

The Idea and Practice of
World Government

GERARD J. MANGONE

New York · Columbia University Press · 1951

This book is dedicated

not to those who cry for peace,
but to those men and women everywhere
who will not let the light of reason go out
nor the fruits of democracy spoil.

Preface

AFTER FOUR YEARS in the Army and two years of demobilization at Harvard, I was confronted with the same questions which every new generation must try to answer: What are "peace" and "justice" and the "good life"? How is political organization to be used to solve contemporary problems? This book is an effort to think through the idea of a world government and its application to our lives today.

A seminar on Immanuel Kant by Carl J. Friedrich at Harvard set my mind off in this direction, but I am chiefly indebted to Rupert Emerson and Payson S. Wild for their guidance, counsel, and encouragement upon such a precarious theme. It should be added that I alone am responsible for all the errors.

My colleagues at Wesleyan University, E. E. Schattschneider, Sigmund Neumann, Victor Jones, Stephen K. Bailey, and Donald G. Herzberg, have all shared vicariously in the production of this book. Their friendship has been an inestimable source of pleasure during the weary days of writing. I am most grateful to the Wesleyan Research Committee for its financial assistance in publication.

My wife, Kathleen, deserves all the credit for the completion of the manuscript. With patience she did the chores and smiled while I poked clumsily through the far-distant clouds.

GERARD J. MANGONE

Middletown, Connecticut
February, 1951

Acknowledgments

I WISH to thank the following publishers for permission to quote passages from books for which they hold the copyright. Appleton-Century-Crofts for Wallas, *Human Nature in Politics*, and Sanson, *Japan, a Short Cultural History*. Jethro-Bithell for a translation of verse from Sir Walter von der Vogelweide. A. & C. Black, Ltd., for Ogg, *Europe in the Seventeenth Century*. Cambridge University Press for *Cambridge Modern History, Vol. XII*, and Russell, *Philosophy and Politics*. The Clarendon Press for Oppenheim, *The Future of International Law*. Thomas Y. Crowell for Wissler, *Man and Culture*, and Robinson, *History of Greece*. Doubleday Doran for Whitman, *Leaves of Grass*. E. P. Dutton for Dante, *De monarchia;* Mill, *On Representative Government;* Rousseau, *The Social Contract;* Sorokin, *The Crisis of Our Age*. Harcourt Brace for Case, *Social Process and Human Progress*, and Sandburg, *The People, Yes*. Harper and Bros. for Angell, *The Steep Places;* Bryson, *Approaches to National Unity;* Doman, *The Coming Age of World Control;* Dulles, *War, Peace, and Change;* De Huszar, *Persistent International Issues;* Johnson, *Religion and World Order;* Laski, *The Dangers of Obedience;* Lucas, *Renaissance and Reformation;* Reves, *The Anatomy of Peace;* Robinson, *Toward International Organization;* Eliot, *Defense of International Order;* Streit, *Union Now;* Welles, *The Time for Decision*. Harvard University Press for Brinton, *From Many One*. A. A. Knopf for Becker,

How New Will the Better World Be?; Spengler, *The Decline of the West;* Seagle, *The Quest for Law.* Little, Brown and Atlantic Monthly Press for Lippmann, *U.S. Foreign Policy* and *U.S. War Aims;* Meyer, *Peace or Anarchy.* Longmans, Green for Barrington, *The Life and Works of Walter Bagehot;* Oppenheim, *International Law.* The Macmillan Company for Acton, *The History of Freedom and Other Essays;* Carr, *Conditions of Peace;* Phillipson, *International Law and Customs of Ancient Greece and Rome;* Ransome, *Studies in Federal Planning;* Spahr, *Readings in Recent Political Philosophy;* Shotwell, *Governments of Continental Europe;* Carr, *Nationalism and After;* Hayes, *Essays on Nationalism;* Jessup, *A Modern Law of Nations;* Kohn, *The Idea of Nationalism;* MacIver, *The Web of Government* and *Towards an Abiding Peace;* Northrup, *The Meeting of East and West;* Shotwell, *The Great Decision;* Stammler, *The Theory of Justice;* Whitehead, *Science and the Modern World;* Zimmern, *League of Nations and Rule of Law.* Methuen for Cole, *Social Theory.* Houghton Mifflin for Rand, *Modern Classical Philosophies;* Eliot, *The Road toward Peace;* Hicks, *A Short History of the American Democracy;* Murphy, *Human Nature and Enduring Peace.* John Murray for Maine, *Ancient Law.* Harold Nicholson for *Diplomacy.* Oxford University Press for *Anarchy or World Order, Problems of Peace;* J. B. Scott, *An International Court of Justice* and *The International Conference of American States, 1889–1928;* Toynbee, *A Study of History;* Weber, *Theory of Social and Economic Organization and Essays in Sociology;* Young, *Federalism and Freedom.* G. P. Putnam's Sons for Angell, *The Great Illusion;* Dewey, *Freedom and Culture;* Peaslee, *A Permanent United Nations;* Vestal, *The Maintenance of Peace.* Random House for Burtt, *The English Philosophers;* Burns, *A Handbook of Communism.* Rinehart for Fromm, *Escape from Freedom;* Sharp and Kirk, *Contemporary International Politics.* Rivingtons for Hassall, *The Balance of Power.* Charles Scribner's Sons for

Taft, *The United States and Peace;* Heimann, *Freedom and Order.* University of Chicago Press for Morgenthau, *Peace, Security and The United Nations;* Cobban, *National Self-Determination;* Chafee, *Government and Mass Communication;* Wildes, *Social Currents of Japan.* The Viking Press for Delaisi, *Political Myths and Economic Realities;* Crankshaw, *Russia and the Russians;* Kirillov, "We" in *Voices of October.* World Peace Foundation for Reinsch, *International Public Unions.*

G. J. M.

Contents

Part One

THE THEORY OF WORLD GOVERNMENT

Chapter 1

To mortal men Peace giveth these good things:
Wealth, and the flowers of honey-throated song;
The flame that springs
On carven altars from fat sheep and kine,
Slain to the gods in heaven; and, all day long,
Games for glad youths, and flutes, and wreaths,
And circling wine.
Then in the steely shield swart spiders weave
Their web and dusky woof;
Rust to the pointed spear and sword doth cleave;
The brazen trump sounds no alarms;
Nor is sleep harried from our eyes aloof,
But with sweet rest my bosom warms:
The streets are thronged with lovely men and young,
And hymns in praise of boys like flames to heaven are flung!

Bacchylides (450 B.C.),
translated by John Addington Symonds

The Premises of
World Government

Is WORLD GOVERNMENT POSSIBLE? Of course it is. But the world wears many faces, some beguiling, like a fresh-painted, dangerous mistress, others curved in angelic sentimentality, still others hideous with the blotches of ignorance, war, and pestilence.

Which of these is the last true countenance? It depends upon the observer; and as man conceives the nature of his society, so does he fashion his plans for its direction. This is the first clue to the meaning of world government, that a particular plan for the rule or coordination of the peoples on this earth is based on a particular comprehension and interpretation of the world society.

Historical literature is starred with a thousand gleaming ideas for the reorientation of political society from the Grand Union of Confucius to the Dumbarton Oaks Conference in Washington, and each is a mirror of the age in which it was conceived. For Dante, in the early fourteenth century, concerned with the destructive rivalries of papal and imperial factions in the shambles of the old Roman Empire,

All concord depends upon a unity of wills. The human race when best disposed is a concord. Therefore, the human race when best disposed depends upon a unity in wills . . . and . . . it is necessary for the best disposition of the human race that there should be a monarch in the world.[1]

The Abbé de Saint-Pierre, observing the incessant dynastic struggles of the European princes in the seventeenth and eighteenth centuries, believed that "the balance of power between the House of France and the House of Austria could not offer a sufficient guarantee for either the Sovereigns or their subjects from the evils of foreign and civil wars" and that a league of Christian princes, solemnly pledged to the five fundamental articles which he proposed, would obtain "perpetual peace both inside and outside their states." [2] And in the nineteenth century an American, William Ladd, commented

nations are considered as individual, moral persons, perfectly equal and independent of one another [and that his plan for establishing a Congress and a Court of Nations] has nothing to do with physical force and leagues offensive . . . but . . . depends entirely upon the influence of moral power. . . . Is it too much to hope that, in this age of reason and philanthropy, the preservation of peace, equity, and justice . . . may be sufficient motive to induce Christian nations to try the experiment . . . ? [3]

Similarly, Emeric Crucé, in an age of mercantilism and divinely ordained kings, emphasized the benefits of developing commerce between nations and the personal responsibility of monarchs for maintaining peace; for Immanuel Kant, when Europe was split by despotism and the fiery principles of the French Revolution, republican constitutions would deprive rulers of their arbitrary decrees of war, and a confederation of republican states was the first approach to peace. In 1916 the League to Enforce Peace, cognizant of the growing success of arbitration among states up to the First World War, believed that a compulsory process of international litigation should be the primary goal, but "in case any nation should feel, after the

[1] Dante Alighieri, "De monarchia," in *Latin Works*, Book 1, chap. xv.
[2] Abbé de Saint-Pierre, "Abrejé du projet de paix perpetuelle," in *Ouvrages de politique*, Vol. I, Second discours et seconde proposition.
[3] Ladd, *Prize Essay on a Congress of Nations*, chaps. i, viii.

adjudication of its case, that substantial justice had been denied, it would . . . be quite at liberty to resort to war for the securing of its rights." [4]

No age has lacked a distinguished advocate for the reorganization of the world political society: Erasmus, Sully, Penn, Rousseau, Bentham, Lorimer, and Bryce have all raised their voices; and no age has lacked ingenious devices.

The blueprints of past ages, indeed, are anachronisms, curious oddities out of tune with the pressure of technological revolutions and the cult of new gods, but they do indicate important characteristics in any scheme: first, an essential relevance to an historical epoch and, therefore, a transient nature; secondly, a crystallization of those social ideals which the planners believe ought to be operative. Such plans are particular constructions of the society from which they emanate, using the contemporary myths and institutions that readily spring to mind and adding the value judgments which are respected by the individuals who engineer the project.

Any plea for world government, then, is a plea for that type of world society desired by the suppliants and formulated within the limited range of their current experience. The saint would seek world order in the souls of men and the beneficence of God; the hero would hammer out a world order by zeal and force; the rational man might institute a logical series of calm acts. In order to meet reality, the efforts of each of these approaches must encompass the techniques and structures which have evolved contemporaneously; but the direction of these instruments will vary according to the desired result.

No modern view of world order, for example, can ignore the impact of industrialization upon society. More efficient utilization of natural resources and improved fabrication processes offer mankind some opportunities hitherto inconceivable. Rapid transportation and communication coupled with surplus products afford leisure time for education, aesthetics, and mo-

[4] Short, *Program and Policies of the League to Enforce Peace,* p. 25.

rality; the same factors, however, make large-scale warfare more feasible. Industrialism is a fact, in either case, but its connotations are different. World government specifically denotes universality, but universality may have very different aspects. World government, then, means a particular kind of government based upon a particular conception of society.

The phenomenon of the nation-state also has a clear historical development and by some political theorists has been regarded as the perfect instrumentality of civilization. Such a view of the nation-state as the ultimate achievement of mankind, a criterion of morality, as in Machiavelli, or a fountainhead of law, as in Hobbes, presents a dark and angry picture of the world community, a hectic panorama of anarchy, but it is this view which many modern "realists" accept. According to this picture it may be argued that since anarchy is intolerably destructive, order must be substituted at any price; the first step, therefore, is the institution of supreme coercive power to guarantee stability and a regard for universal law. Assuming the propriety of the first act, however, a definition of the universal law or its application to a world community remains debatable, for once again it is contingent upon those ideals which the use of force would make effectual.

Hegel, attempting a more general formulation of the existence of society and with striking emphasis upon his own culture, believed:

In order that a truly universal spirit may arise, the Spirit of a People must advance to some new purpose; but whence can this purpose originate? It would be a higher, more comprehensive concept of itself—a transcending of its principle—but this very act would involve a principle of a new order, a new National Spirit.[5]

In this case, conceiving society as the expression of an immanent spirit forever seeking out its universal principles and purposes through the moral constitution of a nation, world government is virtually meaningless. Those nations impelled to

[5] Hegel, *The Philosophy of History*, p. 75.

activity by the World Spirit would attain a hegemony over the peoples of the earth, yet inevitably fade and fail, while no fundamental moral principle could be attained simultaneously by all states to serve as a basis for a cooperative world union. Though some dynamic central authority might dominate the world stage, it would constitute no permanent advance to a stable organization governing the whole of society.

From an entirely different aspect, using a framework of states based upon the principle of "the free federation of the individual into the community," even the anarchist Bakunin had sought a United States of the World. The only authority to be recognized was "human justice," and "the right of voluntary union and the right of voluntary separation are the most important of all political rights." Without these fundamental rights the confederation would merely be a mask for a centralized state. The greatest evil, then, is authority itself: the only integrating principle to be recognized is the development of autonomous parts which do not deny the special rights or interests of any other part. To be sure, in a test with historical reality such a presumption may seem invalid. But the answer of the anarchists to this would be that any other kind of world government is tyranny. They admit that

Unity is the goal towards which humanity irresistibly strives. But unity becomes a menace destroying reason, dignity, and well-being if it is achieved through the authority of theological, metaphysical, political, or even economic ideas.[6]

Whatever the merits of such a proposal, it is patent that world government in this instance is intended to serve a specific end, the voluntary cooperation of decentralized, unbureaucratic, and nonmilitaristic states which serve the interests and needs of individuals. Going back one step further, it is a theory of man, innately and individually good, enslaved by force in social institutions at the command of a group.

[6] Proposals placed before the Central Committee of the League of Peace and Liberty, Berne, 1867—"Fédéralisme, Socialisme, et Antithéologisme," in Bakounine, *Œuvres*, Vol. 1.

To analyze world government is to analyze implicitly the nature of man and the purpose of society, for while universality in the sheer interest of large-scale coordination may provide more efficiency, it is a superficial end in itself. Efficiency must always answer the question Efficiency for what? It is at this point that men surmise the character of society and the best translation of human efforts into human happiness. World government can be regarded as a potential capacity of society, even as an inevitable outcome of society, but an estimation of such a political entity must proceed by reference to the prevailing conception of rights, duties, and desires. And though these attitudes of a particular social order are cast in an obscure hierarchy of values, no diagnosis is useful unless one begins by an "inventory of its system of convictions" establishing "which belief is fundamental, decisive, sustaining, and breathing life into all the others." [7]

The longest exposition of civilized aspirations for the abolition of war does not warrant the unconditional statement that men have always desired something amorphous called peace; instead, they have cried out for minimum physical wants and spiritual satisfactions according to their past and immediately conceivable future experience. For such minimum needs men have been willing and ready to fight. To sift from such standards the decisive and sustaining creed is essential for an understanding of the qualifications inherent in the many demands and entreaties for a world government.

T. D. Weldon refers to such creeds as "first order moral questions," which are not compatible in different communities because of different evolutions. Conceivably a wide area of socio-economic relationships might be sacrificed by a state as the price for security, as individuals are willing to pay for police protection, but some convictions are so essential to the integrity of a people that no compromise is possible. Such an

[7] Ortega y Gasset, *Toward a Philosophy of History*, p. 168.

analysis emphasizes the logic of cooperation on "second-order problems—which are economic and therefore almost always capable of solution by discussion"; [8] it is also neatly fitted to a contemporary supposition that totalitarianism and individualism are irreconcilable.

Whether the first-order moral questions can be deferred requires further investigation, but it seems clear that tacit premises stand behind all views on world government: the ardent propagandists in the United States,[9] for example, who demonstrate in starkly dramatic and telling terms the need for world security, undoubtedly intend to provide for the continuance of free opinion and expression of the Anglo-American sort, at least in this country. Further assumptions immediately rush to mind: the maintenance of approximately the same physical standards of living, a wide area of cultural autonomy, local determination of the division of social efforts and rewards, and so forth. The question "What price security?" has a sequel: "What is worth securing?" Therein lie the powerful motivations toward world government.

The sponsors of supernational organizations, therefore, plan a framework which is in accordance not only with self-preservation but also with a "decent" way of life. Assuredly the high moral tone to the preamble of the League of Nations calling for "open, just, and honorable relations" as well as "a scrupulous respect for all treaty obligations" was as meaningful to Woodrow Wilson as Article 10, the Guarantees against Aggression. Marxists, at the same time, regarding history in the light of class struggle, have proclaimed:

We do not speak of the right of self-determination of nations (i.e. of their bourgeoisie and their workmen) but only of the right of the working classes. . . . Sooner or later we will have the International Republic of Soviets. . . . Therefore, the program of our

[8] Weldon, *States and Morals*, p. 302.
[9] See Emery Reves, Raymond Swing, Owen J. Roberts, Cord Meyer, Jr., and others.

party, which is the program of international revolution, is at the same time the program of complete liberation of the weak and oppressed.[10]

And at San Francisco in 1945 the United Nations were agreed on promoting "social progress and better standards of life in larger freedom," [11] in general terms; but the interpretation of those terms remained with each state, for all matters which "are essentially within the domestic jurisdiction of any State" [12] were excluded from the Charter. Even a positive promise of security from aggression would not be exchangeable for certain habits and creeds which men believe essential to their integrity.

It is more than coincidental that the proponents of leagues, federations, or unitary world states either have a vested interest in the *status quo* or envisage a hegemony within such a structure. If Sparta supported the oligarchies of Tegea and Megara within the Peloponnesian League, no less did the Holy Alliance at Laibach and Verona aim at suppressing popular governments in Italy and Spain; if France cast benign glances upon princely leagues in the seventeenth and eighteenth centuries, no less would the United States today favor a federation following the standards of Western liberalism. The forging of the North German Bund of 1867 by Bismarck meant the supremacy of Prussia within that organization just as an International Republic of Soviets signifies the leadership of Russia within such a conglomeration. And the United Nations in all its one hundred and eleven articles makes no provision for changing the privileged permanent membership of the Security Council. None of the present "Big Five," the grand allies against the Axis Powers during the Second World War, can be deprived of its special status except by its own express permission.[13]

---

[10] Bukharin, *A Program of Communists*, chap. xix.
[11] *United Nations Charter*, Preamble.
[12] *Ibid.*, art. 2, par. 7.
[13] Changes in permanent membership in the Security Council could be brought

The universality of any one of these political groupings is not the point at issue, but rather that a combination is made to preserve or expand some system favorable to the interests of the leading members. If the consolidation is voluntary, however, it must offer some advantages to all its members. The affinity of military alliances and various confederations seems clear; but since the motive for common action originates with the primitive instinct for self-defense, such an affiliation cannot endure after the external threat has been removed unless a stronger motive for concerted action is substituted. Thus, the American Articles of Confederation enacted by the States for "their common defense . . . binding themselves to assist each other, against all forces offered to, or attacks made upon them, or any of them" [14] did not have a substantial warrant for further integration of the people when the immediate danger had passed. But a Federal Government which offered incontrovertible economic benefits,[15] among other common interests, did form "a more perfect union."

The task of world government is constantly to explore those interests about which communities are agreed, and "some coercive power must be provided to coordinate the actions of its members and give their common interests and mutual obligations that firmness and consistency which they never could acquire for themselves." [16] The community of interests which unites any society, however, is not an abstraction, but a dynamic relationship fraught with infinite perils of disintegration. It rests upon daily contacts and reflexes, the economic struggle,

---

about by amendment of the Charter. This would require ratification by "all permanent Members of the Security Council." See art. 109, par. 2.
[14] *Articles of Confederation*, art. 3.
[15] See *The Federalist* (Modern Library Edition), Number 11, by A. Hamilton. "The importance of the Union, in a commercial light, is one of those points about which there is least room to entertain a difference of opinion, and which has in fact commanded the most general assent of men who have any acquaintance with the subject."
[16] J. J. Rousseau, "A Lasting Peace through the Federation of Europe," in Elizabeth York, *Leagues of Nations,*

a never-codified morality, instincts, passions, and harmonizing myths. Like any government, world government would direct these expressions of mankind toward a preconceived goal. This implies the interpretation and evaluation of such activities by a known standard. In the last analysis it means that a philosophy of government must precede any pattern of world government.

Finding a community of interests in the strictly material sense, therefore, is but the first phase of instituting any larger framework of government. The requisites of orderly and successful maritime commerce among various communities, for example, prompted the ancient Rhodian Sea Law, the medieval Consolato del Mare, and the modern Paris Declaration of Maritime Law in 1856. Other coordinated activities in economic and social welfare have led to innumerable pacts, commissions, and joint administrations. So long as a fixed benefit accrues to each of the members at no expense to any other predilection, the union is secure and, in fact, requires no coercion.[17] The important factor in all pledged cooperation, however, is the unwillingness of the signatories to subscribe their forms and uses of power to an ever-changing relationship, yet this is the stuff of politics.

It is on this level, the willingness to enforce continuously, on the basis of general principles, a whole interplay of social cooperation that a genuine community of interests is to be sought. Only such an agreement will yield a stable and enduring union.

Early in the operation of the League of Nations, by way of illustration, an International Blockade Commission was established to settle a general plan for the application of economic sanctions under Article 16 of the Covenant, one of the means by which the League had pledged "to enforce their will by effective action on any particular country which . . . defies

[17] The Universal Postal Union and the World Health Organization are the best illustrations.

the general verdict of the world." [18] As Lord Robert Cecil admitted, "It is indeed one of the vital, the cardinal, provisions in the whole Covenant, without which you would not have the final material guarantee which in human society is no doubt necessary for the enforcement of even the most beneficent code." [19] But the three Scandinavian states proposed that exceptions be made for some Members whose application of sanctions "might entail serious danger." The Netherlands went even further, insisting that each state be its own judge in the matter. Austria, Cuba, Canada, Uruguay, and others joined the chorus attaching reservations to the Article. In 1935, when Italy clearly violated the Covenant in attacking Ethiopia, France found reasons to temporize—and Britain followed. Gradually, in successive commissions, reports, and interpretations, the automatic, instant, and continuous enforcement which had originally been contemplated gave way to a policy of hesitation, quibbling, and deferment undermining and toppling the whole cardboard structure.

A stable and enduring union, however, merely provides a mold for world government; it is no indication in itself of what is to be made stable and enduring, for this hangs on the meaning of the "general principles" which are to be continuously enforced. Racism and Christianity are incompatible; castes and democracy do not mix; sovereign equality among states has to be reconciled to a patently unequal distribution of resources on the earth; even a "scrupulous respect for treaty obligations," without some mitigation by an appeal to equity, would lead to impossible stagnation.

In other words, What conception of justice will this union follow? What standards will it apply to the determination of truth? What comprehension will it have of the beautiful? A

---

[18] League of Nations, *Records of the First Assembly*, Meetings of the Committees, II, 334 *et seq.*
[19] *Ibid.*, Plenary Meetings, p. 396. See Rappard, *The Quest for Peace*, p. 219 *et seq.*

world government does not require some abstract, eternal, perfect justice, a one and only Platonic "form." The penetrating Pascal wrote:

On what shall man found the order of the world which he would govern? Shall it be on the caprice of each individual? What confusion! Shall it be on justice? Man is ignorant of it. . . . The glory of true equity would have brought all nations under subjection, and legislators would not have taken their model from the fancies and caprices of Persians and Germans instead of this unchanging justice.[20]

Custom and community throughout history have given their consent to more than one type of justice; it is no less a consideration for those who advocate one set of principles or another for world government. This does not mean that men would willingly accept all kinds of justice, for in fact only those ethical standards which, like Stoicism, sweep aside particular societies and look towards universal normative relationships could prepare the way. Pristine Marxism, with its banner "from each according to his ability, to each according to his needs," has a similar catholicity, though perhaps the resulting world government would be very different.

When statesmen or propagandists encourage "world government," the geographical word is of minute importance compared to the political word, though the impression conveyed is often quite the contrary. Wendell Willkie wrote, "First we must plan for peace on a world basis; second, the world must be free, politically and economically, for nations and for men, that peace may exist in it," [21] but obviously the first term is meaningless without a consensus on the second term, "free." This is the ethical impasse. Quite naturally Mr. Willkie believed that America had achieved "the most reasonable expression of freedom that has yet existed in history," and he continued, "Liberty, if it is to be for all, must be protected

[20] *Pensées*, No. 17.
[21] Wendell Willkie, *One World*, in *Prefaces to Peace*, p. 146.

by basic safeguards intended to give it the most general diffusion attainable, and none can expect privileges which encroach on the rights of others." [22] Indeed, it is not the size, or even the monumental complexity which daunts the hardiest advocate of world government, but the conflict of rights and duties, privileges and obligations, all of which are ultimately grounded on nonrational tenets. A resort to simple logic, with contrived premises, can demonstrate natural slavery as easily as natural freedom; one world can be shown to be better than another, if the standards are agreeable.

It is frequently asserted that a "functional" approach [23] would obviate this difficulty: that is, concentration upon the technical problems of transportation, communication, finance, health, and so forth, is the first task of international society. Organizations would be patterned in area and authority according to their specific functions, with no immediate effort to erect an all-embracing political institution. Railways, shipping, wireless, public health, trade, and other communications which span communities could be regulated according to particular grants of power, regionally or universally as the need might require. In brief, it is maintained that a continuous articulation of communities in "practical" undertakings creates the most feasible basis for an eventual super-state government.

Paul Reinsch, struck by the phenomenal growth and success of international public unions between 1865 and 1911, keynoted the functional program:

Without legal derogation to the sovereignty of individual states, an international de facto and conventional jurisdiction and administrative procedure is thus growing up, which bids fair to become one of the most controlling elements in the future political relations of the world.[24]

The argument is persuasive. Perhaps the energies of the League

[22] *Ibid.*, p. 139.
[23] See Mitrany, *A Working Peace System.*
[24] P. Reinsch, *Public International Unions*, p. 14.

of Nations should have been more positively channeled in this direction. This theme will require more probing, but one comment is appropriate here: the goal of the functional approach is the efficient use of resources, material and human, in order to demonstrate to men the value of more extended collaboration. Again the problem is how to determine the ends of such a program. Having achieved a full utilization of resources, how will the social product be distributed? What priority will be given to what social needs? How will penalties and rewards be apportioned? What liberties will be realized? What beauties captured?

A plethora of superficial plans exist today for a world federation to make such decisions, implicitly or explicitly. An examination of the constitutions of such organizations, however, quickly betrays their intellectual womb. One author tries "to work out some form of measuring stick which will, most equitably and wisely, allocate voting power between the various nations; their relative educational accomplishments seem to be such a criterion." [25] Another believes "representation should be . . . in part based upon populations" and that "perhaps such factors as international trade should be taken into account." He concludes that "the central government requires much the same powers as the people of the states have transferred to the United States government." [26]

Such schemes are fashioned from conceptual models of world government designed without reference to critiques of psychology, but simply on the reasoning of the author. The popular way of expressing many contemporary plans has even gone beyond "what ought to be done" to "what must be done." No serious discussion of world government in present-day circumstances deserves ridicule; not only do such expositions provide criticisms of the existing order, criticisms which must be an-

[25] Rider, *The Great Dilemma of World Organization*, pp. 63–64.
[26] Cornell, *New World Primer*, pp. 90, 96.

swered by a severe analysis of accepted values, but they also quicken the imagination, stimulating men to look beyond the exigencies and constrictions of daily life. Nevertheless, their genealogies must be traced, and the values which they purport to be universally desirable and agreeable must be analyzed in the light of their parochial origins.

In a chapter entitled "What Are We Fighting For?" written in the midst of the Second World War, Carl Becker succinctly set forth the heterogeneous values for which the Allied nations were violently expending their treasure and their lives.

. . . they are all fighting primarily for something they have or the recovery of something they have lost—their native soil, their national independence, their familiar institutions and way of life . . . each country is fighting for the particular sort of freedom—the particular set of political and social institutions—with which it is familiar and to which it is attached.[27]

On what basis can it be expected that men will yield quietly and amicably these hard-won "freedoms" to some plan for the transfer of authority either to larger numbers, more ambitious traders, or brighter intellects? While it is understandable that a self-consistent system impresses reasonable men, logical order, of itself, does not indicate a useful or truthful correlation with the existential. The assumption that any ten heads are better than any other nine remains an assumption; the beliefs that commerce and business and enterprise are pecular merits of a community and that scholarly achievement may provide an index to social values remain beliefs. The self-consistent system merely elaborates and embellishes such tenets, spelling out the details in schemes to make that kind of world community attractive.

William James, in his famous "faith ladder," has shown the interesting processes of the mind in first imagining that something "might" be true, then proceeding to believe that it "may"

[27] Becker, *How New Will the Better World Be?* pp. 125–126.

be true, or it is "fit" to be true, gradually asserting that it "ought" to be true, and finally that it "must" be true.[28] Speculation on world government is dominated by this kind of thinking; the subtle distinctions between what is possible, what is desirable, and what is necessary are blurred in either cheerful or dreadful panaceas. It is important, however, to note the last rung of this faith ladder: namely, that when men have convinced themselves that something "must" be true, they begin to act in such a way as to make its supposedly incontestable validity secure. Racists, for example, who rant of "naturally" inferior peoples, demand every means available to compel such a status;[29] the Crusaders, on capturing Jerusalem in 1099, to attest the superior morality of the Christian faith massacred all the Moslems and burned the Jews alive;[30] and Marxists, certain of the inevitable "victory of the proletariat,"[31] are painstaking in their efforts to assure the fall of the bourgeoisie. Similarly many peoples and states, most recently Germany and Japan, have fallen under the spell of some "manifest destiny" impelling them to reach out beyond their accustomed boundaries—not only with the strength at their disposal but also with the ideas, attitudes, and convictions peculiar to their social order.

Governments embrace all types and agglomerations of human beings and, by definition, govern or regulate them. Coercion is, therefore, implicit; but the degree of coercion is dependent upon the willingness to participate in the kind of social order sought by those who command. It is a perennial inverse proportion: the greater the degree of consent, the less need for coercion; the less consent achieved, the more coercion required. Under the most liberal government, some coercion is necessary to channel innumerable conflicting wills, or anarchy would ensue. On the other hand, dictators today require the good will

---

[28] James, *A Pluralistic Universe*, pp. 328–330.
[29] See Grant, *The Passing of the Great Race*.
[30] Reinach, *Orpheus—A History of Religions*, p. 177.
[31] See *The Communist Manifesto*, by Karl Marx.

of their inner party councils or chief military officers as much as the Roman emperors needed the approbation of their praetorian guards or the Egyptian sultans their mamelukes.

If a structure of world government is to be imagined, then its size, shape, and strength will be conditioned by the social order which it intends to establish. Should there be a genuine consensus among the members on the hierarchy of values within such a community, the coercive element will be minimized; if but little consensus exists, an autocratic leadership would be the obvious recourse for universal conformity. The idea of world government, in itself, does not exclude either method or variations of them. Indeed, the states of the world today, whether regarded as the final consolidation of men under government or models of integration to be imitated on a world scale, were forged by a mixture of ruthless coercion and consent, a mixture of quite inconstant proportions. The point is, however, that the degree of consent determines the requisite compulsion, and, at the same time, this does not preclude a totally authoritarian world government based upon an absolute minimum of willing cooperation. The whole matter hinges on the particular social order which is envisaged by the leadership and the acquiescence of the community therein.

World government, to be sure, is possible. But the potential subjects of such an organization ought to inquire: What kind of world will it be? By what tokens shall the purposes of a new political apparatus be known? Max Weber answered in this way.

It is not possible to define a politically corporate group . . . in terms of the end toward which its corporate action is devoted. All the way from the provisions of subsistence to the patronage of art, there is no conceivable end which *some* political corporation has not at some time pursued. And from the protection of personal security to the administration of justice, there is none which *all* have recognized.[32]

[32] Weber, *Theory of Social and Economic Organization*, p. 155.

He went on to say that the only way to define the political
character of a corporate group is by the means peculiar to it,
that is, the use of force. In a sense, furthermore, the means
is identified with the end. Excommunication, interdict, and
absolution from the feudal oath were the repressive instruments
of the medieval church, but these powers are unthinkable without the Christian faith they sought to preserve. The organization of the League of Nations was to be buttressed by collective
security, both the keystone of its power and the purpose of its
existence.

The difficulty of defining a universal end upon which a number of political groups may find agreement suggests not only
the necessity of coercion within world government but also
the close identification of the means sought to bring about consolidation with the character of the social order to be created.
Constitutional government cannot be arbitrarily imposed any
more than imperial administration can burgeon from a free accord.

What seems to follow from this preliminary investigation,
therefore, is that there are alternative kinds of world government possible depending upon alternative views on society and
that any particular kind of government which may come about
by a mixture of consent and coercion will be based upon a
particular conception of the nature and destiny of mankind.
If the universe is regarded as a giant clock unwinding a slow
procession of causes and effects, then the regulation of the system may be demanded by those who declare that they know
the intervals; if the universe should appear as a stage of passion-
ate combat, then the strong will claim the right to rule; if the
universe exists for the realization of ideals, then those who inquire and experiment may presume to teach proper government.

Certainly the various patterns and purposes of society which have threaded history testify to the different postulates upon which communal action has proceeded, and the next chapter will be devoted to some of this evidence.

Chapter 2

A noiseless, patient spider,
I mark'd, where, on a little promontory, it stood isolated;
Mark'd how, to explore the vacant, vast surrounding,
It launch'd forth filament, filament, filament, out of itself;
Ever unreeling them—ever tirelessly speeding them.

And you, O my Soul, where you stand
Surrounded, surrounded, in measureless oceans of space,
Ceaselessly musing, venturing, throwing,—seeking the spheres, to con-
    nect them;
Till the bridge you will need, be form'd—till the ductile anchor hold;
Till the gossamer thread you fling, catch somewhere, O my Soul.

                                                    Walt Whitman

The Forms of
World Government

By MARCH, 1945, forty-seven states of the world had each pledged "to employ its full resources, military or economic, against those members of the Tripartite Pact and its adherents with which such government is at war." [1] This was the culmination of six years of violent warfare which had spread with ever-increasing destruction over the face of the earth, but it was also the most shocking testimony of the failure of the League of Nations to achieve international peace and security.

To some who are concerned with world government the new international organization to maintain peace and security seems to embody the same inherent defects and ultimate futility as the old institution, for the United Nations, like the League, is based upon the principle of the "sovereign equality" [2] of states. The shattering disappointment in a confederation of independent nation-states, moreover, has driven many people to the conclusion that some means must be found to transcend national boundaries and authority in the interests of peace, or annihilation will be the consequence of international anarchy. [3] In the current literature of the Western world the most popular suggestion is a federal union of nation-states to which certain

[1] *Declaration of United Nations*, Washington, Jan. 1, 1942.
[2] *United Nations Charter*, art. 2.
[3] See Swing, *In the Name of Sanity*.

powers have been unequivocally delegated for the prevention
of war, while "the rights of nations which may not be infringed
by any superior international authority . . . should be defined, declared, and reserved to those nations." [4] Even more
explicitly Cord Meyer maintains, "only those functions of government that are determined to be indispensable to the prevention of war need be transferred to the United Nations while
the member nations retain their independence of action in all
other matters," [5] and he cites such federal functions as control
of armaments, direct taxation for financial support, judicial
control over individuals disobeying the charter, and so forth.
By 1949 some seventeen state legislatures had urged the United
States Congress to take first steps toward world government.
A number of resolutions upon developing the United Nations
into a world government were introduced into Congress, and
early in 1950 hearings were commenced before a Senate subcommittee on foreign relations.

Analogy is a common tool of intelligent thinking. Things
similar to one thing are similar to one another. If existing federal unions are able to harmonize different ethnological communities, preventing war while assuring them relative independence in local matters, then a world federal union might
accomplish the same thing for nations. Furthermore, the preservation of independence in domestic affairs is the best possible
way of gaining the voluntary acceptance of the union as the
final arbiter in international relations. So the argument runs,
and very convincingly.

The variations of this theme of delegated powers, limited
federal government, and the retention of local independence
are many, but it is clearly analagous to the constitutions of the
United States and Switzerland. In both states there was a period
of loose confederation, chiefly for defensive purposes, then
a voluntary resolution to unite the several states or cantons into
a strong federal system. According to the advocates of a world

[4] Peaslee, *A Permanent United Nations*, p. 5.
[5] Meyer, *Peace or Anarchy*, p. 151.

federal union, the nation-states of today are floundering through this phase of loose confederation as exemplified by the League and the United Nations. While some writers propose a union of all states, others are inclined to begin with the United States and the British Commonwealth [6] or to organize a number of unions among closely related states on a regional basis.[7] With a few popular writers the idea of a federal union emphasizing law and constitutionalism has assumed shrill tones of self-righteousness.

The idea of freedom within union, basic to the American system, is a universal idea. . . . A solid sense of union among the democracies, with an Anglo-American nucleus, is the voice crying in the wilderness of international politics. . . . America and Britain, champions of constitutionalism, are the guardians of civilization. . . . No nation can be united to the atomic union which is not governed by a Constitution and a Bill of Rights . . .[8]

Whatever the ramifications, the most characteristic aspects of federal union are the attempt to define positively the spheres of superstate and national prerogatives, to enforce this constitution by adequate superstate machinery, and, initially, to secure the voluntary agreement of all the members.

In surveying the record of political organizations which have extended their sway over diverse communities, however, one is led to the conclusion that while a voluntary federal union might be a desirable form of world government, it is only one of the several alternatives, and a rather unlikely one at that. In his monumental study of history, Arnold J. Toynbee writes,

we have now brought a fresh opportunity to attempt this difficult enterprise of abolishing war through a cooperative system of world government . . . whether we in our world will succeed in achieving what no other civilization has yet achieved is a question that lies on the knees of the Gods.[9]

[6] See Streit, *Union Now with Britain.*
[7] See Corbett, *Post-War Worlds.*
[8] Leonard, "Atomic Union Now," *The Christian Science Monitor* (Boston), March 27, 1948.
[9] Toynbee, *A Study of History;* abridgment of Vols. I–VI by D. L. Somervell, p. 285.

19

But the United States and Switzerland cannot be accepted as good analogies for world federal union. It is commonplace to recognize that British America was a single ethnic community sharing the same institutions, manners, and morals [10] for more than one hundred and fifty years before somewhat less than four million people came to a half-hearted agreement on a federal government.[11] For another seventy-two years a large proportion of the population, both in the North and in the South, was dubious about the fundamental character of the union until a decision was made by force of arms. During these two hundred and fifty years, finally, there was a combination of circumstances peculiarly favorable to the development of this kind of union: a republican ideology, a high regard for trade and commerce, which encouraged efficiencies of national transportation and communication, a sprawling frontier, and hostile British, French, Spanish, and Indians to evoke a unified defense.

Switzerland, because it has successfully provided a federal government for three nationalities and two distinct religions, is sometimes a more apt example for world federalists. The first Swiss confederation of three cantons took place in 1291 as a mutual protection against the domination of the Hapsburgs, their feudal overlords. By 1649 the Confederation had grown to thirteen cantons, all German-speaking, and was an alliance of sovereign states with a common foreign policy. The cantonal governments varied from peasant democracies to rigid oligarchies. At the end of the eighteenth century, however, the French Revolution smashed into Switzerland, destroying in particular the historic institutions of an aristocratic or oligar-

---

[10] ". . . Providence has been pleased to give this one connected country to one united people—a people descended from the same ancestors, speaking the same language, professing the same religion, attached to the same principles of government, very similar in their manners and customs, and who, by their joint counsels, arms, and efforts, fighting side by side throughout a long and bloody war, have nobly established general liberty and independence."—John Jay, *The Federalist*, No. 2 (Modern Library).

[11] A switch of six votes among the 168 delegates to the Virginia Convention of 1788, for example, would have defeated ratification in this key state.

chic nature by briefly establishing the Helvetic Republic. With
the downfall of Napoleon and the advent of reaction throughout Europe, efforts were made to recreate the cantonal institutions of the prewar period.

But the basis of modern Switzerland had been firmly laid between
1798 and 1815 . . . moreover, the liberal, democratic, and central-
izing influences, generated during the period when France controlled Switzerland, began to manifest themselves. After 1830 the
power of the aristocracies and the oligarchies was permanently
destroyed . . . and representative institutions of a popular character were universally introduced.[12]

Six of the French and Italian speaking cantons had been added
to the Confederation by Napoleon, and three more by the peace
terms of 1815. In regard to the religious differences, there had
been internecine warfare for three centuries after the Reformation, and as late as 1847 a rebellion of the Roman Catholic cantons had to be put down by force. It was in this manner that
the Swiss were prepared for a federal union, and consequently
they voluntarily approved a Constitution in 1848.

The purpose of this exposition is not to derogate the accomplishments of the Swiss, but to put the federation in proper
perspective if it is to be used as a prototype of world government. Here is a Christian community smaller than Costa Rica,
with a population never exceeding five million, curiously situated on the highest mountain tops, and surrounded by powerful
neighbors, having lived in loose cantonal confederation for
thousands of years, but actually having been molded for union
by the French army. Then, the physical framework of Swiss
government was fashioned by the Napoleonic Wars, and final
coordination was achieved by stamping out the several oligarchies, aristocracies, and a Catholic rebellion.

None of the British dominions now practicing federal government represents a free amalgamation of sovereign states, but

---

[12] Arnold Zurcher, "The Political System of Switzerland," in *Governments of
Continental Europe*, ed. J. T. Shotwell and others, p. 985.

rather colonial consolidation, accompanied in South Africa by
the forceful incorporation of other peoples. As for federal
unions such as Brazil and Mexico, their quasi-decentralized
representative constitutions were born out of revolution after
a unitary state had already been formed.

The federal experience of the United States and Switzerland
indicates the rarity of such occurrences, the need for a set of
fortuitous circumstances and, most of all, association with
democratic institutions. Democratic procedure thrives on tolerance of minority opposition, and, in effect, this is a virtue of
the federal system, which permits a large measure of autonomy
to the minority views of individual states. In both the United
States and Switzerland, as in other modern democracies, it is
the party system which reflects the ability of opposing groups
to work peacefully under agreed principles, for when the principles are themselves at issue the parties become factions, and
civil war ensues. Thus, the Democrats in the United States were
forced to accept the Republican view of the "state's rights"
doctrine as the Catholic Conservatives were compelled to yield
to the opinions of the Liberals and the Radicals in Switzerland.
Only by becoming reconciled to the new principles could the
party system prevail.

Now the inferences which may properly be drawn from
these illustrations are: "it is a painful, paradoxical truth that
world peace and the instrumentalities of world democracy must
be imposed" and that "this process cannot, of course, be expected to be purely democratic," [13] since nothing comparable
to the choice circumstances of the American States of the late
eighteenth century exists on a world scale. Even Emery Reves,
an apostle of world federalism, concludes his book with an eye
to this alternative. "If we cannot attain to universalism and
create union by common consent and democratic methods as
a result of rational thinking—then rather than retard the proc-

[13] Doman, *The Coming Age of World Control*, p. 174.

ess, let us precipitate unification by conquest." [14] Further consideration, nevertheless, suggests that unless those upon whom "the instrumentalities of world democracy" were imposed were soon reconciled to them and willing (or able) to cooperate with them, world peace would be a chimera. Unless it is possible to imagine world political parties which could agree upon a universal framework within which peaceful opposition and an interchange of rule could occur, a representative federal union will bear little resemblance to the models offered. Law and peace are not universal banners to attract the peoples of the world, a standard by which they might form their constitutional organization, as world federalists seem to intimate, for law and peace in a free society are the consequences, not the motivations, of continuous agreement on moral issues, good and bad, right and wrong, which are at root irrational and localized, not absolute and universal.

"Law exists," said Max Weber, "when there is a probability that an order will be upheld by a specific staff of men who will use physical or psychical compulsion with the intention of obtaining conformity with the order, or of inflicting sanctions for infringement of it." [15] Taking the definition at its pragmatic value, the possibility of several forms of world government through various hierarchies or bureaucracies opens a new vista on the problem, for the distribution of power through the administrative staff may be arranged in more than one way to accomplish the same purpose.

The simplest criterion for world government would be its ability to exercise some control over society as a whole, that is, to achieve an order which will be universally upheld. Scanning the experience of hitherto existing societies, we see that ap-

[14] Reves, *The Anatomy of Peace*, p. 269.
[15] From Weber, *Essays in Sociology*, tr. and ed. by H. C. Gerth and C. Wright Mills, p. 180.

parently personal rule through imperial bureaucracies has by
far the longest history and within large areas the greatest success in maintaining peace. The new Egyptian Empire, the
Roman Empire, the Ottoman Empire, the Danubian Hapsburg
Monarchy, the Manchu Dynasty, the Muscovite Czardom, and
other states combined scores of peoples during fairly long
periods of domestic peace. Sheer personal authority, however,
was never sufficient for government; the conquests of Alexander, Timur Lenk, and Attila quickly disintegrated; the Caro-
lingian and Holy Roman Empire were unstable and impotent.

It would be, then, necessary to institutionalize personal authority if it were to be forced upon the world and an endeavor
be made to establish a permanent organization. The Persian
emperors used satrapies to administer the provinces, the Ab-
basid Caliphs bought Turkish slaves and trained them as administrators, the Chinese tested and employed their litterati, the
Roman Republic, as did the early British and Spanish empires,
drew upon its nobility. The task of organizing a unitary world
government in a bureaucratized pyramid would not be insuper-
able, and modern dictatorships have offered one clue to the machinery. Industrialization and egalitarianism have sucked the
masses into the political process, preparing the way for a new
kind of clique which is nurtured by this wholesale political activity itself, namely, the Party.

Robert M. MacIver comments:

. . . leadership and office give men control over the behavior of
other men. This control is more selective in the sense that those
who respond to it are united not so much by a common territory or
common nationality as by a common faith, a common ideology, or
a common mission.[16]

The Soviet Union, for example, has conferred precisely this
selective control upon the Communists, overreaching boundaries, uprooting old ruling groups, and ruthlessly establishing a
dictatorship within the Party within the government, a com-

16 MacIver, *The Web of Government*, p. 89.

bination of Roman proconsuls and medieval church clergy to rule and to teach the people their salvation.

By comparison with the authoritarian, unitary form of world government, the possibilities and practicalities of a federal union, simply on the level of establishing some effective order, are not promising. The scant historical evidence [17] concerning such formations is not of itself conclusive evidence, but prejudicial. The United States as the most successful example, as well as the world's greatest power today, quite naturally harbors many of the arch-exponents of federalism, yet the essential element of the initial success was a willingness to compromise. The Constitution is the apotheosis of that spirit, for it was fashioned by men imbued with the French Enlightenment and English liberties. A world federal union, therefore, must capture a give-and-take mood, unembittered by prolonged warfare, class antagonisms, or racial disdain, admittedly a dubious prospect.

Granting this anomalous occasion, however, it would seem that the structure itself raises intrinsic difficulties. E. H. Carr, in analyzing the interplay of utopian and realistic critiques of international relations, summarizes in part by saying, "to establish methods of peaceful change is the fundamental problem of international peace and morality," [18] but by structure, by the delineation of national and superstate functions in precise terms, it would almost seem that in the federal union scheme there would be a predisposition to tension. If explicit provisions could be drawn for the division of political power, either another agency would be required to act as arbiter in case of dispute, such as the United States Supreme Court, or the judgment of the federal government must be allowed to prevail, as in Canada or South Africa. The first course raises additional problems to be compromised: Who will interpret the constitution and by

[17] See Wynner and Lloyd, *Searchlight on Peace Plans*, Parts IV and V, "Practical Attempts."

[18] Carr, *The Twenty Years Crisis*, chap. xiii.

what principles? The second course enervates the substance of a federal union and could hardly answer the perennial cries for "domestic jurisdiction" raised once again by the Netherlands in the Indonesian situation, by the Chinese and Brazilians in the Spanish question, by the Russians in the Greek question, and by the South Africans in the Indian minorities question, all brought before the United Nations.[19]

Furthermore, as William Fielding Ogburn has pointed out in a sociological analysis of world peace,[20] the two greatest difficulties in any association of nations are the adjustment of the unequal powers and the resistance to change. Perhaps they are one—and follow Carr's prescription. But the inequalities of power may be surpassed by another pejorative factor:

Governments of dissimilar principles and forms have been found less adapted to a federal coalition of any sort than those of a kindred nature. "As the confederate republic of Germany," says Montesquieu, "consists of free cities and petty states, subject to different princes, experience shows us that it is more imperfect than that of Holland and Switzerland." [21]

Finally, there is sufficient evidence that territorial divisions of power under federalism tend to a rigidity that does not respond as readily to the demands of modern economic and social interdependence. Even in the United States the region, for example, New England, the South, or the Midwest, is more expressive of the political relationship than the individual state, and the Constitutional barriers ill-suited to dynamic needs have evoked sufficient criticism [22] to doubt their efficacy on a world scale in constructing an order most likely to be upheld.

"Where Federalism has failed," writes Sir George Young, "the reason generally has been because, as an organization, its authority was insufficiently distributed and delegated, and, as

---

[19] See *International Organization*, Vol. I, No. 1, Feb., 1947.
[20] Ogburn, "The Sociological Problem," in *New Perspectives on Peace*, ed. by G. B. de Huszar.
[21] Madison, *The Federalist* (Modern Library), No. 43.
[22] See Elliot, *The Need for Constitutional Reform*.

an organism, it was not rooted in the people and so could not grow." [23] Institutionally a world federation would be most susceptible to these defects. The extreme disequilibrium of the member states today in power and in their social structure threatens any adequate distribution of authority; the initial preservation of all states depends upon the lack of giants, the slim balance of power each state wields among many conflicting ambitions until a natural integration by party interests (and party protection) takes place. So far as Young's second condition is concerned, not only does the framework, due to the intermediation of states, render a popular basis more difficult, but "no matter how noble its purpose, sane its organization, and vital its function, an agency can only succeed to the extent to which it is rooted in the emotional responses of the people." [24] Peace, as indicated before, is not a universally sustaining aspiration; however, a sense of right and wrong, a religion, a moral code, which has on occasion stirred men beyond their daily limitations, may well be. If any standard is to be a universal determinant, certainly the less rigid the departmentalization of the world, the better, again from a purely technical viewpoint.

To federate the world is not the only alternative to conquering it, for states may continue to pursue their national policies through alliances, balances of state power, international law, and the host of devices which add up to what Rappard has called "international government by persuasion." When it is argued that the latter course inevitably leads to war, increasingly devastating for mankind, it may be replied that nations, like the people who comprise them, often prefer to joust with death rather than submit to what they deem slavery.

But the greatest appeal of federation is the possibility of establishing a world government by consent, a peaceful, democratic way respecting the integrity of nations and, therefore, most likely to be accepted.

[23] Young, *Federalism and Freedom*, p. 10.
[24] Murphy, ed., *Human Nature and Enduring Peace*, p. 193.

A superficial reading of our plan [writes Fremont Rider] might give the impression that all present nations will, as such, cease to exist. . . . It would almost surely be impossible to secure the present acceptance of a new world-state organization by the people of *any* country if it were to be the fact.[25]

Albert Einstein thinks world government will come in any event, though it might be on the terms of the single victor of another world war, but he believes "it can come through agreement and through the force of persuasion alone, hence at low cost."[26]

Two obscurities need clarification here: To what extent is consent an essential part of a workable world government and to what extent is agreement a moral imperative of the federation itself? In other words, does the notion of acceptance meet the reality of the world as units of power, or it is the hope for a universal ethical doctrine.

To begin with,

The role which a state plays in international politics is by no means the result of the exercise of a free and unlimited choice on the part of those who tenant its foreign office. Behind all the vanity of dictators, the caprice of foreign ministers, and the campaign pledges of political leaders, there are certain fundamental forces which influence the conduct of their affairs.[27]

These fundamental forces are the natural interdependence of states in their economic relationship. To speak of free and unlimited choice of sovereign states in their political affairs, therefore, always means within a context of economic restriction, which may be extremely circumscribed. Before the Second World War three countries supplied 70 percent of all the iron ore; four countries possessed two thirds of all the lead; while one country alone produced more than one third of all the copper and two thirds of all the oil. When Clarence Streit

[25] Rider, *The Great Dilemma of World Organization*, p. 71.
[26] Einstein, "Atomic War or Peace," *The Atlantic Monthly*, (Boston), CLXXX (November, 1947), 29.
[27] Sharp and Kirk, *Contemporary International Politics*, p. 41.

proposed his union, in 1939, he noted that the fifteen founders together governed nearly half the human species, owned almost half the earth, ruled all its oceans, had more than 50 percent control of practically every raw essential in peace and war, did 65 percent of the world's trade, possessed virtually all the world's gold, and concluded that "the fifteen have so much power that the problem of ending the present chaos is nothing more nor less than organizing these few democracies." [28]

In the light of the tactics of the Second World War, a different interpretation must be given to such statistics, for the figures are themselves conditional upon a certain organization of the world, but what is significant is that "a reasonable equilibrium in the world distribution of productive power has been lacking since before 1914; as the result of the events of 1939–45, the international economy has been further distorted." [29] The monopolization of resources and industrial power has proceeded to such a degree in the world today that if the few leading powers should consolidate their trade, credit, and communications alone, without any recourse to military intimidation, every other state would be compelled to orient its foreign policy to the new superstate. Agreement, therefore, in respect to a workable world government, is required of a very few leading powers and nothing has illustrated this more clearly than the proceedings of the Security Council of the United Nations.

The actual consent of minor states to a federal union is an ethical consideration based upon the willingness of the major powers to permit, under their own self-restraint, as wide an area of autonomous action to each of the nations of the world as possible, despite the consequent delays, inconveniences, and inefficiencies for the giants. It is an attitude consonant with the democratic process. It is typical of British tolerance of Irish neutrality during the Second World War and American with-

[28] Streit, *Union Now*, p. 75.
[29] Hutcheson, "European Recovery Program," *Foreign Policy Reports*, XXIII (December 15, 1947), 238.

drawal from strategic positions in Panama; domestically it coincides with the status of the Opposition in Parliament or the privileges of the minority in the Senate.

The postulation of agreement or consent as a requisite must always be regarded with a wary eye. In the Union of the Soviet Socialist Republics each Union Republic has reserved the right freely to secede from the federation,[30] but a cursory examination of the national government reveals the utter impracticability of this course. Similarly, in the formation of the German Empire of 1871, the consent of Schaumburg-Lippe, one of the petty principalities, with 45,000 people, was hardly to be withheld in the face of 37,000,000 Prussians. And it would have been extremely inconvenient for Rhode Island to have remained outside the United States after 1790, when she finally agreed to join. Consent, like any election, is a matter of alternatives; the trend of international power toward an ever-increasing concentration over the recent years has gradually constrained the free choice of state action in foreign affairs.

The idea of consent is closely identified with plebiscites and nationalism, the powerful dogma of self-determination which has clamored its way to public attention in the past century, a dogma democratic in its viewpoint, but anarchical in its ultimate consequences.

Self-determination per se [writes G. B. de Huszar] will not realize any of the Four Freedoms. . . . First, the nations in question must carry out a program of internal reforms. . . . Second, self-determination should be granted only on the condition that the nation in question will cooperate economically and politically with her neighbor. . . . The existence of many small nations is not disastrous if there is cooperation among them.[31]

Now, it is apparent that the Soviet Union would affirm these dicta as well as the United States. The Russians have instituted reforms in Eastern Europe and ensured economic-political cooperation among neighbors while permitting the existence of

[30] *Constitution* (1936) *of the Union of Soviet Socialist Republics*, Art. 17.
[31] De Huszar, G. B., ed., *Persistent International Issues*, p. 212.

"many small nations." The United States, using a different procedure to be sure, economic rewards and sanctions, nevertheless has pointed its policy toward the same ends in Western Europe. Both these colossi, within limited areas, already have the power to enjoin participation in cooperative international relations so that in an age of monopoly it is only the willingness to endure criticism, to exercise self-restraint, which permits a few, narrow alternatives. Federal union by agreement is, therefore, a valid condition so long as the controlling power positively adheres to this ethical doctrine, but as a practical necessity it is only relative to the dispersal of resources and industrial power.

"When several villages are united in a single complete community large enough to be nearly or quite self-sufficing," wrote Aristotle, "the state comes into existence for the sake of a good life." [32] The Philosopher was not thinking of the sixteenth-century "stato" of Machiavelli, but the innumerable Hellenic communities of the Tarentine Gulf, the Aegean, and Asia Minor, whose physical and ethical needs were encompassed within separate *polei*, or city-church states. The universal occurrence of totems and taboos among societies of men throws a somewhat different light on the origin of communities by introducing an element of magic and mysticism apart from mere production for sustenance; furthermore, Aristotle's idea of a complete community, already outmoded by Macedonian cavalry victories over citizen soldiers, was static. But this does not diminish the wisdom of perceiving the functions of the "state" as a secular *and* spiritual force, for so long as a government is regulated according to a known law, whether revealed, traditional, or statutory, it proceeds by reference to a "good life," procuring its peace and prosperity via the accepted ethical standards of the most influential segments of the community.

Government has come to man in many guises: the despotisms

[32] *Politics* (The Jowett Translation), Book 1, chap. ii.

of Thutmosis, Darius, and the Incas are starkly similar; in many societies the family or kinship-group has been the nucleus of all social relations, making law, administering justice, disposing of property, regulating marriage, giving charity, and protecting its members from all foreign danger. The modern state has usurped nearly all these functions, and the clans of Scotland and the practice of vendetta in Corsica were recent vestigial traces of this order. Among the Bantus, as with several other primitive peoples, the gentillic organization still prevails.[33] The few wealthy and strong have formed oligarchies in all ages and climes, and in great ages of faith theocracies have flourished among the Hebrews, the East Indians, in Switzerland, Paraguay, and Massachusetts. In rare moments of history some governments have been based upon the opinion of a relatively large number of the citizens, and only since the nineteenth century on any appreciable percentage of the world's population.

The various molds of society are not immutable in themselves. They respond to the economic and psychical needs of the people contained within them, although the changes are constantly opposed by the group which secures the greatest advantage from the established forms. But it is essential to realize that the economic, the material, needs of man are not sufficient inducements to change institutions. "We are dealing partly with education in the formal sense, partly with a system of attitudes and beliefs which we call folklore, tradition or public opinion, partly with unconscious assumptions and dispositions upon which we have as yet focused but little light." [34] To comprehend the power of the state system, therefore, which is a relatively short-lived political organization of the world, or the efforts to substitute a new institution which will supersede this system, it is necessary to account for its satisfaction of emotional as well as economic requirements.

[33] See Levy-Bruhl, *Primitive Mentality;* tr. by Lilian A. Clare.
[34] Murphy, ed., *Human Nature and Enduring Peace*, p. 47.

Though the origins of the modern state are rooted in conquest and the rapacious aggrandizement of kings, concomitantly there was greater security from oppression and arbitrary justice. Under feudalism the individual or town subjected to the rule of the petty lord, unchecked or uncontested by any other power, had no relief from local despotism. In the struggle between the kings and the aristocracies it was the national force which promised succor; moreover, the rivalry enlisted other groups, hitherto repressed, and rewarded their assistance with new privileges. Thus, a Henry Tudor or a Cardinal Richelieu bolstered the mercantile class in their struggles against the nobility. The new state, then, with central leadership and facilities for extensive control, such as gunpowder, the King's Highway, and so forth, met the emerging needs for greater security and justice. Now the dread sovereigns who had vanquished the divisive forces in their kingdoms claimed not only the physical control of their people, but their spiritual guidance, and with the arrival of the democratic state this all-embracing sovereignty, once associated with a personal monarch, was transferred to "the people" or "the nation."

Hans Kohn has pointed out [35] some of the deeply-rooted prejudices of this contemporary nationalism: the belief, extolled by some philosophers, that the nation-state is the ideal form of political organization; the acceptance of nationality as a source of culture rather than the code of a class, such as medieval chivalry or eighteenth-century cosmopolitanism; the feeling that economic well-being is dependent upon a favorable balance of trade for the nation—as preached by mercantilism, which accompanied the rise of its patron; and, finally, the transfer of supreme loyalty to the nation, a recrudescence of the ancient tribal gods. At the same time the industrial revolution generated new needs and motivations which could not be met by a passive state, but required an increase in the power of the

[35] See Kohn, *World Order in Historical Perspective.*

agent of social action so that it might not only satisfy the economic welfare of its citizens but also answer their yearnings for security, equality, and unity.[36]

In stating that the rigid national state arose as a protection against the risks of an anarchical world society, David Mitrany is quite correct. He then goes on to posit that "the first institution to be redeemed for the sake of our own ultimate freedom is the national state," since it is strong enough to enslave us, but too weak to secure us equality.[37] And another, who would deliberately federalize all states as well as federate them to achieve a weakening of the nation-states, writes:

The real problem, therefore, is how to redistribute governmental power through the whole pyramid of relationships between man and man. How to convert that centralization of sovereign authority into a decentralization of sovereignty and a system for collective security.[38]

Can one institution, one division of power, be substituted for another by some *deus ex machina?* The important point is that institutions grow out of social relationships, not purely economic ones, and that as long as an institution satisfies the beliefs of a people it will be maintained. The nation-state has a specific historical development which has embodied spiritual values not easily altered in time or to be dismissed by the most logical of plans. The most cherished traditions and values for the great mass of politically conscious people still reside within their native land. To argue that "world institutions must be created" is to assume that men are utterly free beings. Man, to be sure, creates with his mind, but only after long tedious experience, and then in concert with some impulse of conduct that reaches out to a better life. He is a limited being, bound by his environment, his faith or superstitions, forever struggling under the weight of the existing social relationships. The state

[36] For a discussion of this phenomenon see Simon, *Community of the Free,* chap. iv.
[37] Mitrany, *The Progress of International Government,* p. 136.
[38] Young, *Federalism and Freedom,* pp. 20–21.

today, therefore, ought to be considered as the political manifestation of that kind of life and subject to the same inertia.

To discount the pervasive influence of the nation-state upon
the ordinary feelings of its citizens would be utterly naïve. The
state is a concrete unity; its people are visible and can communi-
cate with one another directly; they are bound by the same law
and share at least vicariously the same traditions, symbols of
authority, and reverence. Indeed, they enjoy a proud distinction from foreign citizens. The very word "alien" has connotations of hostility—even for college students.[39] On the other
hand, the plan for world government is an abstraction, and

What is abstract secures less allegiance than what is steeped in the
emotions proper to time-honored custom. Law and custom remain
psychologically the servants of a concrete culture, a body of common goods so commonly enjoyed that their protection has become
second nature.[40]

Not only affection for the state is in the balance, but also
jealousy. Although the citizens as a whole might gain peace
by means of a world government, the agents of state power, the
policy-making officials, and the top-ranking bureaucracy
within the state would have their authority curtailed. The lati-
tude of decision on interstate policy would inevitably be nar-
rowed, and consequently the domestic influence of such officers
would be reduced. Yet they are the same individuals who
would negotiate a voluntary world union. With such a paradox
in mind, Hugo Krabbe has advocated that some body within
each state be divorced from national law interests and that the
state government's monopoly of knowledge regarding international relations be broken.[41] But this again is a purely logical
construction. So long as state governments are believed to be
the best defenders of the values cherished by the citizens, the

[39] See Lippmann, *Public Opinion*, p. 50.
[40] William Ernest Hocking, "Cultural and Religious Organization in the
Future," in Howard Robinson and others, *Toward International Organization*, p. 179.
[41] Krabbe, *The Modern Idea of the State*, chap. x.

ultimate responsibility for protection is theirs, and no derogation of their authority in international relations will be tolerated.

From the foregoing remarks, however, it should not be assumed that the state is indispensable, for this would belie all
historical experience. It is only contended that its form and
function answers profound psychological needs, which cannot
be superseded by sheer logic. A world government established
by force could brusquely sweep aside the political barriers to
its authority and integration, while permitting as much local
autonomy as does not interfere with the order it requires. This
was the system of the Romans. When Christ was accused of
"perverting the nation, and forbidding to give tribute to
Caesar," [42] Pontius Pilate could evade the trial no longer, for
this matter touched the rule of empire. The Soviet Union, with
relative success, has attempted to dissociate statehood from
both nationality and race, and within the essential elements of
its state policy it has encouraged the development of the many
local cultures within its borders by guaranteeing the minority
their languages, schools, customs, folkways, and so forth.[43]

The crux of the matter for world government is the minimum superstate order to be observed and the alternatives open
to the nationalities which the union embraces. For the imposed
government the problem is simplified, but federation is a peculiarly difficult structure, since it signifies a substantial degree of
acquiescence to the regime. One presumption is that a viable
division of authority can be made, that

there should not be any one State so much more powerful than the
rest as to be capable of vying in strength with many of them combined. If there be such a one, and only one, it will insist on being
master of the joint deliberations; if there be two, they will be irre-
sistible when they agree; and whenever they differ everything will
be decided by a struggle for ascendancy between the rivals.[44]

[42] Luke 23:2.
[43] See Kohn, *Nationalism in the Soviet Union.*
[44] John Stuart Mill, *On Representative Government*, pp. 367–368.

The contemporary distribution of power in the world between the United States, the Soviet Union, and few others almost appears to thwart such an approach. Linked to this condition for federalism is the ability of states themselves to continue satisfying the material and psychical needs of their inhabitants. Without a capacity to maintain a semi-autonomous existence within the union, federalism would be a quick entry to a super-state of uncontemplated powers and policies. Moreover, "a federal polity is necessarily a legal polity," [45] a constitutional order in which the definition of rules, principles, and standards enforceable and to be enforced is a necessity. A union which would allow secession would be no union at all, yet final agreement to renounce the right of secession must entail the additional burden of clearly defined rights and liabilities.

K. C. Wheare, in his excellent study of federal government, believes that it is not only desirable that the majority of the federating units should at least have similar social and, particularly, political institutions, but "it is essential that these institutions should not be autocratic or dictatorial." [46] In the last analysis federation must elicit a high degree of moderation, a circumscribed area of what may be done by the federal government and the individual state governments with due respect to each other. It is simply not the nature of autocrats or dictators to brook limitations; inconvenience, delay, even some frustration are the price of the democratic process, and these are exactly the handicaps imposed by a federal system.

World government may be organized, then, in a number of patterns which are closely related to ideologies. If security from foreign aggression at the present time were the only criterion of political value, a superstate founded on force and dictating a minimum universal order might be the most expedient institution. But if the particular claims of nation-states are to be answered, and a willingness to share authority exists

[45] Pound, *Federalism as a Democratic Process.*
[46] *Federal Government*, p. 47.

among them, federalism offers a delicate and tenuous balance. The intricacies of each solution in a dynamic world situation, the possible modifications, and the consequences for both large and small democratic and dictatorial nation-states must be faced next.

Chapter 3

Awake! The day is coming now
That brings the sweat of anguish to the brow
Of Christians, Jews, and Pagans all!
Many a token in the sky
And on the earth shows it is nigh:
Foretold in Holy Writ withal.
The sun no longer shows
His face; and treason sows
His secret seeds that no man can detect;
Fathers by their children are undone;
The brother would the brother cheat;
And the cowled monk is a deceit,
Who should the way to Heaven direct;
Might is right, and justice there is none.
Arise! we slept, nor of the peril recked.

Sir Walther von der Vogelweide (13th century),
translated by Jethro Bithell

The Consequences of
World Government

CONTEMPLATING the tempestuous gulf between the loose-jointed United Nations and the glittering vision of world federation, more than one propagandist for peace on earth has set his sights on a less difficult target. The advocate of a more modest approach to world government would strive to organize those states which have particular interests and affiliations with each other into blocs or regions under a common roof, providing for local diversities as much as possible, but delegating responsibility for a whole area to some regional government. Ely Culbertson, for example, would divide the world into eleven groups of states, such as the Pan-American, British, Latin-European, Germanic, Russian, Chinese, and so forth, provide for an "initiating" state with the largest population in each bloc, and give it special privileges and responsibilities.[1] Coudenhove-Kalergi crusades for a Pan-European federation to be eventually united with other regional federations,[2] and W. Ivor Jennings has written a detailed plan for a Western-European government.[3] Disregarding geography and emphasizing similarity of institutions, both Lionel Curtis and Clarence Streit have proposed a bloc of democratic states.[4]

[1] Culbertson, *Total Peace*.
[2] Coudenhove-Kalergi, *Crusade for Pan-Europe*.
[3] Jennings, *Federation for Western Europe*.
[4] Curtis, *Faith and Works*, and Streit, *Union Now*.

It remained for Walter Lippmann, however, in a hard, positive advocacy of the regional concept, to reveal inadvertently the fundamental limitations of this approach to world order and peace, for while attempting to formulate a "practical" foreign policy for the United States, he has carried the zone idea to its inevitable and dangerous conclusion. What he suggests is an Atlantic Community, a Russian Orbit, a Chinese Orbit, and eventually an Indian Orbit, "for these regional groupings already exist, particularly in our own region, and they are forming elsewhere . . . only by perfecting these regional groupings can we hope to make any progress towards stabilizing international relations." [5] None of the groups should attempt to interfere with the other's internal organization. It is not suggested that this is the ultimate goal of world society, but that the United States, for its own security, must realize how far its effective action can carry and where its words are merely full of sound and fury, signifying nothing.

Now it must be admitted from the outset that the organization of the world into blocs enjoys a historical coincidence. A few great powers, with their satellites huddling behind, characterize in part the modern state system, and this disposition is undoubtedly more favorable to regionalism than a total world organization. The satisfactory integration of some sixty or seventy states over the face of the globe presents a far more arduous and complicated task than the effective coordination of either contiguous or philosophically congenial nations. Yet having stated a prevailing possibility of world organization, the inherent problems of the nation-state system are magnified, but unanswered; the dilemma of securing world peace without tyranny in an age of superpowers and mixed ideals still confronts society.

While the Federal Constitution of the United States is used as a model for world federalism, to some extent the inter-American system of the Western hemisphere is used as a model for regionalism. Since 1890 the twenty-one American republics have

[5] Lippmann, *U.S. War Aims,* pp. 188 *et seq.*

been conferring regularly on hemispheric problems of health, trade, communications, agriculture, transportation, international law, and security, to name a few subjects, and have established a permanent secretariat, the Pan-American Union, to publish statistics, furnish reports, centralize correspondence and documents, arrange conferences, and assist in drafting international conventions to implement the purposes of the collaborative system.[6] But Sumner Welles writes of inter-American consultation with commendable candor:

The system can worthily serve as a successful example of what free peoples can achieve. . . . But it cannot be taken as an exact model for an effective international organization since the inter-American agreements now in effect include no provision for the use of force to prevent or check war . . . there is no provision as to when, or how, or if, force is to be used to repel either an extra-continental aggression or aggression arising within the hemisphere itself.[7]

A notable advance in inter-American regionalism was taken at Quitandinha in the state of Rio de Janeiro, Brazil, in 1947, when the members of twenty Western Hemisphere states signed a treaty for reciprocal assistance in the event of threats or acts of aggression, either among themselves or from some non-American state. But while the Organ of Consultation under the Pact may by two-thirds vote decide upon measures such as recalling chiefs of diplomatic missions and interrupting economic-communication relations to restrain aggressors, such decisions to be binding on all signatories, there is no general police force available, nor is any state pledged to supply troops for punitive action without its express permission.[8]

The innumerable conventions on economic-social-legal mat-

---

[6] See the *Act of Chapultepec*, Inter-American Conference on Problems of War and Peace, Mexico City, March 3, 1945, for a restatement of the basic principles of the system. See also text of Charter of Organization of American States adopted at Bogota, Colombia, April, 1948. The pertinent articles on collective security are Nos. 24–25. New York *Times*, May 3, 1948.

[7] Welles, *The Time for Decision*, p. 369.

[8] See "Inter-American Treaty of Reciprocal Assistance," *Part* 3, Appendix 1, of the Final Conference Documents, especially arts. 3–22. Department of State, Publication 3016, International Organization and Conference Series 2, American Republics 1, April, 1948.

ters of common interest which have been initiated through the American conferences represent a genuine achievement, but it would be difficult to maintain that the system is responsible for peace without recognizing that extremely unstable state governments, sparse populations, and agrarian economies have made modern international warfare in this area less feasible, especially with the all-decisive power incumbent on one giant member to the north. Border disputes, nevertheless, have flared into open conflict from time to time,[9] and the Chaco War was fought between Paraguay and Bolivia from 1932 to 1935, with an estimated loss of 100,000 lives despite regional collaboration.[10] The growing power of the ambitious Argentine nation, which has almost quadrupled its population since 1900 and increased its physical volume of mining and industrial production 100 percent between 1935 and 1946 [11] has already been reflected in increased tension within the inter-American system, and this heralds further strains upon an embryonic regional arrangement.

Turning from a presumably existent regional system to a hypothetical one—such as Europe—it is even more apparent that any bloc organization of the world must face in each of its components some of the same tantalizing problems of universal organization. "There are in Europe," writes Carl Becker,

twenty distinct nations differing in racial origin, language, social customs, national character, and in many cases animated by mutual rivalries and animosities deeply rooted in past experience . . . the various peoples of Europe are not, and have never thought of themselves as being one nation, nor have they ever desired to be united under one government . . .[12]

Again the predominance of a single member, such as prewar Germany, haunts any voluntary union; the problem of har-

[9] Costa Rica and Panama, 1921; Peru and Colombia, 1932–33; Ecuador and Peru, 1938.
[10] M. W. Williams, *The People and Politics of Latin America*, p. 657.
[11] Holmes, "Latin America and the United States," *Foreign Policy Reports*, XXIII (January 15, 1948), 262–271.
[12] Becker, *How New Will the Better World Be?* p. 183.

monizing dictatorships, peasant oligarchies, and democratic republics under one government is no less difficult because the states neighbor one another; and there is no more evidence of emotional response by the ordinary citizen to "Europe" or "Pan-America" than to the League or the United Nations. Can it then be argued that "communities" exist in the Near East or in the Far East or in Africa? Let us suppose Europe to be further subdivided into Scandinavian and Germanic and Atlantic Lowland and Latin-European regions in order to eliminate the most radical differences of ideals or institutions. In 1905 Norway deliberately broke its union with Sweden; Austria was willing to join with Germany after 1918, but none of their neighbors could tolerate the federation for fear of losing their own independence; Eire has stubbornly cut its way out of the British Commonwealth of Nations; French-speaking Belgium shows little inclination to attach itself to France, and reconciling Italy and Spain under one government seems incredible. Indeed, if the division is too narrow, it will be found that the subscribing countries offer no protection to each other, and the slight benefits derived from common government may not outweigh the intense desire for self-rule.

Ideological blocs, too, have gained little ground. All the importunities of rabid American nationalists have not evoked the slightest evidence that the Canadians wish to merge with their closest friend, the United States. On this subject of fraternal organizations E. H. Carr comments: "The popularity recently enjoyed by schemes for the incorporation of Great Britain and the British Dominions in the American federation or for still wider unions with foreign states should not mislead the observer to take them seriously." There is, he maintains, a common strain of idealism and caution mixed in Anglo-American politics, "so that while idealists are listened to, applauded, and supported morally and materially, caution plays a far larger part in the eventual decisions." [13] It is curious to note that three

[13] Carr, *Conditions of Peace*, p. 180.

months before Pearl Harbor, when the democracies were struggling for their last breath, less than 7 percent of American public opinion favored an ideological federation, while more than 83 percent advocated something between "minding our own business" to taking a place of leadership in organizing world peace, "but form no actual ties with other countries." [14] Despite the experience of the Second World War and the new attacks of communism on the Western liberal order itself, in 1947 only 17 percent of the American people felt that its government should "*start plans* for a world government in which *various* countries will become member states," while the bulk of opinion supported the United Nations, and some 10 percent were still content with simple alliances.[15]

The most tenacious root of the difficulty in partitioning the world is the uncertain and disputable criterion to be applied in defining a region or a community. Some areas are economically related; some countries have firm cultural ties with others; geographical affinity or institutional similarity is an additional guide to regional orientation. When Walter Lippmann now speaks of an Atlantic Community or a Russian Orbit or a Chinese Orbit it is obviously an area deemed important by the leading powers within each of these spheres by virtue of its "defensibility" or military considerations. Yet this contradicts his own position in an earlier book which contains what seems a more logical answer.

Nor could the nuclear allies divide the globe into spheres of influence which each was free to dominate and exploit separately. For no spheres of influence can be defined which do not overlap, which could not therefore bring the great powers into conflict.[16]

And in an earlier passage:

The will of the most powerful states to remain allied is the only possible creator of a general international order.[17]

---

[14] Survey of Public Opinion, *Fortune Magazine*, XXIV (August, 1941), 78.
[15] Survey of Public Opinion, *Fortune Magazine*, March, 1947. (Italics mine.)
[16] Lippmann, *U.S. Foreign Policy*, p. 172.
[17] *Ibid.*, p. 166.

If the measuring rod of regions is the defense of great powers, who shall decide the place of the Scandinavian states, Germany, the Middle East, Korea, to name but a few places, where the interests of large powers impinge upon each other so heavily that genuine regional incorporation would be intolerable to the defense of one or the other bloc.

There is, indeed, a large and undemonstrated assumption that nation-states are willing to choose sides, yet in many cases it is the competition of the rival powers which supports state independence and profits its government. Turkish foreign policy for decades had been based on the natural contention between Russia and Britain; the independence of Poland was tenable as long as Germany and Russia could not agree; Switzerland, Belgium, and Sweden, surrounded by encroaching seas of enmity, strove to maintain an impeccable neutrality. States have frequently pursued indecisive tactics as an aid to their international bargaining power, and Argentina, China, Iran, India, and Ethiopia may gain more through intermediate policies than by outright commission to one or another bloc.

Economic ties are also confusing guides to regional formations. Aside from their irrelevance to geography, culture, and institutional brotherhood, they fluctuate with the tides of power. Hemispheric solidarity of a kind, for example, links Pan-America, but prior to the Second World War, Britain and the states of Europe accounted for approximately 45 percent of Latin American exports and imports.[18] In 1937 the United States and Germany alone sold more than 25 percent of Czechoslovakia's imports for consumption; moreover, the United Kingdom supplied six times the value of Russian imports to the Slavic nation and bought more than eight times the value of exports purchased by the Soviet Union.[19] Fifty-

[18] Holmes, "Latin America and the United States," *Foreign Policy Reports*, p. 264.
[19] *Foreign Commerce Yearbook* (Washington, D.C., U.S. Government Printing Office, 1939). See pp. 16, 121, 247, 293, and 298 for pertinent statistics; percentages are based upon dollar values of products.

seven percent of Turkish imports were secured from Germany and the United States in 1938, whereas neighboring Greece, Syria, Bulgaria, and the Soviet Union together supplied less than 5 percent by value. In the Far East, Japan and China have never constituted an economic unit, and in the South Pacific, before 1939, both New Zealand and Australia secured slightly less than half their imports from their mother country, the United Kingdom. The channels of trade have been radically altered by the defeat of Japan and Germany. To define a region in economic terms is a slippery task.

Beyond this obstacle, however, no region can be fully "self-sufficient," for as long as the globe contains additional resources which enhance the power and welfare of men there will be an incentive to inter-regional trade; but economic blocs with political power could monopolize their resources more effectively and restrain inter-regional trade with as heavy a penalty on the local nation-state as is imposed upon the individual consumer under high tariffs, domestic monopolies, and unregulated international cartels. Dr. Hubert Ripka, former Czechoslovakian minister of state, has made a stirring defense of the small nation. He pointedly answers the critics who maintain that "balkanization" is the root of economic nationalism and political selfishness leading to conflict by a comparison of those same qualities in large states and their particular responsibility for outbreaks of world wars. On the problem of economic regionalism he notes:

The artificial creation of groups of nations and federations, far from solving the economic problem, would merely aggravate it. Just because the resources at its disposal are less limited a federation would be more readily tempted than a small country to become self-supporting and to pursue an economic policy which is purely national. . . . The remedy is to be found in organizing economic collaboration on the world scale in which large and small nations can participate. . . . While the federation of a certain number of small states brings with it no solution whatever of the economic problem, it can in certain cases, actually hide a danger . . . as a pretext for an expansionist Great Power which, by encouraging the federation of a certain region, would more easily dominate the countries which form a part of it.[20]

Another writer who has made a comparative study of organizations in actual existence finds that the regional groupings "have been no more successful on the whole than the universal unions" and "not only is regionalism a reactionary principle . . . but it also tends to sanctify, crystallize, and institutionalize elements of selfishness and opposition to the general welfare which, if not thus dignified, might gradually be eliminated or assimilated." [21]

The mere fact that regional economic or ideological associations seem easier to obtain is no indication of their superiority over universal organization, for in fact it must be recognized that they do not answer the fundamental problem of establishing a world-wide law. Instead, they tend to promote semi-rigid divisions of moral and economic life and to demarcate the rivalries of the international scene more sharply. Two equally balanced monster blocs are in no way more conducive to peace than are several fairly strong units. A balance of power must be created under any system of government in order to deter arbitrariness and despotism, and it is strongly suggested that an equilibrium of regions may be less stable than a world with a few dozen relatively independent states.

As an analysis of regionalism proceeds, gradually penetrating to the core of the problem of world organization, it becomes evident that the proposed blocs must have recourse to some machinery beyond themselves to coordinate their inescapable relations. But as soon as this is admitted, world society is returned to the fundamental problem of agreement upon an om-

[20] Ripka, *Small and Great Nations*, pp. 10–11. Dr. Ripka supports his thesis that the rise of new smaller states in Central Europe neither brought about nor increased economic difficulties in Europe or the world by analyzing and comparing the foreign trade and agricultural-mining-industrial production of Austria-Hungary with the Succession States.
[21] Potter, "Universalism versus Regionalism in International Organization," *American Political Science Review*, XXXVII (October, 1943), 856–858.

nipotent arbiter who will justly settle the arguments generated by such a dynamic community. "Anything less than a universal order," says Robert MacIver quite bluntly, "is no order at all. Anything short of a universal order is doomed from the start." [22] Regions may rightly be regarded as a useful means for the decentralization of world government; but whatever authority is constituted to govern all the regions must, on the one hand, be able to permeate through the group government to the citizens of the bloc and, on the other hand, overrule the regional governments on several important matters. The two conditions are intertwined and indispensable.

In a chapter on the conditions and methods of lasting peace Sir William Beveridge has ably expressed the familiar doctrine of the necessity for a world-wide rule of law; this, in turn, signifies the establishment of some agency for its declaration, with power to enforce its judicial decisions. Those who wield such force "must regard themselves as trustees for international order, not as agents for any particular nation." [23] Now, whether the participating unit of a world order be a state or a group of states, the armed forces which are to insure this order must derive their authority, their sustenance, their equipment, their bases from the whole community; otherwise they have no choice but to serve as particular agents of their local creators, suppliers, and administrators. In this sense there never has been an "international army," although collaboration, joint strategy, and the pooling of resources have been quite common, for the ultimate authority and disposition of national armies depends upon nations acting through their governments. Blowing this apparatus up to regional size, substituting regional armies, does not change the principle with regard to world law enforcement.

It is the Federal Government in the United States which has power to provide for the common defense, raise and support

---

[22] MacIver, *Towards an Abiding Peace*, p. 135.
[23] Beveridge, *The Price of Peace*, p. 54.

armies, provide and maintain a navy, provide for organizing, arming, and disciplining the militia, and which exercises authority over all places, once purchased by consent of the states, to be used for forts, dockyards, and arsenals.[24] The Swiss Confederation, which is forbidden to maintain permanent troops, nevertheless limits the cantons to three hundred men each, makes military service compulsory, has the right to dispose of the army and war material, the exclusive right to dispose of all military resources in case of danger, and is responsible for the military instruction and armaments of the army.[25] A world army needs just such grants of authority. Since it must reach down through regional governments to individual enlistment and discipline, and have a virtual monopoly of fighting equipment and the control of innumerable bases in all locations, the organization will have to transcend boundaries, direct and judge personnel without regard to their local governments, and establish independent facilities unrestricted by state or regional law. Nor is this all. "The fighting force of your *international* police force would be worth absolutely nothing . . . unless it had behind it that industrial power which in the last analysis can only be national." [26] Put in this light, a world army demands an integrated economy responsive to the regulation of one government, a government enabled to exert war powers over industrial and labor mobilization similar to the practices of modern industrial nations in times of emergency. Accompanying these potentialities would be the necessary measures of central intelligence and propaganda, all part and parcel of any effective security force in contemporary political life.

Certainly none of these tremendous transfers of function from state or regional governments to world agencies begins to be possible until the various peoples of the world are willing to divide their allegiance between local and universal govern-

[24] *U.S. Constitution*, art. 1, sec. 8.
[25] *Federal Constitution of the Swiss Confederation*, art. 13-20.
[26] George Fielding Eliot, "Defense of International Order," in Robinson and others, *Toward International Organization*, p. 102.

ment, deciding, in some instances at least, that their blood and treasure should be dedicated to the larger purpose, regardless of or despite the decision of their more proximate community. Imperceptibly, but surely, the problems of regionalism creep back to the problems of federalism, for they both face the greater issue of pouring mortar into the numberless interstices of a new world structure which requires indivisible strength. In 1920 Colonel Vestal summed it up this way.

The government of the world, like that of each country, must be able to address itself to the hopes and fears of individuals; and to attract to its support those passions which have the strongest influence on the human heart. It must, in short, possess all the means and have a right to resort to all the methods, of executing the powers with which it is entrusted, that are possessed and exercised by the governments of the earth today. It must be capable of living and carrying on its functions without the aid or intervention of any subordinate government.[27]

To speak of "international government," therefore, is as paradoxical as "international armies," and Leonard Woolf correctly drew the distinction between an international state or Bundesstaat and a confederation of States or Staatenbund. Admitting that the nation for a long time would remain the nexus of patriotic sentiment, he nevertheless reasoned that "the most vital interests of human beings are hardly ever national, almost always international." [28] Such interests Mr. Woolf—with his fellow Fabians—construed to be economic. The solution, then, was to have one international organization, based upon states, in which the majority might bind the minority except on questions of independence, territorial integrity, or alteration of domestic laws. At the same time various public unions, based upon "international interests" such as communications, transportation, trade, credit, and so forth would continue to develop their practices of fulfilling the needs of the community, miti-

[27] Vestal, *The Maintenance of Peace*, p. 85.
[28] Woolf, *International Government*, p. 354.

gating economic-social conflicts, and building a solid, functional basis for a new world order.

There is no objection to this view as long as its inherent dichotomy and limitations are recognized. In many respects the League and the United Nations have proceeded along such lines. But world government, unitary or federal, cannot tolerate a separation of economic from political powers as, indeed, no modern government can, for decisions about communication facilities, transport, trade, and monetary matters on a hustling, crowded planet cannot fail to invade the sanctified zones in which states claim omnicompetence and independence. H. G. Wells gives a good illustration of this symbiotic relationship when he probes Mr. Streit's blithe assumption of a common money for his federal union.[29] National credit manipulation, they agree, is a major source of international conflict, but in a union, unless the whole fiscal policy is controlled by one government, the same abuses are immanent; moreover, a common money is impossible unless its purchasing power is nearly equalized, but this, in turn, calls for a comparable economic system, else money, subject to different profit rates, would assume different values; in addition, the danger of vast world monopolies under private ownership and the incompatibility of such free enterprise with a mass democracy indicates far-reaching government regulation beyond the present experience or expectation of the liberal states.

The sharpest objection to obscurities in defining world government and its implications is the false expectation aroused by the splendid verbiage in which international organizations are clothed and the subsequent embittered chagrin when their feeble structure collapses under an intolerable burden; there

[29] Wells, *The New World Order*, chap. 7, and Streit, *Union Now*, "The monetary problem, now so perplexing from a short range view, would be among the easier problems for The Union. It would be mainly a question of establishing a common Union currency and pooling behind it the existing reserves of the member democracies . . ." p. 216.

is, too, the calamity that may befall those who are lured into shallow security by the proud emblems of a new organization, only to meet an unexpected crash when hidden conflicts break through the surface of peace; finally, there is the blind labor toward a world government which, undefined, may be a Frankenstein monster, created for good, but turned to evil.

Professor Rappard, in his lecture to the Geneva Institute of International Relations in 1931, devoted much of his time to a clarification of terms, arguing that if a nation does yield to the authority of another government, international government is not the correct description. "Either there is a government, and then it is not international, but supernational . . . or there are independent nations and then there is no international government." [30] This does not preclude international cooperation and international organization, with its concomitant rules of international "law," but thrusts the whole discussion of what has been done, can be done, and ought to be done for world government into its true perspective. No one disputes the commendable achievements of the International Labor Organization, for example, and its provision for the direct representation of labor and management as well as governments in its conferences is a cheerful omen. Before World War I only two labor conventions had been effectuated in a whole generation whereas five years after the establishment of the ILO by the Versailles Treaty sixteen conventions were in operation among several states. But it must be noted that any convention to become effective requires ratification and enforcement by the national government within its own borders. Furthermore, although sixty-seven conventions had been approved by conferences up to 1946, only thirty-two states had ratified more than ten of them, and apart from remonstrances for bad faith no device for enforcing such treaties is available. For example, the 1937 Conference of the ILO approved a convention fixing the

[30] William E. Rappard, "The Beginnings of World Government," in Geneva Institute of International Relations, *Problems of Peace*, Fifth Series, pp. 9 *et seq.*

minimum age for employment in industrial occupations at fifteen. Four years later, only China and Norway had ratified this convention.[31]

Whatever form or force world government may take, the organization will be an integrated one, united in the purpose, scope, and execution of its principles, for anything less will not be world government, but an alliance or a retractable agreement among states. The next step, once this simple but essential point is clarified, is to recognize how thoroughly such integration may extend and under what circumstances it may be accomplished.

In all societies unification is sought for some purpose. The joining of private industrial enterprises is directed toward cheaper production and larger profits; consumers combine in cooperatives to increase purchasing power and reduce prices. Philatelists meet to trade stamps, and politicians adhere to parties to secure public office. The association of men in an organization—whether economic, cultural, or political—presupposes a common object, and the attainment of this object has prior claim over individual aberrations. In his analysis of the pluralist concept of society, de Maeztu wrote,

For what is the common characteristic of all societies, be they States, limited companies or football clubs? That men are associated for a common object. . . . It is only because there is a thing which several men find good that associations are possible.[32]

The state, however, is a special kind of organization, since its purposes are more extensive and encompassing than those of any other. It provides the loom upon which the materials of daily life are woven. It permits or ignores or forbids the economic and social life of its citizens within the framework of its constitution, but upon certain points it is resolute, for they

---

[31] Otis E. Mulliken, "Labor," in De Huszar, ed., *Persistent International Issues*, p. 200. Also Hudson, *International Legislation*, VII, 783, for descriptions of this convention and details of ratification.
[32] De Maeztu, *Authority, Liberty, and Function in the Light of War*, Part II, chap. iv, reprinted in Spahr, *Readings in Recent Political Philosophy*, p. 521.

are the marrow of the constitution itself. In one state the parliamentary process may be the root of society, in another the primacy of one class or group, in another certain institutions may be inviolable. If the constitution is democratic, the people as a whole reject or approve these tenets, while under an authoritarian regime the élite which operates the mechanism of coercion perseveres in its chosen program. People, to the best of their ability, merge their wills and fortunes to carry out some purpose in all such associations; if they fail to find a suitable program, separation, discord, rancor, or civil war must follow —depending upon the extent of the breach. It may then be asked, what definition of purpose has been elaborated or proved acceptable for world government?

One author writes, "The purpose of federalism is wider union for wider power for wider law for wider order and planning," for once we have controlled all the markets, distribution facilities, trade, finance "such a mighty economic instrument supreme in the world can advance democracy in a widened radius to be regularized later on by any constitutional changes thought necessary"; [33] and K. Zilliacus declares, "there should be no fooling around. . . . This time we must have a single, comprehensive world organization that absorbs and integrates all international institutions serving any useful purpose." [34] These comments are like many other glib assertions that the "democratic order" is to be extended once a wider union and wider control is invested in some central authority. The democratic order is rarely dressed in precise terminology applicable to particular states, but, beyond this, the notion hinges on some tacit assumptions about the nature of the executive power and its manner of regulating huge enterprises. If the atmosphere for the operation of this mechanism is sought, there are several constant but vague references to "international justice and fair

[33] Mousley, *The Democratic Advance*, pp. 153, 165.
[34] K. Zilliacus, "World Government and World Peace," in Ransome, *Studies in Federal Planning*, p. 352.

play." [35] A harping on hackneyed phrases like "justice under law," democratic processes," and "peaceful order" and then a hasty plummet into details of structure may be dramatic, but not too helpful in solving the problem of finding a substantial agreement or platform for a world association.

Indeed, governments have found narrow programs upon which some concerted positive action could take place: for example, the International Sugar Convention between 1903 and 1913 could, by majority vote, compel the alteration or modification of sugar tariffs by its members; and the Rhine treaties of 1804, 1815, 1831, and 1868 all followed the principle of an international commission to hear appeals from local Rhine courts in complaints regarding river navigation, tolls, and so forth.[36] But a world government needs a much broader consensus, for in addition to the simple economic and productive associations which may be formed as nuclei of specific agreements, there is required some all-embracing agreement on procedures for improving, directing, and altering the entire system and on the social goal to be attained. To do this, however, introduces indispensable political and ethical factors, for apropos of creating political institutions for international life, Norman Angell correctly observes that "the acceptance of the principles of third party judgment . . . is the only possible basis of peace; that even that cannot operate until there is some agreement as to 'what is right.' " [37] The formulation of consent to a common objective is hardly enough; there must be an understanding on the means of procuring it. A thief and a merchant may both pursue similar economic satisfactions, but the difference in procedure brands one as an outlaw; he is ar-

---

[35] For example, Lord Lothian writes in the vein of those who deplore the anarchy of international life, traces its cause to the sovereignty of states, and blandly pleads for an organism representative of all, acting for the benefit of all, under one law, "based on moral principle," uniting and governing the whole earth—without ever inquiring into that moral principle. "The Ending of Armageddon," in Ransome, *ibid.*, pp. 8–9.

[36] See Sayre, *Experiments in International Administration*, especially chap. v.

[37] Angell, *The Unseen Assassin*, p. 106.

rested by the police for his refusal to recognize society's agreement on "what is right."

If the local police act in consequence of a common agreement on the state level, no less is it true that a world police is impossible without a consensus on standards to be enforced under all circumstances by the combined strength of the world.

> There cannot be an "international police" until there is an international executive. The police everywhere is merely the arm of the executive authority; it is a perversion of sense to try to provide the arm when the body to which it is to be attached, and by which it is directed, does not yet exist.[38]

Such an executive, moreover, would be animated by a common goal and means of achieving that goal; it would have a plan for society and a mode of implementation; the world executive would need not only agreement on what "functions" are to be raised to world control, but in what manner the ordering of the universe should be conducted. In essence, the world executive, gradually extending its regulations to commerce, finance, communications, natural resources, and so forth, would personify a single philosophy of government.

This begins to be dangerous. The philosophy of government which the available force supports may not coincide with the values dear to a particular people. It is in this light that Percy Corbett writes, "I would have grave misgivings about any monopoly of force in a universal government until we have gone much further in the development of common values,"[39] for it soon becomes evident that the operative ideals in any government will depend upon those who wield power. In a literal sense, might does make right: that is, they who control the force of any society set the standards of conduct for their association, and there is the threatening likelihood that once a giant network of universal economic-political control is established, the mechanism may be more easily captured and

[38] Royal Institute of International Affairs, *International Sanctions*, p. 130.
[39] Percy E. Corbett, "Power and Justice," in H. Morgenthau, *Peace, Security, and the UN*, p. 23.

dominated by a single government completely alien to the traditions and beliefs of other regions.

This contingency has been effectively prevented thus far by the state system which strives to divide power. At the same time, and this is the frightful dilemma, it is the division of power which makes the emergence of common ethics more difficult. In the old Roman-Christian family of nations, at least there was some consideration of the universal Law of Nature, the moral imperative which rational men are bidden to observe, but the expansion of the community to include Prussia, Russia, Turkey, and the Orient, and the impact of industrial-nationalism jarred this feeble concept loose. "Legitimacy" of 1815 and "self-determination" in 1919 were superficial rallying cries, but hardly pervasive principles of human conduct. On this subject Martin Wright posed a puzzling question: "the idea of a common interest can never have much vitality if it is separated from a common obligation. . . . It may, indeed, be asked whether an effective common ethos is likely to grow up again without an effective common government." [40]

If the monopoly of force, however, is achieved by an authoritarian, dogmatic government, it may be an effective government, and peace, in the short run, will be more likely, since integration will proceed to the most minute details: every aspect of the world economy or social life would be under constant surveillance, precluding the likelihood of all combinations, either material or moral, which might successfully wage war. "If you are out to produce a dead world, a mechanical world, that system may work, but if you are out to produce a world which has more life in it, more personality, more happiness, you have to set to work in a different direction." [41] In effect there must be some safeguard for the existence of different values, though not at the sacrifice of an all-inclusive principle upon which a universal society can be built. The world

[40] Martin Wright, *Power Politics*, pp. 63–65.
[41] A. E. Zimmern, "Education for World Citizenship," in Geneva Institute of International Relations, *Problems of Peace*, Fifth Series, p. 309.

federalists attempt to secure this guarantee by a structural manipulation, but, as has been indicated, it was not the federal structure which established the American or Swiss or Australian "compromise, conservatism, and legalism—at once the virtues and vices of federal government," [42] but those historical attributes which coalesced into a federal system. For example, many of the new Latin-American states which achieved their independence between 1810 and 1825 modeled their constitutions on the United States' instrument of 1787, but the operation of these paper documents, leading to a succession of military dictatorships, indicates that the real source of democratic government lies in the capacity of the citizens to govern in both a uniform and self-restrained manner regardless of forms.

Unless it is possible for states to unite on a principle of government (rather than a form) which tolerates heterodox values, but insists upon a fundamental morality, world government may well come in the guise of imperium or dictatorship. The difficulty of modern government, even in the most liberal states, in giving free play to dissenting opinions and private opposition to the public demand is apparent. Zechariah Chafee writes:

> Modern democratic society is in the greatest crisis of its history, because new conditions have been rapidly created by a technical civilization. The issue is whether the old ideal of a free society can be maintained against the hazards presented by these conditions. Men are constantly called upon to learn over again how to live together. It is a hard task. When unprecedented disputes and difficulties confront them, they repeatedly turn for help to the government, as the recognized umpire. All the traditional liberties are subjected to novel strains. . . .[43]

The desire for efficient mass production has its concomitants of single-purpose direction (bureaucratization) and the outpourings of material wealth potentially available for all who are willing to oust old ethical traditions for new economic

---

[42] K. C. Wheare, "What Federal Government Is," in Ransome, *Studies in Federal Planning*, p. 37.
[43] Chafee, *Government and Mass Communication*, pp. 10–11.

evaluations. A world government faced with the coordination of vast resources, a myriad of communication and trade facilities, and other giant economic challenges which must be met by general solutions will certainly be subject to the same tendencies to stereotype its society by constantly widening the sphere of world jurisdiction at the expense of local predilections. Only the positive affirmation of a way of life which includes self-restraint and a high respect for individuality actually demonstrated by the conduct of those states whose force is requisite to establishing such a universal order can lead directly, though not necessarily, to a liberal world government.

Assuming that such an integration can take place, however, the consequences of world government are not guaranteed peace, for peace is not an objective in itself, but the result of continuous skilled adaptation to the dynamic processes of life. If world government turns international war into an anachronism by abolishing nations, it by no means eliminates the natural functions of life and the normal instincts of men. Frictions will always appear in the process of change; government is an instrument by which man can implement his self-denying propensities and mitigate such frictions. If such moral qualities exist in a society and world government were directed as an instrument of compromise, the possibility of peace would be enhanced; if not, cataclysmic civil wars, fragmentation, and anarchy can result from world government as well as any other.

The mere prevention of war is scarcely enough. An immediate remedy for war can be found in transferring all power to absolute government or following a course of nonresistance. But though there may be nothing pleasant about war in its actual process, nevertheless it serves an important and indispensable function in a society which cannot agree upon its hierarchy of values, a society which refuses to suit the exigencies of moral or material changes. Men count their genuine achievements, indeed their happiest freedoms, on a long calen-

dar of rebellions, revolutions, and full-scale wars. "The meek
do not inherit the earth," wrote Harold Laski, "unless they are
prepared to fight for their meekness. Justice does not come to
reign unless those who care for its coming are prepared to insist
upon its value." [44] One British philosopher, although a pacifist
by inclination, concludes a paper by saying that

Liberalism . . . is the only philosophy that can be adopted by a
man who . . . demands some scientific evidence for his beliefs
. . . and . . . human happiness. . . . For without these beliefs
life on our politically divided but technically unified planet will
hardly continue to be possible.[45]

In this way he rallies his sympathetic fellows to a banner which
they will gladly carry into battle, seeing war, not as a vicious
practice of mankind, but as a great and necessary crusade for
a "better" world.

World government, with or without war, can be better only
insofar as it meets criteria which may be universally agreeable
and are implemented by corresponding institutions. Unless all
parties start their measurement of progress from the same point,
it is simply impossible to gauge what practice of government
is superior to another, and before one can discuss the applica-
bility of a single basing-point to historically heterogeneous
populations, there are more prying questions: What guides to
the amelioration of mankind's lot are available? What signposts
of progress should world government follow?

[44] Laski, *The Dangers of Obedience*, p. 29.
[45] Russell, *Philosophy and Politics*, p. 21. See *Which Way to Peace* for Mr.
Russell's pacifist sentiments.

Part Two

THE PROGRESS OF WORLD GOVERNMENT

Chapter 4

Nature and Nature's laws lay hid in night;
God said: "Let Newton be," and all was light.

Alexander Pope

The Idea of Progress

THE CLEAREST DIVERGENCE of modern society from the past ages is shown by the idea of creating a better world on this earth. Not merely the restoration of some golden age or the incarnation of an immanent order of the universe, not a resignation to the cyclical upswings and relapses of history, perhaps retarded or softened by some wise legislator, but an actual accretion of knowledge utilized for the constant improvement of all mankind distinguishes the approach to the problems of life some time after the Renaissance from the speculations of the medieval period and classical antiquity.[1]

When René Descartes, early in the seventeenth century, wrote,

[1] See, for example, the search for absolutes in Plato, especially the *Republic*, the *Symposium*, and the *Phaedo;* Aristotle's preoccupation with ideal states and revolutions in the *Politics;* Polybius speaks of "the regular cycle of constitutional revolutions, and the natural order in which constitutions change, are transformed, and return again to their original stage" in his *History* (Book 6, sec. 9); Lucretius concludes the fifth book of *On the Nature of Things* with, "time by degrees brings each several thing forth before men's eyes and reason raises it up into the borders of light . . . until these have reached their highest point of development . . ." but his writings on the whole emphasize the fruitless, ephemeral qualities of life—so evident in his poems, "No Single Thing Abides" and "Against the Fear of Death"; St. Augustine warned, "the earthly city . . . shall not be everlasting . . . the peace which we enjoy in this life . . . is rather the solace of our misery than the positive enjoyment of our felicity" (Book 15, chap. 4, and Book 19, chap. 27), and this dirge was followed by subsequent churchmen; even in sixteenth-century Machiavelli there is still the yearning for one wise legislator, reiterations on the cyclical theory of governments, and omnipresent uncertainty personified by the goddess, Fortune (chap. xxix, *Discourses*).

The long chain of simple and easy reasonings by means of which geometers are accustomed to reach the conclusions of their most difficult demonstrations, had led me to imagine that all things, to the knowledge of which man is competent, are mutually connected in the same way . . .

he was stating the possibility of ascertaining truth by the application of sound reasoning, essentially a deductive or mathematical process, to the immutable basic laws of nature. The novelty, of course, was the complete disregard for the canons of ancient authority and the exposition of a way, open to all thinking men, by which it would "be possible to arrive at knowledge highly useful in life . . . and thus render ourselves the lords and possessors of nature." [2]

Cartesianism was a method for advancing knowledge; yet if rationalism could be used for adding to mankind's intellectual reservoir, why could not the searching inquiry of a disciplined mind be turned on the foibles, the prejudices, the ignorance of society itself? Why could not this method penetrate not only the wonders of the physical universe but also the causes of human misery? Enlightenment, then, in the eighteenth century, was to be the clue to progress, and Diderot, d'Alembert, and Holbach responded to the challenge. Voltaire, the great iconoclast of the age, wrote to Frederick of Prussia, "We are not born solely to read Plato and Leibnitz, to measure curves and to arrange facts in our heads; we are born with hearts which must be filled, with passions which must be satisfied . . ." [3] One more question remained: Was human nature malleable? The mere elaboration of hitherto obscure facts about the processes of life outside man and relating to man was useless for improving society unless man himself could profit from his experience, unless his nature, long perverted by its past en-

[2] René Descartes, "Discourse on Method," in Commins and Linscott, *The Philosophers of Science*, pp. 172, 203–204.
[3] *Letters of Voltaire and Frederick the Great*, tr. by R. Aldington, p. 64. This letter was written April 17, 1737.

counters, could respond to a new environment. For this obstacle to progress John Locke, among others, had an apt answer:

Let us suppose the mind to be, as we say, white paper, void of all characters, without any ideas. How comes it to be furnished? . . . Whence has it all the materials of reason and knowledge? To this I answer, in one word, From *experience* . . .[4]

Or, carried one step further by a contemporary who foreshadowed the utilitarian school of philosophers which was to emphasize "greater happiness" as a principle of progressive legislation,

. . . though it be necessary to solve the principal actions of human life to suppose a moral sense . . . and also public affections; yet I deny that this moral sense, or these public affections, are innate or implanted in us. They are acquired, either from our own observations or the imitation of others.[5]

The philosophy of the eighteenth century, therefore, was pregnant with the perfectibility of man and the elevation of society. Progress was in the air—spiritually, economically, politically. The devastating shafts of Holbach, Diderot, and Voltaire were piercing the orthodox religions.[6] The physiocrats were joined with Adam Smith in saying that laissez faire, laissez passer, would enable "the progress of society towards real wealth and greatness." [7] In America a new kind of commonwealth had been established. In France the Great Revolution fanned the imagination of Europe to heated speculation on the emerging freedom of man. Condorcet had no doubt that the

[4] John Locke, "Essay on Human Understanding," Book 2, chap. 1, sec. 1, in Rand, *Modern Classical Philosophies*.
[5] John Gay, "Concerning Virtue or Morality," Conclusion, in Burtt, *The English Philosophers*. See also E. B. de Condillac, *Treatise on the Sensations*, for a French representative of this approach.
[6] See Voltaire's *The Questions of Zapata* or Diderot's *Conversation of a Philosopher with the Marechale de X* or Holbach's *System of Nature* for typical illustrations.
[7] Adam Smith, *Wealth of Nations*, Book 4, chap. 9.

human race would continually improve itself through its intellectual achievements and the realization of natural rights,[8]
while Kant, though disdaining "happiness" as a motivation,
nevertheless postulated a *telos* for society in which the moral
freedom of man would be realized under law, since the inherent
conflicts of nature impelled man to establish a universal, peaceful constitution.[9]

The nineteenth century was prepared to test the hypothesis
of progress, and its amazing record of intellectual advancement,
technical improvements, and increased comforts for mankind
buttressed the idea in unmistakable terms. Even the most scanty
description of the innovations between the Napoleonic Wars
and 1913 is remarkable: the railroad, the steamship, the motor
car, the airplane, the telegraph, the wireless, the electric motor,
the gas stove, the dynamo, the incandescent lamp, the camera,
anesthetics, and antiseptics are but a few. Physics, chemistry,
and astronomy began to fill in their huge gaps of ignorance;
geology, archaeology, anthropology, and psychology as organized sciences were born.[10] New agricultural and industrial
techniques coupled with cheaper transportation-communication facilities promoted exchange and multiplied wealth. A. N.
Whitehead wrote that the process of change in the nineteenth
century was different from all the past in that it was quick,
conscious, and expected. "The greatest invention of the

[8] Jean de Condorcet, "Outlines of an Historical View of the Progress of the
Human Mind," Tenth Epoch, in *Contemporary Civilization Source Book*,
Part I, sec. 9 (New York: Columbia University Press, 1941): "Will not every
nation one day arrive at the state of civilization attained by those people who
are the most enlightened, most free, most exempt from prejudices, as the
French, for instance, and the Anglo-Americans? Will not the slavery of countries subjected to kings, the barbarity of African tribes, and the ignorance of
savages gradually vanish? Is there upon the face of the globe a single spot the
inhabitants of which are condemned by nature never to enjoy liberty, never
to exercise their reason?"
[9] See Kant's essay "Eternal Peace," in Friedrich, *Inevitable Peace* and *ibid.*,
chap. 5, "The Idea of Progress," for Kant's position.
[10] For a magnificent survey of nineteenth-century achievements in fourteen
fields of human endeavor see Wallace and others, *The Progress of the Century.*

19th Century was the invention of the method of invention. ⌐
. . . It is a process of disciplined attack upon one difficulty after another" not only in technology but, as the Germans of the period demonstrated, in scholarship itself.[11]

The profound reaction to the new industrial civilization, with its increasing army of wage earners, of course, was socialism; but despite its radical attacks upon existing institutions, it fastened itself quite naturally and enthusiastically to the creed of an emerging, beneficent social order.

National differences and antagonisms between peoples are daily more and more vanishing, owing to the development of the bourgeoisie, to freedom of commerce, to the world market. . . . The supremacy of the proletariat will cause them to vanish still faster.[12]

Two difficulties for the concept of progress remained. First, the phenomena of change and advance were manifest, yet could anyone predict, as in the other sciences, the rules governing society itself, the stages through which mankind advances, and thereby utilize the evidence of progress? Comte, following Saint-Simon, replied that the present disorder of society was caused by the simultaneous existence of three incompatible philosophies—theological, metaphysical, and positive, that knowledge passes through these three stages and positive philosophy is bound to prevail.

It is time to complete the vast intellectual operation begun by Bacon, Descartes, and Gallileo, by constructing the system of general ideas which must henceforth prevail among the human race. This is the way to put an end to the revolutionary crisis which is tormenting the civilized nations of the world.[13]

[11] Whitehead, *Science and the Modern World*, pp. 141 *et seq.*
[12] Marx, *The Communist Manifesto*. The philanthropic, humanitarian approach to elevating society is represented by Robert Owen, *A New View of Society;* the extremely radical, anarchistic view is represented by Piotr A. Kropotkin, *Conquest of Bread,* chap. 2, sec. 1: "Well-being for all is not a dream. It is possible, realizable, owing to all that our ancestors have done to increase our powers of production." Reprinted in Spahr, *Readings in Recent Political Philosophy*.
[13] Comte, *The Positive Philosophy*, translated by Harriet Martineau, Vol. I, chap. 1.

In other words, social relationships can be subjected to the same analysis as natural phenomena, their laws formulated, and their activity controlled for the continued advance of civilization.

The second difficulty of early nineteenth-century optimism was the want of a satisfactory explanation for the very process of change. The inertia of an original creation of species idea, essentially a theological dogma, weighed heavily on the reflection of most people when it came to imagining a genuine metamorphosis of either individuals or society. Darwin's theory of evolution clinched the argument for the possibility of mutation. Nevertheless, as Bury has pointed out,[14] evolution, applied to society, does not necessarily mean the amelioration of man's lot—unless it can be demonstrated that social life actually obeys the same evolutionary principles as nature and that it also signifies an increase of human happiness. Darwin, however, finished his work on an optimistic note.

. . . as natural selection works solely by and for the good of each being, all corporeal and mental endowments will tend to progress toward perfection. There is grandeur in this view of life . . . from so simple a beginning endless forms most beautiful and most wonderful have been and are being evolved.[15]

And Herbert Spencer, the most popular English philosopher of the late nineteenth century, widened the principle of evolution to embrace the whole of society. For him, evolution meant advance from the simple to the complex, "from an indefinite, incoherent homogeneity to a definite, coherent homogeneity." He believed that a giant orderly plan was gradually emerging from the adaptation of all organisms to their environment, tending toward a complete development of their potentialities and a successful harmony of life.

. . . it is seen in the evolution of humanity, whether contemplated in the civilized man, or in the assemblage of races; it is seen in the

14 Bury, *The Idea of Progress*, pp. 335–336.
15 Darwin, *The Origin of Species*, pp. 428–429.

evolution of Society, in respect alike of its political, religious, and its economical organization.[16]

At last the gospel of Progress knew no limits. Reason had first opened a vast, inexhaustible treasure house of knowledge, then directed its intelligence toward the nature of society, and found human nature plastic and responsive. From this it was a short step to either "Social Physics," as Comte called it, or a magnificent panorama of life unfolding its complicated, adaptable, harmonious mechanism to the demands of the environment.

International political relations were no less a part of this balmy atmosphere of progress. Above everything else the intellectual-economic revolution of the eighteenth-nineteenth centuries stimulated trade, widened markets, and prompted those agreements among nation-states which would facilitate commerce. As early as 1804 France and the moribund Holy Roman Empire entered into a treaty fixing uniform tolls on the Rhine River traffic instead of the many irregular local levies which hamstrung shipping along that route.[17] In 1815 the General Treaty of Vienna dealt extensively with the free navigation of rivers in Poland (Article XIV), the commerce of the Ems and port of Embden (Article XXX), navigation of the Po (Article XCIV), and in addition declared that "the powers whose states are separated or crossed by the same navigable River engage to regulate by common consent all that regards its navigation . . . the Rivers . . . shall be entirely free, and shall not, in respect to commerce, be prohibited to anyone." [18]
Under Articles 15 to 18 of the Treaty of Paris, 1856, the prin-

[16] Herbert Spencer, "First Principles of a New System of Philosophy," chap. xv, sec. 126, in Rand, *Modern Classical Philosophies*, p. 723.
[17] See Sayre, *Experiments in International Administration*, pp. 132–141, for a history of Rhine River administration through the nineteenth century, as well as other international river commissions.
[18] Articles CVIII, CIV, General Treaty between Great Britain, Austria, France, Portugal, Prussia, Russia, Spain, and Sweden, signed at Vienna, June 9, 1815, reprinted in Oakes and Mowat, *The Great European Treaties of the Nineteenth Century*, pp. 37 et seq.

ciples of the Vienna Congress were extended to the Danube, and a European Commission was established to improve navigation on this main artery of trade. The Congress of Berlin, in 1885, opened the Congo to all commerce on equal terms, while the Treaty of Constantinople three years later defined the international character of the Suez Canal by declaring its passage open to all vessels at all times without distinction.

By 1852 all the European states had agreed to cooperate in the regulation of telegraph tariffs and services; between 1875 and 1878 the General Postal Union was expanded to embrace thirty-two states and colonies; an International Union of Railway Freight Transportation serving Europe was formed in 1893; the signal code for sea traffic adopted by Britain and France in 1864 was recognized by some forty states just prior to the First World War; and by 1911 at least seventeen countries had acceded to a general convention protecting patents and copyrights.[19] It is significant that a paid consular service was not organized in Great Britain until 1825, in France until 1833, and in the United States until 1852,[20] for the exigencies of international trade had been amply satisfied hitherto by the sporadic employment of foreign citizens. But the emergence of large-scale, continuous traffic geared to modern communications and mass production required the speedy and calculable exercise of official administration with as commodious an arrangement among political organizations as possible for products and services which recognized no boundaries but the market place.[21]

These thrusts of international regulatory commissions were

[19] Statistics compiled from Reinsch, *Public International Unions.*
[20] Bowden, Karpovich, and Usher, *Economic History of Europe since 1750*, p. 742.
[21] "Normally, the very large, modern capitalist enterprises are themselves unequalled models of strict bureaucratic organization. Business management throughout rests on increasing precision, steadiness, and, above all, the speed of operations."—Weber, *Essays in Sociology*, tr. by H. H. Gerth and C. Wright Mills, p. 215. See especially chap. vii, "Technical Advantages of Bureaucratic Organization."

not limited to communications, industry, and commerce, but were also directed toward public health problems and the peculiar difficulties of arresting crimes which transcended national frontiers. Rapidity in communication, while bringing cheap, raw materials closer to Europe, also carried disease more quickly. Cholera entered Europe in 1830, crossed the English Channel in 1832, and then jumped the Atlantic to America. Sixty years and six epidemics finally convinced the European powers of the need for the International Sanitary Conventions of 1892 and 1895. At the Conference of Brussels in 1889 and 1890 eighteen states agreed to establish an International Administration for the suppression of slavery in Africa; between 1902 and 1910 a number of conferences were arranged to work out means for international police cooperation in apprehending organizers of the white slave traffic.[22] Tariff and agricultural statistics, scientific measurements, the opium trade, submarine cables, and fisheries, all came into an ever-growing area of human activities subject to some international regulation. One author claims that between 1864 and 1914 two hundred and twenty-eight multiparitite treaties and conventions dealing with the common interests of man came into existence.[23] The whole tone of the century was resonant with progress in working out common economic and social problems through cooperation. Paul Reinsch opened and concluded his study of the new internationalism on this sanguine note.

There are in existence over forty-five public international unions, composed of states. . . . When once we appreciate the scope of the forces involved, we are impelled to the conclusion that world organization is no longer an ideal, but is an accomplished fact.

The growing unity of the world . . . rests upon the technical advances made in communication and industrial processes during the last 100 years.[24]

[22] See Woolf, *International Government*, Part Two, chap. iii, for a lucid account of these developments.
[23] Randall, *A World Community*, p. 203.
[24] Paul Reinsch, *Public International Unions*, pp. 4, 5, 186.

There was something else to accentuate this apparent progression toward concerted and harmonious international action, something more tangible for the average European than conventions or treaties, and that was the relative absence of widespread total warfare on the Continent during the nineteenth century. Contrary to some current intimations, the years from 1815 to 1914 could scarcely be considered an age of peace. Following the protracted and exhausting Napoleonic Wars, the chancelleries of Europe feared a resurgence of republican government within their borders more than national rivalries, and strong military forces were everywhere employed in quelling domestic turbulence.[25] The Crimean War in 1856 succeeded the revolutionary upheavals of 1848; the French allied with Piedmont against Austria in 1859; the Germanic states overwhelmed Denmark in 1864; Prussia defeated Austria in seven weeks during 1866, then turned and smashed France in 1870–71. Yet none of these engagements embroiled all the Great Powers simultaneously or for a long period. Moreover, the main stage of Europe was clear of battling armies from 1871 to 1914. Wars continued, but the struggles had been removed to more distant horizons:

The clashes occurred in exotic and distant countries, not only in the Balkans, in Turkey, or in Persia, but in Afghanistan, in Tibet, in Manchuria, and in China, as well as in the most inaccessible regions of Africa, on the marshes of the Bahr-el-Ghazal or near the falls of the Zambesi River.[26]

[25] For example, there were revolutions in Italy during 1820, 1821, 1831, 1832, and 1848; in Spain during 1820; in France during 1830, 1832, 1848; in Belgium, Poland, Brunswick, Saxony, Hesse-Cassel, and two Saxon duchies during 1830; in Prussia and throughout the Austrian Empire during 1848. See C. D. Hazen, *Europe since 1815.*
[26] Delaisi, *Political Myths and Economic Realities*, pp. 283–284. See also Hobson, *Imperialism; a Study.* "The decades of Imperialism have been prolific in wars. . . . Every one of the steps of expansion in Africa, Asia, and the Pacific has been accompanied by bloodshed. . . . The pax Britannica, always an impudent falsehood, has become in recent years a grotesque monster of hypocrisy . . ." pp. 119–121.

The increasing appetite and complexity of capitalist enterprise had not only diverted the attention of the leading states to more remote sources of raw materials and markets, but also popularized the idea that the flow of goods and services based upon sound credit among the civilized nations of the world transcended narrow, selfish political allegiance, that international capitalism dedicated to a practical task of producing cheaper commodities and improving trade created a common interest among all men which was making international war a fruitless interruption to progress and as costly to the victor as to the vanquished. The division of labor carried to the entrepreneurial level had brought about specializations in factories as well as jobs. Some plants supplied one part of a manufacturing process, and others finished the work; but considerations of cost due to location of resources, availability of labor, skill in production, propinquity of the market, and other factors, often placed these factories within different political borders. Similarly, capital in the form of bonds, stocks, and notes followed the desire for profits regardless of national politics. During the Crimean War, for example, the Russian government punctually paid the interest due on loans from English investors.[27] Freedom of the seas and neutral privileges in trading with belligerents reached a new, lenient interpretation during the nineteenth century. Except for a brief list of war contraband, the cargos of neutral ships, regardless of ownership, were not liable to seizure nor was neutral cargo subject to capture when discovered aboard belligerent vessels.[28] Perhaps nothing illustrates better the sprawling links of commerce among the leading powers than the phenomenal growth of their foreign trade: between 1873 and 1914 French foreign trade increased 205 percent, English 214 percent, Italian 276 percent, German 347 percent, and American 400 percent![29] Part of the increment,

[27] J. W. Headlam, in Marvin, *Unity of Western Civilization*, p. 220.
[28] Declaration of Paris, 1856.
[29] Delaisi, *Political Myths and Economic Realities*, p. 102.

to be sure, was due to imperialism; nevertheless, the bulk of business was transacted among the great nations themselves. On the eve of the First World War, for example, Germany was the best customer of Russia, the second best customer of Britain, and the third best customer of France.[30] Finally, the impact of finance capitalism on the world economy had transferred ownership across political boundaries to an even larger extent than merely efficient production, so that foreign holdings swelled in the hands of investors, creating a property interest which did not share patriotic limitations. In 1893 British financiers and rentiers had loaned some 525 million pounds to foreign countries other than British colonial possessions. In addition, more than 248 million pounds were tied up in foreign noncolonial railroads, and another sum of 540 million pounds had been poured into overseas banks, lands, mines, and so forth.[31] By the incontestable demonstration of such economic interdependence, war was revealed as a folly, a great illusion,

because of this delicate interdependence of our credit-built finance the confiscation by an invader of private property, whether stocks, shares, ships, mines . . . anything, in short, which is bound up with the economic life of the people—would so react upon the finance of the invader's country as to make the danger to the invader resulting from the confiscation exceed in value the property confiscated.[32]

There were dire warnings, too, about the culmination of international monopoly capitalism from both evolutionary and revolutionary socialists, but, on the whole, a hopeful attitude toward the unifying elements of big business prevailed. The solid *Cambridge Modern History* thoroughly reflects this view.

No power, no person, is too great, no man too humble, to be reached by the pervasive and unseen pressure of financial interests and financial authority. This force, non-moral as it is, sordid as it

[30] Keynes, *Economic Consequences of the Peace*, p. 17, and chap. ii, "Europe before the War."
[31] Quoted by J. A. Hobson, *Imperialism*, p. 56.
[32] Angell, *The Great Illusion*, p. 32.

may seem, is a growing factor in European politics and, as a rule, it is exercised for the preservation of peace.[33]

Confirming this sentiment was the manifest advance of the nineteenth century toward humanitarianism. The religious reformation and the intellectual revolution of the preceding era had turned the inquiry of reason toward man as an individual, as a human being with a dignity of person deserving respect. Slavery slowly disappeared from the civilized world: the British Empire forbade the practice in 1833; the Czar emancipated the Russian serfs in 1861; the United States ended involuntary servitude in 1865; Brazil curtailed the debasing institution between 1871 and 1888, while an elaborate international commission began to suppress the slave trade in Africa after 1890. With regard to warfare, there was similar compassion aroused among the peoples of Europe and America. Actually the Crimean War and the sufferings at Solferino were no more horrible than previous military engagements, but the same technical changes which made the telegraph and the camera available for spectacular communication to the people at home also suggested the possibility of relieving pain through anesthesia.[34] Bureaucratization of large armies provided specialists. Foraging, spoliation, draft labor were less effective than organization and discipline; in addition, the goal of warfare was envisaged as defeating the enemy without ruining him, imposing one's will upon the government without damaging the source of mutual wealth. For a combination of these reasons, therefore, the nineteenth century nurtured a genuine effort to regulate the conduct of war and a decided mitigation of human suffering. Numerous Peace Societies flourished in the United States, Britain, and France from 1815 onwards. The Geneva

[33] *Cambridge Modern History*, XII (1910), 15.
[34] The first use of the telegraph in combat operations, the first military photographs, and the first war correspondents appeared with the Crimean War (1854–1856). On October 16, 1846, Dr. John C. Warren first performed a major surgical operation without inflicting the slightest pain, at the Massachusetts General Hospital, Boston.

Convention of 1864 founded the International Red Cross. A Convention of the Hague in 1899 prescribed a detailed code for the proper conduct of war, and at the same time a Permanent Court of Arbitration was formed to encourage the promising habit of arbitrating international disputes, a habit which the preceding century had fostered.[35]

The proliferation of capitalist enterprise, the remoteness of business wars, the budding spirit of humanitarianism, all these manifestations of nineteenth-century life cajoled men into the magic chambers of progress. For the ardent patriot, however, nothing could corroborate this vision more perfectly than the exalted idea of nationalism. The old regime in France had been toppled from its rotten structure, and all Europe was awakened by the clarion of liberty: "The nation is essentially the source of all sovereignty; nor can any individual, or any body of men, be entitled to any authority which is not expressly derived from it." [36]

To make the world a more free and equal place by proving the right of self-determination for all peoples was as much the mission of the new French nationalism as the establishment of a republican government,[37] and the seminal ideas bore fruit. Belgium and Greece struck for independence; Italy, Bulgaria, Rumania, and Serbia emerged as states; Hungary demanded and won its own parliament; Poland and Bohemia chafed under foreign rule. Nationality became the lodestone of justice and the moral foundation of world order, so that the slogan "self-determination" rang out through the decades to reach a crescendo at Versailles in 1918. The extinction of time-worn,

[35] There were 177 cases of arbitration from 1794 to the end of 1900. "This number shows that the inclination of States to agree on arbitration has increased and there can be no doubt that arbitration has a great future . . . arbitration is an established force which daily gains more power and influence." L. Oppenheim, *International Law*, 2d ed., 1912, pp. 22–23. Incidentally, there are no traces of these optimistic phrases in the corresponding sections of the 5th ed., 1935.
[36] *Declaration of the Rights of Man and of the Citizens*, art. iii.
[37] See Hayes, *The Historical Evolution of Modern Nationalism*, especially chap. iii, "Jacobin Nationalism."

enfeebled dynasties unresponsive to the changing climates of opinion and incapable of filling the iron mold of industrialism was only part of the sincerely democratic aspirations of nationalism. What was more impressive, however, was the grand conception of brotherly nations marching forward under a universal banner of democratic government. Perhaps no one preached this sentiment more passionately than the arch-patriot Mazzini. In truth, this fervent advocate of Italian unity invested the nation with the sublime qualities of a mystical organism divinely selected as the distinct organization of mankind, and he emphasized the sense of duty to the nation as the source of individual rights, yet he embraced no clique, no clan, no elite, but representative republican government. Most significantly, moreover, he stressed the duties of nations themselves as part of a greater humanity, that the moral law of the nation applied to individuals must apply equally in its international relations.[38]

In the eyes of many historians before the First World War the most remarkable phenomenon of the nineteenth century, in fact, was the steady progression of Europe toward democratic government. There was a shimmering faith, which today seems naïve, that the slow but sure advance of the principle of representative government over the face of the earth augured an era of good feeling and fraternity which only kindred institutions and the relief from despots could give to international life.

In France a democratic autocracy was replaced by a democratic Republic. . . . The German Empire was established . . . on a democratic basis. The Italian Kingdom has a democratic constitution. The franchise has been considerably extended in Great Britain. . . . Bulgaria, the latest addition to European states, is controlled

[38] "The *end* of politics is the application of the moral law to the civil constitution of a Nation in its double activity, domestic and foreign. . . . And what is true for one Nation is true as between Nations . . . Nations are individuals of humanity. . . . International policy (is) to be governed by the moral principle that rules the Nation." There can be no doubt as to Mazzini's program being "liberal." See "To the Italians: Program of the Roma del Populo" in Mazzini, *Essays*, tr. by T. Okey, pp. 139–176.

by popular suffrage . . . also the other independent polities of the Balkan peninsula . . . universal suffrage was adopted by Austria . . . in Hungary (it is) under consideration. In Russia . . . there seems to be an advance. . . . Even Turkey is making the democratic experiment . . . and all the self-governing European communities beyond the seas have adopted democratic government.[39]

Such was the philosophical and historical background for nineteenth-century progress! Such was the miraculous confluence of scientific, humanitarian, and political advances in the nineteenth century! To imagine mankind gradually progressing toward world government in brilliant stages of technical and social integration did not seem fantastic. Even when the seething forces of nationalism and economic rivalry, ambition and fear, erupted in 1914, the conflict could be aptly translated as the inevitable frictions between free and autocratic institutions, and "the question of more public liberty, the question of civilization developing under the forms of free government," wrote Charles W. Eliot, "is the real issue this war is to decide." [40]

Two world wars have since punctured the balloon of inevitable democratic progress, and the hissing sound of escaping hope has been the tune for not less than twelve dictatorships on the European scene since 1918. The forms of republicanism on other continents, moreover, have been slavish imitations of a design often ill-suited to the history, economics, and temperament of the community and therefore doomed to woeful failure. Still the bland comparisons of society to a healthy biological organism growing to a more perfect shape as it solves the conflicts of its environment have not been silenced. Even the imaginative tale of a splendid advance from families to tribes to communes to nations and consequently to world government under justice, law, and peace still persists.[41]

[39] *Cambridge Modern History*, XII (1910), 5–6.
[40] Eliot, *The Road Toward Peace*, p. 190.
[41] See Newfang, *World Federation*, chap. i; or Brewer, *Permanent Peace*, p. 15.

Evidence of greater, more complex political structures developing from the embryonic nation-state is easily marshaled: the two thousand petty states of Europe have virtually disappeared; perhaps only three states in the world today can fight an extensive war.

Almost half the world's industrial capacity is in the United States. Of the balance almost half is in the U.S.S.R., and much of the remainder is in the British Empire. All the world, like Caesar's Gaul, in tres partes divisa est. . . . In the language of Oswald Spengler, we are passing out of the Epoch of Contending States into the Age of World Empires.[42]

The experiences of 1914 and 1939, moreover, have not halted the steadily mounting piles of pacts, covenants, treaties, conventions, agreements, and charters among nations,[43] each paper document a new pledge, a new restriction, a new obligation on the modern shibboleth "sovereignty," and the tentacles of an octopean world communication and commercial system still reach out to every portion of the earth, stereotyping, combining, familiarizing the cults and characters of many peoples with one another. The weight of nineteenth-century experience bears heavily on the plans for world government, and the old vision of progress through the institutionalization of the co-operative nation-state family was crystallized by both the League of Nations and the United Nations.

What truth, indeed, can be drawn from illustrations of growth and the increasing complexity of human relationships? How valid is the idea of progress applied to an expanding web of interstate functions, the expectation of increasing adaptability to environment, and the prospect of larger areas of life under larger forms of government?

[42] Schuman, "Regionalism and Spheres of Influence" in Hans J. Morgenthau, *Peace, Security, and the United Nations.*
[43] At the end of 1945, for example, the United States, an old symbol of "isolation," was participating in 143 international agencies and 48 bilateral committees, commissions, etc. See *International Agencies in which the U.S. Participates* (Washington, Public Affairs Press, 1946).

Unfortunately the shortsighted exuberance which points out the federalism of the United States, Switzerland, and Germany overlooks the fact that historically political structures have tended toward fragmentation quite as much as toward integration. If small communities have been united either by force or by other compelling circumstances, empires, too, have been splintered in the same way. Without probing antiquity for illustrations, it is seen that the Spanish Empire, the Ottoman Turkish Empire, the Austrian Empire, and the British Empire have been dismembered since the seventeenth and eighteenth centuries. Now it may reasonably be argued that vital economic interdependence and weapons of mass destruction make political separatism physically impossible in the twentieth century, but this is not the same thing as saying that nations will be "progressing" by yielding their powers and functions, even in a limited sense, to a superstate, no more than the Athenians would have been progressing by succumbing to the Achaemenian Empire, than the cities of Florence, Milan, or Siena would have benefited under the French Kingdom of Charles VIII after 1494, than the United Provinces of Holland would have gained under the Spanish Empire or the domination of Louis XIV, or the Swiss Forest Cantons would have advanced under the Austrian Hapsburgs. There is by no means conclusive evidence that people would be more imaginative, more creative, more industrious, or more satisfied under world government than they would be when subject to tribal states, town meetings, church canons, or national administrations. Unless man is inspired by larger forms of government, increasingly loyal to a wider structure than his present concrete experience, devoted, in short, to the kind of life the bigger political administration will yield, the mere extension of political functions may incorporate more misery than merit.

There is another consideration to be applied to the parallel use of natural evolution and the progress of political integration. Evolution stresses adaptability to environmental conditions, that is, the external challenge to any form of life. Political societies, it is said, being an expression of man's experience on earth, must respond to the climate created by dense populations, the wireless, airplanes, and atomic bombs; they must, in brief, either organize their structures to meet the impact of these factors upon civilization or perish. However,

Those who are given to such reasoning assume constantly that progress is necessarily implied in the evolutionary processes of nature, failing to recognize that the latter may involve a degradation of type and form of life just as easily as approach toward more "perfect" forms.[44]

For example, if the earth should begin to lose its heat very rapidly, a race of men which could grow a heavy fur might prove more adaptable to the new conditions, but not necessarily "better" men in the customary sense. In his analysis of growth in societies, Mr. Toynbee has given a wealth of citations from reptiles to British industrialism suggesting that a response to one challenge of the environment may ruin the possibilities of further and more valuable advances.[45] In the change of forms, political or otherwise, there is, of course, the explicit meaning of "difference," for better or for worse, depending upon the standards sought. But, as Mr. G. D. H. Cole has pointed out, the glib analogies comparing society with a mechanism, or an organism, or a person, or even a God confuse the issue. "The mechanical and organic analogy have been alike definitely harmful for they both invoke a material analogy in what is essentially a mental or spiritual study." [46]

From another point of view, Hans Kohn commented: "It is frequently assumed that man loves in widening circles—his family, his tribe, or clan, the nation and, finally, humanity and the supreme good." But obviously the connotation of each of these social units for the individual varies immensely. Neither

[44] Case, *Social Process and Human Progress*, p. 39.
[45] Toynbee, *A Study of History*, abridged by D. C. Somervell, chap. xvi.
[46] Cole, *Social Theory*, p. 14.

Sparta nor the sixteenth-century Ottoman Empire nor the Third Reich cherished family ties to any degree commensurate with the Roman Republic, sixteenth-century Flanders, or Ibero-America. The knights of the Crusades, medieval church-men, humanists, eighteenth-century philosophers and twentieth-Century Trotskyites either disregarded or disdained the claims of nationality in preference to their class or humanity as a whole. Despite the efforts of diverse periods to fix godliness on imperium, the state, or a particular group, there seems to be nothing sacrosanct about social forms of organizing political life itself. There is some general agreement that in past ages there have been both good and bad empires, nations, ruling classes, tribes, and families. One of the new contenders for man's affection is the union of nation states in a world government.

In his philosophy of federal union Mr. Joad begins:

It cannot, I think, be reasonably denied that a further stage of integration lies before mankind which is some form of World-State. . . . Federal Union, which is the first step beyond the Nation State toward the World-State, is thus in the direct line of evolutionary advance.[47]

He then proceeds to attack the "wicked," "aggressive," "anachronistic" state, implicitly giving this form of social organization the real personality which he denies it has. Nor does he confine his diatribe to the poor adaptability of the national political structure to the economic requirements of the world, but adds that "in the power of the State is to be found the peculiar and distinctive enemy of the happiness of contemporary man." Such a philosophy fails, incidentally, to distinguish the state as a social configuration from its government which may employ the political apparatus in many ways, and it unintentionally repeats the cant that a federal union which sets up a supreme authority coinciding with economic patterns is in-

[47] C. E. M. Joad, "The Philosophy of Federal Union," in Ransome, *Studies in Federal Planning*, p. 50.

trinsically "good," thereby solving the problem of a family of "bad" states. Later, it turns out, this new form of government must be Christian and democratic, but nowhere is there an analysis of how this moral metamorphosis, which is the crucial factor, will take place. The insistent point of this criticism is that larger forms may facilitate the expression of several different human motivations and that reliance upon a harmony of economic interests does not by itself warrant the assumption that any world government is necessarily better or even a first stage of advance beyond the nation-state.

Progress toward world government on the basis of ability to articulate the mechanical components of life through larger political units, it would seem, is a specious postulate. It signifies, in fact, a potentiality for doing more things in less time and commanding a wider direction of both human and material resources, so that any political undertaking will be more thorough in its nature, more pervasive in its influences. In this sense, then, world government becomes a technique, neutral in itself and applicable to various purposes, an organization which must be judged on other criteria than its streamlined affinity with the wireless and the airplane, or even its ability to throttle nation-states. If world government is better government for the universe than a society of nation-states, it should display some tokens other than size and complexity and gigantic control over modern technology. It should, it seems, be a form of government preferable to the current organization of the world by virtue of the satisfactions it brings to the basic, irreducible unit of society, man himself. An examination of such possibilities is the subject of the following chapters.

Chapter 5

We, the countless, redoubtable legions of Toil,
We've conquered vast spaces of oceans and lands,
Illumined great cities with suns of our making,
Fired our souls with proud flames of revolt.

Gone are our tears, our softness forgotten,
We banished the perfume of lilac and grass,
We exalt electricity, steam, and explosives,
Motors and sirens and iron and brass . . .

Our souls fused with metal, part of our engines,
We unlearned to wish for and dream of the sky.
It is here on this earth that we want to be happy,
To feed all the hungry, to hush their long cry . . .

                                                    Vladimir Kirillov

World Government and Economic Progress

THE IDEA OF PROGRESS is an exciting lure for the exponents of world government. It suggests the inevitable development of society into larger and more competent political forms. Without this intriguing analogy of society to a growing organism, moreover, an insight into the nature of world unification becomes not only more perplexing but certainly less optimistic. Instead of depending upon evolution as a guide to world government, however, it seems more reasonable to maintain that social relationships, like the needs and attitudes of the men who make them, are always in flux—and that political processes have the same character. If this is true, government has no ultimate form, nor are political problems ever "solved" for

whenever men discover new resources or build faster ships or invent power engines, or harness electricity or dream new dreams they are thrown into different relationships than before and thereby the problem of government is changed.[1]

Today the task of political organization is dramatized by a global economy in which warfare has become almost totally destructive, and the natural response to these new conditions has been a groping for some means of controlling interstate relations. Just as the feudal order failed to satisfy the dynamic

[1] MacIver, *Towards an Abiding Peace*, p. 154.

social relationships of its period, the nation-state may also be collapsed by a tempest of universal demands for a different economic-spiritual pattern of government. But this is change, which is the substance of all life, and demonstrates an adaptation of the political apparatus to different contingencies; it need not evoke any overtones of progress, of evolution toward a greater good, or of a general amelioration of mankind due to an increasing complexity of its historical contacts. What such change does suggest is simply modification of the forms of government to meet new exigencies of human life.

The mere act of integration, of course, gives no promise that the new political organization will be more or less competent to deal with the special problems it has to face as a whole and which the very act of integration raises. Czarist Russia, for example, represented nearly four hundred years of imperial expansion—from the time of John the Great to Alexander II. During this period the Duchy of Moscow swallowed a vast territory stretching from Austria-Hungary to Alaska, from Sweden to Japan, and it extended its rule over almost two hundred different ethnic groups.[2] Many provincial frictions, indeed, were definitely terminated by the amalgamation, but obviously the new state, in turn, generated its own domestic tensions and irritations, and on a more explosive level. Every society, as Quincy Wright has observed in his study of war,[3] is continually on the brink of conflict and must constantly adapt its organization and policy to changing conditions of internal opinion and external pressures. The degree of response to the ever-fluctuating social pressures of men in action, the ability to adjust frictions, balancing and harmonizing the teeming wants of society, can be viewed as a positive or negative value of government in itself—regardless of the scale of operations. Thus, if any criterion for "progress" is to be sought, it may be found

[2] See Pares, *History of Russia*, especially pp. 100–101.
[3] Wright, *A Study of War*, II, p. 955.

in the fact, not of larger forms, but of larger opportunities to serve the perpetual needs of more people.

Harold J. Laski framed the economic problems of this century as succinctly as possible when he stated that many countries, such as India, China, Rumania, and Yugoslavia, can advance the material well-being of their citizens only by a rapid industrialization.

But, as they do so in the age of horizontal expansion, they intensify the difficulties of the well-established industrial powers or they run the grave danger of accepting aid for their economic development in such a way as to become a political dependency of the power from which they accept it.[4]

Although this is only restating the impact of the industrial revolution upon the nation-states of the world, it does set down in clear and unmistakable terms the inherent frictions and consequences of a system built on competition and exploitation of natural resources, a system which tore the vision of Heaven from the misty skies and affirmed the possibility of creating a prosperous, happy life on earth. This ideal, it should be noted, is not the precious property of capitalism, but is equally claimed by socialism.

The industrialization of nation-states throughout their brief period in history, moreover, was an unplanned and uneven process, creating grave disparities between the states which had revolutionized their economies and those which had not. From England extensive manufactures had spread to western Europe; as late as the Exposition of 1851, German finished products were still looked upon as a curiosity rather than a potential threat to London industrialists. Only in the twentieth century have Japan and Russia turned to the machine in earnest. Now, one by one, those Eastern countries which were indolent, slumbering peoples, living in an ancient tradition of rigid hier-

[4] Laski, "Crisis of Our Civilization," *Foreign Affairs*, XXVI (October, 1947), 41.

archy, agrarianism, and meditation, have been goaded by their predatory neighbors to break the bonds of the past, take up the techniques of industrialization, and claim their share of the world's wealth. Thus, the uneven and unplanned process has moved and is moving as far as one can see relentlessly onward, constantly generating frictions as the ambitious peoples press upon the more contented ones, as those who have partially won their satisfactions resist the efforts of the indigent or greedy to widen their economic horizons. And though the scientific revolution of our modern era has produced infinite treasures for society, famine and poverty still stalk every land on earth, ever ready to break out into domestic commotion.

Even in boom years [writes Eugene Staley] and in the most advanced countries, the production of clothing, of housing, of protective foodstuffs, of medical services . . . has not been enough to satisfy the aspirations of the people or even to cover "necessities" as defined by modern standards.[5]

The requirements for an economically more satisfying world seem plain: "to further the enjoyment by all States, great or small . . . of access, on equal terms, to the trade and raw materials of the world which are needed for their economic prosperity," [6] the channels of commerce ought to be freed of their obstructions by reducing tariffs and stabilizing monetary exchange; opportunities for migration have to be provided for a better distribution of human resources; and international communications, transportation, cartels, and commodity agreements should be put among the public services.[7]

But what becomes immediately apparent is that while cooperation among nation-states can carry the community a certain distance toward these goals, at some point in the dynamic system of mass production, communications, and trade a real

[5] Staley, *World Economy in Transition.*
[6] Declaration of Principles, known as the Atlantic Charter, by the President of the United States and the Prime Minister of the United Kingdom, August 14, 1941.
[7] See Finer, *The United Nations Economic and Social Council,* especially chap. ii, "Functional Problems to Be Solved."

loss will be suffered by one or more of the favorably situated nation-states, and that it, or they, will take steps if unopposed to rectify the balance. It is at this point that retaliation begins and conflict breaks out. If the conflict is serious enough, it is translated into war. The force of some encompassing government, therefore, must come into play before the fuse is ignited by unilateral action.

One of the greatest cooperative economic schemes of all time, for example, has been the European Recovery Program. Its objective is "to achieve lasting economic recovery for western Europe: recovery in the sense that, after our aid is terminated, the European countries will be able to maintain themselves on a sound economic basis." [8] Yet it must be obvious that a Continent which had an income of 2.1 billion dollars in 1938 from services and investment, some of which represented centuries of saving, and in 1948 had a .6 billion dollar deficit from these same items, can only hope to achieve a living standard roughly similar to the past by increasing its productivity far beyond the old record, and then selling its commodities abroad. The United States, as the best possible market for European products, should concomitantly reduce its tariffs and permit a large-scale introduction of foreign goods. [9] But some domestic prices will therefore be driven downward, thus reducing profits for domestic producers and creating some unemployment. If the American bloated economy were slowly deflated, then the political agitation for national protective devices might be resisted. Yet considering the stakes involved for Europe—and the world—to rely upon one nation's discretion is a risky procedure, and the repercussion may always break into new conflicts. This, in truth, is the operation of the international cooperative system, tempered, to be sure, by valuable, painstak-

[8] Statement of George C. Marshall before Senate Committee on Foreign Relations, Jan. 8, 1948.
[9] See J. H. Williams, "The Task of Economic Recovery," *Foreign Affairs*, Vol. XXVI (July, 1948), for an interesting analysis of the European Aid Program, pp. 616–631.

ing reports, the efforts of good statesmanship, and a more profound knowledge, generally, of the consequences. Nothing, however, could sum up better the attitude of the nation-states toward their obligations to the Economic and Social Council of the United Nations, which is the epitome of the cooperative effort, than this commentary on Article 55.

It pledges the various countries to cooperate with the organization by joint and separate action in the achievement of the economic and social objectives of the organization without infringing upon their right to order their national affairs according to their own best ability, in their own way, and in accordance with their own political and economic institutions and processes.[10]

Furthermore, Wellington Koo, Jr., in his study of voting procedures in international political associations, has shown how

the degree of importance which great powers in fact assign to any organization may be measured in proportion to the degree to which their special positions in the world community are protected in the text of the agreement or the treaty [11]

and that principles of equality will vary in inverse ratio to the extent that the organization functions within an important sphere of international life. Thus, the Security Council is virtually impotent without the unanimous consent of the five Great Powers, while, at the other end of the scale, the Universal Postal Union can take effective action within its limited scope of international activity by a simple majority vote. UNNRA, the International Monetary Fund, and the International Bank for Reconstruction and Development have given special privileges to the larger, wealthier powers in view of their heavier responsibilities; the International Civil Aviation Organization and even the International Labor Organization take account of the commerce and productivity of the leading states by affording them some prerogatives. Per-

[10] *Report to the President on the Results of the San Francisco Conference,* June 26, 1945, U.S. Department of State, Publication 2349.
[11] Wellington Koo, Jr., *Voting Procedures in International Political Organizations,* p. 39.

haps nothing reveals the farce of the Economic and Social Council better, as Mr. Koo illustrates,[12] than the easy solution of candidacy and voting principles for the organization; despite the elegant phraseology and the high purposes of its objectives, the acquiescence of the Great Powers to the provisions enabling any eighteen members of the United Nations to be elected by the General Assembly to the Council and permitting decisions to be made by a majority vote clearly betrays the inadequacy of that organization as the instrument for cutting out the cancer of economic nationalism.

The most ambitious and wholesome effort of the nation-states to "facilitate through the promotion of mutual understanding, consultation, and cooperation the solution of problems relating to international trade" [13] has been the signing of an International Trade Organization Charter at Havana in April, 1948. The document is explicit about the noxious trade practices which have imperiled the free and rapid transit of goods and the remedies to be achieved by collaboration. But there are "special provisions," standard safeguards of the nation-state system, which tip off potential dangers:

If, as a result of unforeseen developments and of the effect of the obligations incurred by a Member under or pursuant to this Chapter, any product is being imported into the territory of that Member in such relatively increased quantities and under such conditions as to cause or threaten serious injury to domestic producers . . . the Member shall be free . . . to suspend the obligation in whole or in part or to withdraw or modify the concession.[14]

These illustrations are not meant to derogate the commendable efforts of nation-statesmen, but only to throw into focus the framework of self-interest within which such attempts must be viewed.

[12] *Ibid.*, pp. 257 *et seq.*
[13] *International Trade Organization Charter* (U.S. Department of State Publication #3117, Commercial Policy Series, released April, 1948), chap. i, art. 1, par. 6.
[14] *Ibid.*, chap. iv, sec. F—Special Provisions, art. 40.

Finally, does the gradual transformation of the nation-states from capitalism to socialism augur a more harmonious collaboration? This shift within an economy is a structural reformation affecting the distribution of the total national economic wealth, but it scarcely changes the vital requirements of the state as a whole: disabilities in the way of raw materials, scarce commodities, over-population, remain; need for credit and trade continues; the change does not satisfy either the state's security aims or its military ambitions. Socialized Eastern Europe, perforce, has transferred the bulk of its trade from Germany to the Soviet Union, yet its international economic problems are not very different. In 1948 Poland had twelve agreements for exchange with countries outside the iron curtain and Czechoslovakia about nineteen—despite their political complexions.[15] A new Conservative government in Britain would certainly face difficulties similar to those of the present Labor administration in either restoring a favorable balance of trade for its people or else depressing their living standards. It is fatuous to disclaim any connection between the "expanding and aggressive" foreign policy of the Kremlin and the imperialism of the czars.

Autarchy, or economic isolation, sometimes advanced as a way of avoiding conflict, is completely unrealistic in a century which has above everything else demonstrated the economic interdependence of the world. Peaceful and far-sighted collaboration among nation-states, with self-restraint and self-sacrifice on the part of the more fortunate, can accomplish much in relieving acute distress and building confidence, the basis of a more prosperous community.[16] But no one can shirk the realization that if larger opportunities to serve the economic needs of more and more people are to be opened, it will require

[15] See Vera Micheles Dean, "Economic Trends in Eastern Europe," *Foreign Policy Reports*, April 1 and April 15, 1948.
[16] For a prewar but not out-dated discussion of this problem see "Economic Cooperation as the Basis of Economic World Order," by Dr. M. J. Bonn, in Geneva Institute of International Relations, *Problems of Peace*, Tenth Series.

physical compulsion—or its threat—to check national arbitrariness in times of crisis. This does not mean that any world
government will automatically provide those opportunities
better than the moderate, genuine achievements of the several
nation-states, but that only world government can further
widen the economic horizons of the world. Crane Brinton
struck the right chord when he wryly commented:

If our sentiments and habits cannot adapt themselves in time to the
political and economic needs of large-scale industry, then it always
remains possible that we shall have to abandon large-scale industry.
This possibility is shocking to those brought up in the faith of the
necessary progress toward bigger and better things; but it is in no
way inconsonant with the record of the past.[17]

What are the prospects, then, of a world government which
would facilitate the attainment of a high economic standard
for its multitude of citizens? In stark terms, a universal polity
today would commence with an appallingly poor society in
which there existed a maldistribution of resources, skills, and
equipment beyond the most harrowing contrasts within any
one nation-state. Moreover, due to the concentration of wealth
and power among a few Great Powers, the claims and pressures upon any central directing political organization would
be intensely unequal. The most obvious trap for the world is
that the same states which lead the international community
out of the wilderness of anarchy might become the true in-
heritors of the earth, that the inequities caused by the pre-
ponderance of the giant industrial states over the lesser members of the community might be formalized by government
rather than assuaged. Free trade, by way of illustration, would
be conducive to peace, since it would stimulate commerce, remove the pique of tariff barriers, fasten together the various
parts of the society in a sound interdependence and make all resources more available.[18] But unless a concomitant freedom of

[17] Brinton, *From Many One*, p. 92.
[18] See Jacob Viner, "The Economic Problem" in De Huszar, *New Perspectives on Peace*.

movement is permitted among the various populations and a general economic planning is enforced for the equal benefit of all, the overpopulated, unindustrialized areas might well remain miserable and subordinate to other sections of the world—even within a single polity.[19] Furthermore, the absolute release of commerce from national barriers, as illustrated in Ralph Barton Perry's chapter on a world economy, is not enough.

A merely permitted (economic) freedom of a nation through non-interference may mean nothing, owing to its ignorance and incapacity; the first steps toward its effective freedom may have to be taken elsewhere in the areas of education and welfare or in associating freedom with power through political emancipation.[20]

To expect that this transition on a world level can come about without detriment to any state is to discount all the lessons of redistributing wealth among the citizens within local economies. It is no poor comparison to paint the strong nation-state as the potential economic royalist of any world government and to cast about for the same correctives to this monopolistic system on the world level that have been employed in domestic affairs. In other words, what is sought is some kind of strong, universal political organization which will satisfy the need for a more equitable distribution of this planet's quite limited wealth among all the nation-states in the same manner as a progressive local government strives to assist its citizens in a fair distribution of the economic product.

Mr. Stassen was correct in not advocating any sudden at-

---

[19] "The sudden development of the aeroplane industry in Southern California has not been at the cost of the workingman in New York where the industry first developed; it merely means that he has moved to another State where conditions for doing this kind of work are more favorable. This continual shift of population has therefore reduced inter-state jealousies to a minimum." A. L. Goodhart, "Constitution of the United States" in Ransome, *Studies in Federal Planning*, p. 267. Two qualifications need to be added: first, there was a real cost to the workingman who had to shift into another location or another occupation; secondly, there must be a high enough standard of living, including accessible transportation, to enable migration.

[20] Perry, *One World in the Making*, especially chap. v, "World Economy."

tempt to make trade universally free, but rather to begin economic reconstruction by a general tariff structure which "should not be arbitrarily raised without the consent of the United Nations government." [21] The right of consent is complementary to the ability to forbid—even at the personal hardship of any one state, no matter how large and powerful. Now this is, in essence, the dilemma: to obtain a government with sufficient power to accomplish the planning and channeling of economic resources on a broader basis requires the concerted action of those nation-states which would be most privileged in a world government. This grievous situation has initiated all kinds of acrobatic tricks to divide voting power and influence within some council on the basis of size, population, education, trade, and so forth, but only by trusting in a superlative and rarely visible magnanimity among great nations not to exploit their favorable positions can it be expected that sheer military power will not eventually claim its place. Enough evidence on the character of international organizations is already available to indicate the position of the powerful communities in respect to the common welfare, and if world government is to be born peacefully from the maze of agencies, unions, councils, and commissions now devoted to economic affairs, its machinations would indubitably bear the same stamp.

Once it is recognized that great force will be necessary to break the chain of economic strangulation and that a host of vying states have stubbornly refused to cooperate on that job at the most critical moments, the next alternative is the quest for one state which may accomplish the task as a kind of "chosen instrument" for humanity. An ever-interesting lesson of Walter Bagehot is that anarchic peoples need legal fiber before anything else. Since the nations of the world are so often given a choice of "peace or anarchy" in these days, his comment seems appropriate.

[21] See Stassen, "We Need a World Government," *The Saturday Evening Post*, CCXV (May 22, 1943), 11.

What are called in European politics the principles of 1789 are therefore inconsistent with the early world; they are fitted only to the new world in which society has gone through its early task; when the inherited organization is already confirmed and fixed; when the soft passions of youthful nations are fixed and guided by hard transmitted instincts. Till then not equality before the law is necessary, but inequality, for what is most wanted is an elevated elite who know the law; not a good government seeking the happiness of its subjects, but a dignified and over-awing government getting its subjects to obey; not a good law, but a comprehensive law binding all life to one routine . . .[22]

For in the beginning it is the quantity of government that counts more than the quality, and what is most desirable is some comprehensive rule that a bewildered group will follow, not a fine description of the niceties of freedom. The French nation, for example, was not born in the impassioned years after 1789, despite the sweeping claims of the revolutionaries; rather, it was the slow, cumbersome process of war, intrigue, and good luck on the part of the Ile de France and the Capetians which absorbed the several feudal units and created the consolidated area into which the firebrands of liberty could be hurled. At the time of the social upheaval the overwhelming number of Frenchmen were still loyal to the king as the symbol of unity.[23]

How far can the "chosen instrument" approach be followed? At this moment in history it seems to some observers that only two states of the world could establish a yoke for the anarchic collection of nations. James Burnham pursues this line, and, of course, prefers the United States in the role of guardian-director to the Soviet Union since the American republic is not "inherently totalitarian." [24] Frequently, indeed, the particular interests of a leading power do coincide with a fundamental need of the world community: the institution of free trade by indus-

[22] Bagehot, *Physics and Politics*, reprinted in *The Works and Life of Walter Bagehot*, ed. by Mrs. Russell Barrington, VIII, 20.
[23] Brinton, *From Many One*, chap. ii, pp. 49 *et seq.*
[24] See Burnham, *The Struggle for the World*.

trialized Britain in a world of agricultural nations, or the initiation of a disarmament conference by Russia in 1899 when the expense of her own equipment was staggering the treasury, or the support of a strong, international civil aviation board by France to allocate routes and eliminate waste in view of the deterioration of her own airlines, or the transfer of huge capital sums to Europe for economic reconstruction as a partial thwart to communism by the United States, these are all national interests saddled to an international economic need. But to secure the confidence and cooperation of lesser states in the organization of a world government by one Great Power would be another matter. To trust in the opportunistic altruism of any single nation is demanding a great deal of people when all experience reinforces Lord Acton's dictum that "absolute power corrupts absolutely."

The economic foreign policy of the United States at this moment, does, indeed, offer laudable prospects.

Our policy seeks to break down governmental, intergovernmental and private barriers to the flow of goods among nations. Our financial and monetary policy seeks to ensure adequate money and loans to facilitate the flow of international trade. Furthermore our policy seeks to promote the adequate development of transportation and communication facilities and to insure their equitable use.[25]

Few will quibble with President Truman's words that the United States cannot avoid the role of leadership. "We are the giant of the economic world. Whether we like it or not, the future pattern of economic relations depends on us." [26] Much of the heartiness of the contemporary American attitude, however, must reasonably be attributed to the expanding economy of a state which in 1946, the first year of peace, had an agricultural production almost a third larger and a physical manufacturing volume almost double its 1935–39 averages. Employ-

[25] U. S., Dept. of State, *Aspects of Current American Foreign Policy*, Publication 2961, released November, 1947, p. 38.
[26] Address by President Truman, Baylor University, Waco, Texas, March 6, 1946.

ment rolls have climbed to sixty million, while the increase of goods produced for export has been much greater relatively than the domestic turnout. Whereas the exports of the United States for a six-month period averaged $1,462 million from 1936 to 1938, the total value of exports for January–June, 1949 was $6,645 million and for January–June, 1950 $4,838 million. The steady use of foreign markets is of tremendous importance to the American economy as a whole.[27]

To include this economic giant in a government of the world, however, is not the most promising vista for its neighbors; should its wealth be translated into political control, its paramount position might be fortified indefinitely. A republican government at the capital, moreover, is no indication of how republican policy may operate in the provinces. Clearly, democratic states such as the Netherlands, Belgium, France, and Britain have not always aimed at a more equitable distribution of their economic gains with the weaker colonies under their sway. Even Burnham admits the danger of tyranny in a world led by the United States, but he, unlike the nation-states, is willing to risk this eventuality rather than abide in a dangerously unsettled world. It seems erroneous, also, to assume that any one power could of itself tie the world together with a tight dollar—or rouble—string. Some sixty-odd states of the world do not rank with the Titans, but they are not impotent dependencies either. The wealthiest of the family, the United States, has no tin, only synthetic rubber, no chromite, antimony, or manganese; it is deficient in nitrates, bauxite, wool, potash, tungsten, and mercury;[28] it must depend upon the good will of many nations for its far-flung military bases; and moreover it is divided by a party struggle at home which makes its foreign policy vacillate.[29]

[27] *Foreign Commerce Weekly*, XL, 10.
[28] John B. Whitton, "Peaceful Change and Raw Materials," in Mantoux, *The World Crisis*, p. 306.
[29] For a brief comment on "imperial idealism," particularly the lack of it by the Americans, see Luigi Sturzo, *Nationalism and Internationalism*, pp. 236–239.

On the other hand, Hitler's attempt to create a National Socialist world merits attention as the most ruthless effort of modern times to introduce an "order." But the defeat of Britain and the paralysis of Russia, had they been accomplished, would still have left an undigested Western Hemisphere and an aggressive partner in the Far East demanding a "settlement." Despite the atomic bomb, it would still appear that the problems of a straight one-power rule are virtually insurmountable. The experience of two world wars, moreover, has sharply confirmed the opinion of economists that coercion cannot appreciably advance the economic welfare of either the conqueror or the conquered,[30] for wealth today is not plundered gold and jewels, slaves, or the few useful and beautiful objects which could be seized by marauders, but mass productivity and services which depend for their worth upon a willing organization of skilled men.

Mr. Toynbee, in a short talk at Harvard in 1947, suggested that the chief obstacle to a European federation was simply that the European nations do not want to be thrust into the same cage with the larger and more voracious German people.[31] Some of this aversion, at least, would be felt about a union led by either the United States or Russia. To widen economic opportunities requires a close admixture of force and consent within a world government, but the issue here is whether a single power, acting as the keystone of the organization, will long tolerate a rule of peaceful change which, over the course of time can only be antithetical to its established superior economic position. If the past relationships of states are any guide to the future, it would seem that "the prosperity of all nations does not come about through the enlightened selfishness of any

---

[30] Quincy Wright, *A Study of War*, p. 858.
[31] ". . . if Europe were to federate it would willy-nilly be tantamount to the delivery of its nations to political control by the Germans, not because of any superiority on their part, but because of their number, geographical position, traditional combination of business and politics, plotting temperament, etc."— R. Raestad, "The Myth of Europe," in the *Norseman*, Vol. I, No. 1, London, 1943, quoted by Firsoff, *The Unity of Europe*, p. 92.

one nation, but through the counter pressures of selfishness tempered by a sense of fairness and resolved by a compromise." [32]

The anguish of the United States, torn between the huge material interests which have built and maintained its thriving dominion and its new responsibility as the leader of an international organization, testifies to the immense difficulty of any state to tolerate encroachment upon its power. In its singular way, the British Empire, since 1783, has expressed just such tolerance, with the consequent peaceful unfolding of the Commonwealth. But since so much of the original integrity has been sacrificed in the process, the analogy cannot be carried too far.

Economic unions are often regarded as hopeful precedents of political unions, yet again it is the relative strength of the participants which furnishes an important clue to the operation of the organization. Germany is a common example of a state forged out of many principalities through economic cooperation. The first Zollverein was established by Prussia for all her territories in 1819. Gradually she extended this customs union, and by 1844 the organization included all Germany except Austria, Hanover, Oldenburg, Mecklenburg, and the Hanse cities.[33] By 1849 the Prussian bureaucracy was ready to attempt unification of a German state within the Hapsburg Empire, but the opposition of Austria forced the Prussians to wait. The Zollverein tariffs were then reduced to a point too low for Austria to bear, thwarting her efforts to join the association; nor could her pleas to dissuade the other South German states from their membership lure them from the lucrative northern markets. By 1853 the whole of non-Austrian Germany was included in the Zollverein.

Despite these auspicious beginnings, it required almost twenty more years, two full-scale wars, and the most skillful

---

[32] Perry, *One World in the Making,* p. 159.
[33] See Gonner, *Germany in the Nineteenth Century.*

diplomacy to accomplish the political unification of these linguistically and economically related peoples. Austria was per-
emptorily driven from the German Confederation by Prussia in
the War of 1866. Prussia then embraced her allies, the northern
states of Germany, in a quasi-federal union; to the Austrian
allies, Bavaria, Baden, Hesse, and Wurttemburg, she offered
generous terms in exchange for an alliance against France—and
four years later the Franco-Prussian War drew these territories
further into the Prussian orbit. The brilliant Bismarck thereupon negotiated separately with each state to enter the German
Reich, granting concessions, yielding terms, but never deviat-
ing from the object of one strong nation under Prussian leadership.[34] The economic union, therefore, was not only preparatory to political amalgamation, but a political instrument of the
process. Through Prussia's dominance of common economic
machinery, she secured a lever to the opposition of Austria and
succeeded in utilizing her smaller neighbors for an ambitious
autocratic foreign policy. In her relations with large, rival
powers, however, Germany took another tack, for after the
financial crash of 1873 she rapidly abandoned her free-trade
tendencies for national protective duties. The sequel to this
example of economic exploitation was furnished by Hitler's
Germany. Penetrating the Central European market, the Third
Reich, by sharp, purposeful business tactics coupled to its
dominant industrial position, maneuvered the small nations into
a position of complete economic dependence upon Germany.
Though the mechanism was not the same as Prussia's (that is,
economic-political federal union), due to differences of nationality and the sledgehammer methods of the Nazis, the results
were similar: Prussian hegemony over Germany was replaced
by German hegemony over Central Europe.

A customs union or close economic intertwining by agreement may be a bright entrance to world government too, but
it seems wise to scan the division of power within the arrange-

[34] See Dawson, *The German Empire and Unity Movement*.

ment to ascertain whether the economic ties do not presage a political connection monopolized by one power. Though a monopoly of power may lead to vigorous action, it is not ordinarily responsive to the perennial dynamism of economic life, since the paramount state dictates its own ambitions and policies to the whole community. What is required is the mobilization of adequate power by a collection of states in a common political undertaking, willingness to use force or persuasion as the situation warrants, but assurance that no one of the constituents could ever dominate the organization. The United Nations, indeed, was formed with this in view:

> When universal agreement to the Charter was achieved, the strength of the major powers in relation to one another was such that no one of them could safely break the peace if the others stood united in defense of the Charter. Under existing world circumstances the maintenance of a comparable power relationship is fundamental to world security.[35]

But the United Nations can hardly do more than express the sentiments of the three superpowers, since China and France are feeble attendants of the Security Council; and there is no universal willingness in the organization to use force, because no definable ideal which transcends every national interest is accepted by all—or nearly all—the members. By contrast, the American union of 1789, laying aside the continuity of language, custom, and republican government, was an unusually well-balanced array of power as the apportionment of representatives to the first Congress reveals: Virginia, 10; Massachusetts, 8; Pennsylvania, 8; New York, 6; Maryland, 6; Connecticut, 5; North Carolina, 5; South Carolina, 5; New Jersey, 4; New Hampshire, 3; Georgia, 3; Delaware, 1; Rhode Island and Providence Plantations, 1.[36] Thus, Virginia, the greatest unit of the new republic, held less than one-sixth of the lower house while standing on a par with Rhode Island and Delaware in the Senate.

[35] Marshall's Statement to House Committee on United Nations, May 6, 1948.
[36] United States Constitution, art. 1, sec. 2.

Moreover, the problems that faced the American states were increasingly national in character. The conflicting interests of debtors and creditors cut across state lines . . . commerce vied with agriculture, but most of the states were neither strictly commercial nor strictly agricultural.[37]

Besides the absence of that clear-cut economic sectionalism which was to split the union in 1861, the population was well-dispersed along the coastline, for the census of 1790 indicated 1,968,000 persons in the North and 1,925,000 in the South. The first economic hardship indirectly imposed on one district for the benefit of the whole nation, the excise tax on whiskey, was resisted, and Washington summoned 15,000 militia to disperse the Western Pennsylvania farmers.[38] In 1832 the vigorous action of Jackson toward the nullification acts of South Carolina on the tariffs of 1828 and 1832, which undoubtedly harmed her local interests, backed up by a strong feeling for preserving the union among the several states and the willingness of all parties to compromise, averted secession. Briefly, the sectional shifts of economic power in the United States from the first excise tax to the ruling of the Supreme Court banning the "basing point" system of pricing steel, have caused constant frictions among its people. The sharing of a common culture and a common ideal have been important factors in mitigating this strife, but the equilibrium of power among many states has been a restraining influence which must be considered in transposing the illustration to a world scale.

The formation of the South African Union, not a federal union and not comprising a homogeneous people, linguistically or culturally, nevertheless had the same characteristics of balanced power mixed with persuasion and compromise—in addition to the common advantages of union in respect to the native (colored) population and the efficient exploitation of

[37] John Hicks, *A Short History of the American Democracy*, p. 117.
[38] See "Washington's Proclamation on the Whiskey Rebellion, August 7, 1794," in *Documents of American History*, ed. by Henry Steele Commager, I, 163.

enormously rich natural resources. The two independent
Dutch republics were forced under British rule by war, but the
peace terms at Vereeninging, in 1902, were extremely generous; in fact, the British government provided 3,000,000 pounds
to repair the war damages and granted loans, interest free for
two years, to the Transvaal and Orange River colonies. Within
five years both former republics had achieved self-government
and, therefore, political equality with the other Cape colonies
under the Crown. Thus, when the Union was formed in 1910,
the representation in the lower house reflected the skillful compromise of different strengths rather than the monopoly of
force by any single group:

(British)	Cape Province	51
(Dutch)	Transvaal	36
(British)	Natal	17
(Dutch)	Orange Free State	17

with the equal representation of all provinces in the Senate.[39]

Under present conditions of monopolized power, the formation of some organization to govern the world—the most em-
brasive of all possible functions—would necessarily incorporate
the dominant roles now played by the present great states in
international economic affairs. At best it would seem virtually
impossible to escape a rule of oligarchs, but if reasonably balanced within some government their many selfish interests
might afford an adequate measure of restraint among them to
permit the inevitable fluctuations of economic growth without
bitter obstinacy. In such a universal government, however, one
theme could not be altered from the beginning: manifest power
would demand manifest privilege if it were to be harnessed to
world cooperation.

The contemporary world offers little prospect of a reasonably weighted world government. On the other hand, by
voluntarily vesting their individual strength in a single large

[39] See Green, *The Making of the Union of South Africa*, especially chaps.
xiv, xvi.

state, in exchange for economic protection, the satellite nations run the dangerous risk of arbitrary political domination, even from an inherently democratic people. Finally, if totalitarian conquest should become feasible, a world state could be hammered out, but the recourse to coercion over industrialized economies would leave for some time a bloody wake of bitterness, depression, and grinding poverty, ill omens for an enduring commonwealth and obviously not "progress" for a large portion of mankind. Perhaps Bagehot's words might then prove true: "Later are the ages of freedom; first are the ages of servitude."

Chapter 6

The people is a tragic and comic two-face:
hero and hoodlum; phantom and gorilla twist-
ing to moan with a gargoyle mouth: "They
buy me and sell me. . . . it's a game. . . .
sometime I'll break loose. . . ."

       Once having marched
Over the margins of animal necessity,
Over the grim line of sheer subsistence
       Then man came
To the deeper rituals of his bones,
To the lights lighter than any bones,
To the time for thinking things over,
To the dance, the song, the story,
Or the hours given over to dreaming. . . .

the people hold to the humdrum bidding of work and food
while reaching out when it comes their way
for lights beyond the prison of the five senses,
for keepsakes lasting beyond any hunger or death.
       This reaching is alive.
The panderers and liars have violated and smutted it.
       Yet this reaching is alive yet
       for lights and keepsakes.

Carl Sandburg

World Government and
Spiritual Progress

ECONOMIC MAN is a sheer caricature, grotesque as a eunuch, stripped of beauty, conscience, and the thousand throbbing passions which move the soul beyond the search for bread. No state, therefore, has ever existed solely to satisfy economic wants, for the sense of community which is the basis of every cooperative political organization is at once economic and spiritual in its associations. What is required of world government is the adequate fulfillment of man's imaginative joys and the gentle release of his emotional tensions as much as the proper balance of economic conflicts. The bright banners of nationalism which crown the battlements of nearly every modern state announce in shrill tones the sentiments of race, language, manners, historical experience, or common institutions which bind peoples together in their daily exchange of tangible commodities.

The words of Aristotle on this subject have a very familiar ring.

Nor does a state exist for the sake of alliance and security from injustice, nor yet for the sake of exchange and mutual intercourse. . . . Such a community can only be established among those who live in the same place and intermarry. Hence arise in cities family connexions, brotherhoods, common sacrifices, amusements which draw men together. But these are created by friendship, for the will to live together is friendship.[1]

The sprawling barbarian empires of the East, a conglomeration of motley tribes subjected to the will of despots, could no more be termed states by the philosopher than the several alliances, compacts, and "international" agreements concluded among nations today, for the bonds of community and the will to live together in friendship were—and still are—absent.

There is some difference from the past, however. The historical improvement in military techniques since the fourteenth century [2] provided a more stable control over wider areas by a central authority, and the subsequent increase of commerce and communications offered the framework for a larger political kinship than the polis of Aristotle or the medieval communes of northern Italy. Over the course of centuries, warfare, trade, and the diffusion of one strong local culture combined to break down provincialism and stimulate men to a sense of larger community in their nation. This new organic composition, however, has frequently been viewed as the limit to which the brotherhood of men can realistically extend: Hegel proclaimed that states were "completely autonomous totalities"; Mazzini regarded the nation as the positive and vibrant intermediary between the individual and humanity; Treitsche opined that it was impossible to conceive of a tribunal above the state. Yet the nineteenth and twentieth centuries have worked miraculous

---

[1] *Politics* Book III, chap. ix. Compare the famous lines of Burke: ". . . the state ought not to be considered nothing better than a partnership arrangement in a trade of pepper and coffee, calico or tobacco. . . . It is to be looked upon with other reverence; because it is not a partnership in things subservient only to the gross animal existence of a temporary and perishable nature. It is a partnership in all science; a partnership in all art; a partnership in every virtue, and in all perfection."—*Reflections on the French Revolution.*
[2] As early as the fourteenth century, peasant and burgher foot-soldiers had defeated armored knights by using the pike. The English longbow at Crécy completed the rout of feudal cavalry, but at Formigny, Normandy, in 1450, two French field guns slaughtered the English infantry. The introduction of hand firearms required professional soldiers and expensive equipment which only a national economy could afford. See Ault, *Europe in the Middle Ages,* pp. 665 *et seq.*

effects upon the associations of mankind; the enormity of war, the absorptions of domestic industry, the catholicism of commerce are perennially corroding the sentimental links of patriotism. With this in mind, Graham Wallas at the close of his study of human nature in politics, some forty years ago, asked:

Will the process of coalescence go on either in feeling or in constitutional forms, or are there any permanent causes tending to limit the geographical or racial sphere of effective political solidarity, and therefore the size and composition of States? [3]

This inquiry for world government is crucial to an understanding of the possibility of a stable and progressive world order, for without the emotional bond which inspires men to grandiose schemes and subdues petty private antagonisms to a larger cause, the hope for cooperative effort in a universal organization pales. Nothing has been more effective in submerging local animosities than the flamboyant appeals of the nation to patriotism, and John Stuart Mill, like other liberals, went so far as to declare that free institutions virtually require a coincidence of nationality and government. [4]

The classic example of international peace, the Roman Empire, was not invested with patriotic populations, for the pride in the capital city and its early struggles, its gods and its legends, so much a part of the ancient republic, could not be arbitrarily shared with Greeks and Gauls, Egyptians and Germans, despite the formal grant of universal citizenship by Caracalla in 212 A.D. During the whole period of the Empire, stretching over fifteen hundred years in the East, no serious attempt to restore constitutional government was made. [5] Rousseau shrewdly perceived the difficulty of maintaining liberty unless the polity was small and at the same time noted the physical weakness of a small state against a large, overbearing neighbor. He intended to examine the possibilities of combining the external strength

[3] Wallas, *Human Nature in Politics*, p. 270.
[4] John Stuart Mill, *On Representative Government*, p. 362.
[5] Bryce, *Modern Democracies*, p. 27.

of a great people with the good order of a small state in federalism, but never got around to the study.[6] Not only does this problem remain for the imperial states of the world today, but it accentuates the profound difficulty of realizing a universal commonwealth rather than a universal dictatorship.

What is unmistakable about the nation-state as a form of social organization is its pervasive noneconomic roots; the collective happiness, pride, sorrow, ambition, and regret of a people. Economic livelihood is entwined, to be sure, around each of these aspects of fraternalism, but the resoluteness, the sacrifice, the will to unified action is drawn from the inner feelings of men, not from their pocketbooks. The political consciousness of national solidarity in the nineteenth century, for example, was marked by a cultural revival—in Italy, Czechoslovakia, Greece, Lithuania, Ireland [7]—rather than by economic dissatisfactions. Once the sense of a distinctive heritage was implanted in the minds of a minority people, their economic and social handicaps in relation to the dominant population found a rationale in the idea of nationality, and the remedy was sought in self-determination, or, in effect, becoming a majority within a separate government. When aroused in earnest, this feeling withstood the most repressive forces as the nation united in a common unrelenting struggle against foreign rule until its distinctive character was recognized through political emancipation.

Not long ago religion served the same political purposes. Thus, the union of Bohemia, Hungary, and Austria was pre-

---

[6] Rousseau, *The Social Contract*, p. 80, Book III, chap. xv. "I will show later on how the external strength of a great people may combine with the convenient polity and good order of a small state," and in a footnote, "I had intended to do this in the sequel to this work, when in dealing with external relations I came to the subject of confederations. This subject is quite new, and its principles have still to be laid down."

[7] See Walter Sulzbach, *National Consciousness*, pp. 23 *et seq.* for some illustrations of literary influence on nationalism. The scholarship of the nineteenth century also made giant strides in the study of comparative philology, anthropology, and law which acted as catalyst for the budding national pride.

cipitated by a common Christian resistance against the encroachments of the Moslem Turks in the sixteenth century. Three centuries later the combination was wrecked by a new faith called nationalism. The immediate cause of the devastating Thirty Years' War which reshaped the map of Europe was an attack upon two churches in Prague. In France, Spain, and Italy the viciousness of the Renaissance was directed against religions, not languages.[8] McCartney points out how the English Queen Elizabeth, facing a struggle with the Roman Church, caused the Bible and Prayer Book to be printed in the Welsh language.[9] Contrast these attitudes with the attempts of the Prussians to Germanize their Polish subjects after 1870 or the Russification program in the czars' empire. The recent history of India shows that internecine religious cleavages rather than national sentiment principally account for the craving for internal political division.

The affection for the fatherland has been aptly described by Carlton Hayes as a new religion.

Nor may the role of the modern nation-state, any more than that of the mediaeval church, be thought of as economic or mercenary; it is primarily spiritual, even other-worldly, and its driving force is its collective *faith*, a faith in its mission and destiny, a faith in things unseen, a faith that would move mountains. Nationalism is sentimental, emotional, and inspirational.[10]

The point here is *the cohesiveness of sentiment*, whether in the guise of tribalism, religion, or nationalism. It would be fool-

[8] "Meanwhile Germany was drifting toward revolution. Luther had sensed this as he rode homeward from Worms . . . German knights were dissatisfied because town and urban economy were making vast gains at the expense of this class . . . the unsatisfactory economic position of the peasantry made it equally ready for some kind of blind revolt . . . strange doctrines were readily accepted by the unfortunates . . . the simple peasant was ever prone to appeal to some of the basic ethical appeals of Christianity when he sought fairer economic treatment. Taking religion literally and seriously often led to social and political radicalism in the eyes of both Church and State." Henry S. Lucas, *Renaissance and Reformation*, pp. 452–455.
[9] McCartney, *National States and National Minorities*, p. 42.
[10] Hayes, *Essays on Nationalism*, p. 106.

hardy to assume, therefore, that some such emotional stock is
not essential to the attainment of a universal polity; it would
be more insensate to deny the validity and persistence of nationalism by referring to economic statistical abstracts.[11]

What history teaches in all-too-tragic tones is that sentiment
is both a slave and a master of human will. The same idealization
of religion which brought forth the art of Giotto, Fra Angelico,
Raphael, and Michelangelo and created the cathedrals of Notre
Dame, Rheims, and Le Mans fell into the toils of the Inquisition;
the same affection for the fatherland which inculcated heroism
and sacrifice for liberty has driven nations into a blind ambition
for prestige and power.[12] Nationalism is today the whipping
boy for schemes of world government, but its evils are merely
tokens of the seething prejudices which press upon the community and require a never-ending adjustment. To liberate the
immanent values, to develop the substantial virtues of the nation is one task of world government; to create a larger loyalty
as the basis of a strong regulatory administration which can
check the excesses of particularism is the complementary need.
There is a taut rope forever stretched between liberty and authority, and "the task is not to abolish the tension, but to establish equilibrium between the two dynamic poles of the

[11] "By the identification of nation and state . . . the cultural and emotional
life of the masses has become closely integrated with the political life. Any
change in the principles of political organization will therefore encounter the
strongest resistance, which, against considerations of the national and universal good, will appeal to deep-rooted traditions."—Kohn, *The Idea of Nationalism*, p. 23.

[12] "But if politics seizes this notion of nationality and makes of it an absolute
principle, without limits or controls, then it becomes, like all other absolute
political principles which have no counterweight or measure, a vehicle of
oppression, of tyranny, and of gangsterism. Under the pretext of giving
to a nation the place in the world which will allow it to develop all its worth
and its power and to go to the very end of vital expression which it claims
for itself, the morality of nationalism justifies all atrocities and legitimizes the
worst tyrannies." Quoted by Sturzo, *Nationalism and Internationalism*, p. 37
from "Enquete sur le nationalisme," ed. by Maurice Vaussard (Paris, Editions
Spes, 1924), p. 25.

relationship . . . to combine supra-national order with national freedom." [13]

Nationalism has accentuated diversity, and in doing so has extolled individual character. It offers to its citizens the sense of participating in a common endeavor which has distinctive qualities apart from the herd of mankind, and in a mechanical age which has destroyed the supernatural it furnishes a "spiritual consolation" which touches the deepest need of the individual. Alfred Cobban writes:

> Western civilization owes much of what is best in it to the mutual influence of its different nations, with their varying traditions and outlooks, upon one another. The elements making for uniformity are so many and so strong that we cannot afford to reject any force that holds out a hope of keeping them in check.[14]

The dullness and dreariness of a world government which implied the molding of all peoples into one character for the sake of uniform control and the parceling of economic wealth would signify little progress towards opening wider opportunities to that distinction which men seem to crave. Furthermore, it would throttle the stimulating effect of cultures as they have impinged upon one another in the past and as they are initiated, improved, and passed on in more useful or beautiful forms. Worst of all, the natural antipathy of all peoples to the extinction of their manners, habits, and social consciousness, even for the sake of physical protection, would evoke rebellion in itself.

The complete integration of local areas by the modern state is fortunately an incomplete process: Welsh and Scottish children can still learn their native languages in Great Britain, and the Channel Islanders, the Manxmen, and the Ulster Orangemen are not English; Catalonia continually defies a lumping with Spain, and Sicily with Italy; France has her Basques and Bretons, quite apart from the Parisians. Hugo

[13] Heimann, *Freedom and Order*, pp. 9, 20.
[14] Cobban, *National Self-Determination*, p. 139.

Preuss once thought the Kaiser and the princes of the Reich were artificial obstructions to the single voice of the German people, yet

> Kaiser and Princes vanished overnight, but the particularist boundaries did not vanish with them. The unit in terms of which many thought and acted tended to be rather the local republic than the German Reich.[15]

Canada and Czechoslovakia, South Africa and Yugoslavia are amalgams. The federalism of the United States and that of Switzerland are testaments of a compromise on diversity, and the highly publicized cultural freedoms within the Soviet Union are in keeping with recent trends of imperialism.

The problem has then been the subordination of insularity to the minimum political requirements of a state without losing the intimate ties of the native to his language, his religion, his customs, and his countryside, without destroying those important psychological bonds which, unloosed, would produce unhappy mobs of either mentally or physically uprooted people stereotyped by an alien culture and devoid of communal responsibility.[16]

Leonard Hobhouse, in a brilliant course of lectures at Columbia University in 1911, formulated the development of the state

---

[15] Emerson, *State and Sovereignty in Modern Germany*, p. 237.

[16] The problem of the "déraciné" individual of industrialized society has caught the attention of a number of writers. Ortega y Gasset's "Revolt of the Masses" is an indictment of stereotypes. Erich Fromm writes: "Vastness of cities in which the individual is lost, buildings that are as high as mountains, constant acoustic bombardment by the radio, big headlines changing three times a day and leaving no choice to decide what is important, shows in which one hundred girls demonstrate their ability with clocklike precision to eliminate the individual and act like a powerful though smooth machine . . . these and many other details are expressions of a constellation in which the individual is confronted by uncontrollable dimensions in comparison with which he is a small particle. All he can do is fall in step like a marching soldier or a worker on the endless belt. He can act; but the sense of independence and significance has gone."—*Escape from Freedom*. To some extent the encouragement of particularism would act as a brake upon monotony, insecurity, fear, and the mad flight to slavery disguised as a blatant cure-all.

in three phases: the tribal stage, first, which is compact and enduring, but ill-adapted to an advanced economy or art and inherently hostile to outsiders; the weakness of the tribe, then, in the face of larger populations and improved civilization yields to the authority of imperialism; finally, the principle of citizenship which, incidentally, few peoples have attained, makes possible the practical governance of wide areas while preserving the organic vitality of the clan.[17] Hobhouse did not subscribe to any assumption that civilization as a whole was progressing through such an evolution, for clearly the Greek polis [18] and the Roman republic moved from citizenship to authority, while only recently the German state reverted to a fanatical tribalism; but what he did argue was that citizenship offered a balance between freedom and authority, between the expression of diversity essential to a happy human existence and the necessary subjection to a common will. G. D. H. Cole has elucidated the task of big government in the same context of ideas by advocating the decentralization of national administration into regions. He vehemently asserts that

the vital importance to the larger community of the maintenance of strong local life and feeling throughout the smaller communities within it. Only if men learn the social spirit in their daily contact with their neighbors can they hope to be good citizens of the larger community.[19]

[17] Hobhouse, *Social Evolution and Political Theory*, pp. 139 *et seq.*
[18] As Athens expanded from a city-state to an empire, she pursued a mixed policy of imperialism (authority) and citizenship. Her imperialism at times was harsh. Thus, she slaughtered the men of Melos and sold their wives into slavery in 416 because the Melesians had paid a tribute to Sparta while nominally in the Athenian League. But subject states were normally free to manage their own affairs, although Athens insisted upon a democracy and "instead of the usual futile bickerings between state and state, peace reigned in the Aegean. Unity was never achieved on so grand a scale until imposed a hundred years later by the Macedonian conquerer." There was little disaffection in the transition from League to Empire, and at the beginning of hostilities with Sparta, in 431, the Athenian allies were completely passive to Sparta's entreaties to revolt against the capital city. See Cyril E. Robinson, *History of Greece*.
[19] Cole, *Social Theory*, p. 169.

The distinction between cultural freedom and political freedom begins to fade under these assaults. The Constitution of the Austria-Hungarian Empire promulgated on December 21, 1867, for example, provided equal rights for all the jumbled peoples of its domain: native languages were taught in the primary schools, imperial officials were required to be fluent in the tongue of their areas, all persons were entitled to the same protection by the law, and public office was open to everyone, regardless of nationality. Yet the policy of reasonable tolerance, of liberty within authority, was not rooted in the people themselves, largely due to historical circumstances and the new blindness of nationalism. The actual inequality of the mixed nations, moreover, placed an additional burden on its healthy operation. Comprised of Germans, Czechs, Slovaks, Poles, Ruthenes, Slovenes, Croats, Serbs, and Italians, the polyglot empire in practice saw the Germans, Poles, and Italians far advanced in culture over the other peoples and the Germans, Jews, and Italians more prosperous than their neighbors.[20] Without a supreme loyalty to the system which permits the co-existence of divergent cultures, a common citizenship is a farce; and without the impartial promotion of a vigorous and distinctive local life, such allegiance is an impossibility. By the same token, progressive government is simply not a matter of benevolent despotism or even majority votes. It is the acceptance of diversity and, therefore, articulate criticism of wholesale policies. All these remarks applicable to national development are the more cogent for envisaging a universal organization in which the most varied languages, laws, religions, and customs are to be gathered, for the harmonization of these differences without their utter annihilation must be considered a prerequisite for a "better" arrangement of world society.

One of the fascinating curiosities of history is the development of Chinese philosophy in the sixth century B.C.—at a time roughly coincident with the burgeoning of Greek thought,

[20] McCartney, *National States and National Minorities*, p. 140.

the inspired ethics of the Hebrews, and the beginnings of Jainism, Buddhism, and Zoroastrianism. The succeeding ages of Chinese intellectual brilliance, moreover, were accompanied by a political rivalry among several strong states. Then, almost exactly contemporary with the Roman hegemony over the Western world, the Ch'in and Han dynasties overthrew the feudal states and forged a united, imperial China; but a "composite Confucianism" became the inflexible guide to official policy, and orthodoxy put an end to the stimulating clash of free expression. Domestic peace was temporarily achieved at a high cost to genius.[21]

Now the history of Western civilization from the period of Descartes to the combined talents of those who developed the idea and execution of an atomic bomb is far too fresh in the pages of judgment to permit anything but the most tentative speculations, but the general congruity of the intellectual flowering and the presence of a group of independent nations, none of which positively forbade the migration of ideas, furnishes some clues to the trend of world government. Partly for this tendency to stimulate thinking by the free impingement of one culture upon another, the nation has had its earnest advocates. Lord Acton, for example, deplored making the state and nation commensurate, for this implied the subjection of all other nationalities within an essentially political boundary. He rightly perceived that a state which labors to expel or extirpate or simply absorb different "races" may destroy its own vitality. The political state is a crucible in which the vigor, the knowledge, and the capacities of one nation, sect, people, or race may

[21] "In establishing this composite Confucianism as the leading philosophy of the state and making its texts the subject of study in the schools of the Empire and the basis of civil service examinations, the Han monarchs were promoting the cultural unity of their domains. The very syncretism which so characterized both the Han—as contrasted with the distinct philosophic divisions of Chou times—both reflected and contributed to the political and cultural imperial structure now achieved. The Han not only welded China into a political empire. They found its solidarity upon a more lasting basis, that of one civilization and theory of life." Latourette, *The Chinese, Their History and Culture*, pp. 132–133.

be communicated to another for the mutual benefit of all.[22] Hobson carried this thesis one step further, as a footnote to his scathing criticism of imperialism.

The hope of coming internationalism enjoins above everything else the maintenance and natural growth of independent nationalities, for without such there could be no gradual evolution of internationalism, but only a series of unsuccessful attempts at a chaotic and unstable cosmopolitanism. As individualism is essential to any sane form of national socialism, so nationalism is essential to internationalism: no organic conception of world politics can be framed on any other supposition.[23]

The toleration of diversity means the restrained use of power; it involves politics, with its elements of lurking brute force. The continence of states is not to be sought in their enlightenment alone, for if the weight of economic necessity presses upon a strong people, how much more will the zealousness of their most intimate ideals and customs sway them from a course of moderation? Tolerance or apathy on the part of a single ruling power may confer limited privileges upon the peoples of an empire and in the short run ease the primary emotional conflicts of a subjugated group. In such a scheme, however, cultural tolerance becomes a route of despotic expediency for the dominant group, for unless the independence of language, religion, and folkways can eventually find a political expression, it fails to engender a responsibility to the whole community, an equal respect for the principle of free expression, and the necessary ability to maintain such a government.

The Ottoman Turks, as an illustration, inherited the Byzantine Empire and continued its autocratic rule over the odd collection of religions and peoples within the borders. By the "millet" system [24] non-Moslem communities secured the free

[22] Lord Acton, *The History of Freedom and Other Essays*, p. 290.
[23] Hobson, *Imperialism*, pp. 318–319.
[24] A millet or religious community was placed under an ecclesiastical leader whose powers extended far beyond purely religious affairs in local administration.

practice of their faith and maintained their customs and their local laws. In the early period of the empire the Janissary was a zealous band of disciplined soldiers, the personal guard of the Sultan and recruited solely from Christian families. In the declining years of Turkish rule the declaration of Hatti Humaium, in 1856, pronounced the equality of all sects, the opening of public schools to all peoples, and the principle of mixed nationality courts. Nominally the appointments to imperial offices were shared by all without regard to religion. But from infancy to death every man and woman was considered the slave of the Sultan no matter how high his rank. The enforcement of toleration, moreover, was impossible to realize under the Moslem strictures which recognized only "conversion, tribute, or the sword." [25] What the Osmanli actually demanded in his seeming tolerance was "tribute," and the crude politics of the empire struggled along on this basis. Neither did there exist a larger loyalty to a community which would permit free opinion, nor was a competence to organize and govern such a polity created. In many respects, indeed, the Christians feared the possible oppression by their Christian neighbors within the empire more than they feared their Moslem masters. [26]

How is the equanimity of all states and nationalities to come about? In the final analysis it is a sentiment, and no specific form of government, no constitutional mechanism, no itemization of rights and duties can create *ex vacuo* such a feeling. No proper analogy, in fact, can be drawn between formulation of this mood and overcoming the perverse obstacles of the physical world. [27] Involved here are all the unknown appetites and

[25] See Creasy, *Turkey*, p. 471.
[26] Luke, *The Making of Modern Turkey*.
[27] For a provocative article on this subject see Hans Morgenthau, "The Scientific Solution of Social Conflicts," in Bryson and others, ed. *Approaches to National Unity*, p. 419. The problem of world peace, like other social problems, Mr. Morgenthau finds, "depends essentially on three factors: social pressure which is capable of containing the evil tendencies of human nature within socially tolerable bounds; conditions of life . . . which tend to minimize psychological causes of social conflict . . . and finally, the moral

fantasies of man, his prejudices, his ambitions, and the faint glimmering of reason which occasionally pierces the black forest of savagery. Yet some barometer for the climate of social cooperation is available. For example, the presence of an ethical system which is universal rather than particular, which posits an underlying kinship of all men, which advises the moderation of desire by the good works of friendship is an index to the social harmony which can be encouraged. Not only Christianity, but Buddhism, Taoism, and Confucianism have such qualities—whereas tribal cults stress the peculiarity and absolute distinction of one people from another. Away from the theological plane, exclusive sectarianism has found its defender in rampant nationalism, which places the universal good in a position subordinate to the state and whispers "raison d'état" as an excuse for any policy of government. In other words, a way of thinking which places the advantage of the part continually above the welfare of the whole, or which claims the absolute possession of truth, or which, in brief, denies the responsibilities of one man to all men, breeds a plague of hostility. The meaning of democracy, according to Heimann, is that it "does not claim to be just, but only to strive for justice," [28] and Dewey notes that "an anti-humanist attitude is the essence of every form of intolerance. Movements that begin by stirring up hostility against a group of people end by denying to them all human qualities." [29]

But ethics do not exist in space. Preachments of conduct have frequently required assistance, such as Frederick of Saxony for Lutherans, Spanish conquistadores for Catholics, and English Roundheads for Puritans. The implantation of fraternity requires more than a bare statement on the worth of men, for such an expression remains inaudible unless the use of force can

---

climate which allows man to expect at least an approximation to justice here and now."
[28] Heimann, *Freedom and Order.*
[29] Dewey, *Freedom and Culture,* p. 127.

be checked long enough to assure a receptive hearing. Once again it is the availability of sufficient counterbalances in naked strength which forces upon men a moment's hesitation in the infinity of time, a halt to action and a minute for reflection in which the tuggings of the soul may be felt. Put in bald terms,

Freedom has always, both within and as between states, rested upon the possibility of resistance to dominant power . . . in the international field, where there is no international government . . . the only possibility of freedom lies in the existence of some power of resistance or possibility of resistance to external power.[30]

The creation of a world government to satisfy the urgings of men for a creative life, for liberty within order, and for diversity within unity presupposes a moral climate from which intransigence has been removed and in which mutual respect flourishes, but it is suggested that to adjust continually the innumerable frictions arising from the natural envy, despair, or inertia of any such society, a stop-gap of time for compromise must be available and that this may or may not be furnished by the array of force both within and between nations at some particular time.

A fleeting glance at the nation-states of the world, with their internal discords, bitter intolerance, and absolute claims, is sufficient to expose the rancor that pervades international society. Remarkably few peoples have yet found a stable basis for the peaceful day-to-day conduct of their domestic difficulties. Civil war has in recent years struck Spain, China, Greece, and India, while constantly harassing a dozen Latin-American states; colonial revolutions have flared in Annam and Indonesia; the Arab states have been incensed by Israel; neither France nor Italy has a stable government; Hungary, Rumania, Poland, Bulgaria, Czechoslovakia, Yugoslavia, Albania, and Russia are police states—relying upon unswerving zeal and cold ruthlessness for effectuating government policy. The picture is somber and the débacle of freedom seems certain. When rivalries become so

[30] Angell, *The Steep Places*, p. 140.

intense as to defeat all cooperation, then the cry for the dictator mounts. Has civilization, in fact, ebbed to this point, and viewing the impact of domestic turbulence upon international relations, is there no alternative to the iron fist of imperialism?

David Dallin bluntly carries the analysis back to the freedom within the nation-state in maintaining that real progress can be achieved only through the internal evolution of each nation.

Freedom is no absolute remedy against warlike tendencies, but lack of freedom promotes the growth of the martial spirit. Dictatorship is the high road to war. Conversely the existence of political freedom and civil liberties acts as a brake on tendencies toward conquest and subjugation of alien nations.[31]

The idea that emerges in this connection is that world government, far from being a definable institutional structure for abstract states, must indeed be determined by the kind of universal citizenry the nation-state will allow to develop.[32] The statesmen who carry the spirit either of tolerance or of aggression into world councils must inevitably be the product of their native institutions,[33] and if world government is to be reached by agreement, it will be these same statesmen who reach an accord. The immediate difficulty for the transposition of the national system to the supra-national state is not so much the lack of an international community as the want of stability and liberty within the nation.

The central idea of Woodrow Wilson, under the prodding

[31] Dallin, *The Big Three,* p. 283.

[32] For an interesting insight into the development of truly international civil servants and the influences of their nation-states upon them see Ranshofen-Wertheimer, "International Administration; Lessons from the Experience of the League of Nations," in *The American Political Science Review,* XXXVII (October, 1943), 872–887.

[33] The curt, inhospitable language of Soviet envoys, for example, which so dismays Western diplomats is only explicable by Russian theology—"And a good envoy of this new young Communist school would no more dream of insisting that the Kremlin should change the tone or substance of its message . . . in deference to the strange mental habits of his auditors, than the Christian missionary . . . It is, when all is said, the word of God." Edward Crankshaw, *Russia and the Russians,* p. 164.

of Colonel House, for a League of Nations was mutual guarantees of political independence and territorial integrity under republican forms of government,[34] guarantees undertaken by states which had achieved a measure of orderly intercourse among their citizens and were responsible to popular judgment. With Germany defeated and Russia near anarchy, it could, at first, be said that the leading powers of the League met democratic standards. But the collapse of the League later was only partly due to the march of the dictators within some states; it was also due to the weak or nonexistent allegiance of the democratic states to an international system of peaceful change. That is why Sir Alfred Zimmern wrote in 1936:

If the free states can overcome their anarchistic tendencies and learn to act together, they will not need to be too exclusive in admitting partners since the spirit of freedom is infectious. But if on the contrary they remain divided and the machinery of international cooperation is left to the control of men who do not know what freedom means, then the movement for world order will be divorced from the idea of progress, and it will be necessary to start fresh upon new foundations.[35]

The close of the Second World War, however, found a United Nations organization dependent upon the most totalitarian of nations—an impossible foundation for a towering edifice of cooperative world government.[36] The dilemma revolves about

[34] On December 16, 1914, House suggested to Wilson that he formulate an inter-American agreement of mutual guarantees under republican forms of government as an example to Europe for peace-making. Wilson was excited by this. The negotiations for a Pan-American pact balked, but Wilson never lost sight of the ideal. Zimmern, *The League of Nations and the Rule of Law*, pp. 217 *et seq.*

[35] Zimmern, "Liberty, Democracy, and the Movement Towards World Order," in *Problems of Peace*, 10th Series, p. 151.

[36] By contrast, the "Wilsonian" world order actually desired by Roosevelt is shown in his "Four Freedoms" speech: "Since the beginning of our American history we have been engaged in change—in a permanent peaceful revolution—a revolution which goes on steadily, quietly adjusting itself to changing conditions—without the concentration camp or the quicklime ditch. The world which we seek is the cooperation of free countries, working together in a friendly civilized society." *Message to Congress on the State of the Union*, January 6, 1941.

the internal constitution of the state; so long as the ruling elements are obsessed by an absolute idea and their power is unlimited by forces within the country, it seems sheer fantasy to suppose an "international consciousness" can be manufactured, for such a mind requires a pliant and inquiring disposition which yields to the force of argument rather than the force of armament.[37] Democratic states have also demonstrated irresponsibility in foreign affairs, but the opportunities for hearing evidence, for rectifying errors and checking military forces do seem better. The grim specter of clustered dictatorships with their brazen orthodoxy throughout the many states of the world, however, has some compensating articles for faith in emergent freedom. In retrospect, there has been not so much a loss of democracy as a reformulation of democracy throughout the world; the emphasis on political liberty has yielded little by little to the quest for economic and social equality.[38] The short-sighted observer who scans the international scene through the glasses of Anglo-American history fails to recognize just how far removed from his brand of political liberty the peoples of Europe, not to mention Asia and Africa, have been. Some mention of the Austro-Hungarian[39] and Ottoman empires has already been made. The imperial rule of Russia needs no comment. The Second German Reich fell a victim to its own lack of responsible government. In Italy, under the symbol of parliamentary practice, Giolitti manipulated the elections of 1892, 1904, 1909, and 1913, and democratic principles were subverted by the most flagrant corrup-

[37] "Whenever a single definite object is made the supreme end of the state, be it the advantage of a class, the safety or the power of the country, the greatest happiness of the greatest number, or the support of any speculative idea, the State becomes for the time inevitably absolute." Acton, *The History of Freedom*, p. 288.
[38] For a brief, scintillating analysis of "political democracy" vs. "social democracy" see Carr, *The Soviet Impact on the Western World*.
[39] For an eyewitness account of Austrian parliamentary behavior prior to 1914 see Wolf von Schierbrand, "Austria-Hungary; The Polyglot Empire," reprinted in part in Scott and Baltzly, *Readings in European History since 1814*, p. 327.

tion many years before the appearance of Mussolini.[40] Spain lived under the dictatorship of Rivera from 1923 to 1930 before the fascism of Franco, and the short-lived republic of 1931–36 scarcely caught its breath in the foul air of Iberian politics. Great wars may dethrone rulers and bring forth shiny new constitutions, but only creeping time and constant exertion can implant friendship in the hearts of men.

But if totalitarianism has sacrificed aristocrats, intellectuals, property owners, churchmen, and sturdy individualism, it has also smashed economic barriers and social stigma for the over-whelming mass of peoples who were denied and are still denied an ultimate political control of their governments. With suffi-cient time and the continued maintenance of democracy by those states which have blundered into it, the turtle-like tread of freedom may yet be charted. Dewey has remarked that with proper selection one can make out a case for history as a move-ment toward freedom, but a more sober view indicates that a very fortunate conjunction of circumstances brought about the nineteenth-century achievements in democratic progress: "what was won in a more or less external and accidental manner must now be achieved and sustained by a deliberate and intelli-gent endeavor." [41] It is this conception of "progress" toward world government, neither automatic nor, in truth, highly probable, which seems most meaningful.

While economic centralization under industrialism has im-posed serious threats to individual freedom not only in totali-tarian societies but also in planned democratic states, it has also been the impetus on a world scale to well-coordinated empires.

---

[40] For the best annotated account of Italian democracy before the First World War see Margot Hentze, *Pre-Fascist Italy*. In some respects Croce presents a more balanced picture, for he paints on a larger canvas of social-economic-aesthetic achievements. Even so, "Her free institutions had behind them no long history of varied trials and manifold labors and vicissitudes; they had been given all at once, like an abundant and beneficent rain sent in answer to prayer. Hence the failure to realize their value, or the labor which had been put into them."—Croce, *History of Italy, 1870–1914*, tr. by Cecilia M. Ady, p. 103.
[41] John Dewey, *Freedom and Culture*, p. 173.

In some respects this has reduced the burden of imagining a world government which might give to local administrations the free exercise of their language, customs, laws, and traditions while generally pledged to a larger system providing economic and military benefits. In varying degrees the United States, Britain, and the Soviet Union are traveling along this course within their expansive realms; nor can the distinction between "colonies" and independent states be regarded as vital in an age where small states cannot isolate themselves from the struggle of Titans.

Russia encourages cultural diversity through its autonomous republics and regions, while insisting upon the economic and military integrity of the Soviet Union. The "right of secession" [42] accorded the Union Republics is a token of partnership, if not a feasible practice, for the nationalities under the Red flag. Furthermore, the Czechs, Poles, Hungarians, Rumanians, and Bulgarians have been left as independent states in the Russian sphere of influence, but a strong elite, loyal to the economic and military requirements of their giant neighbor, has been vigorously supported.[43]

The British have a long history of creating self-governing states within their anomalous commonwealth which has been described as "the only practical experience men have had of an enduring and peaceful association among sovereign states." [44] The Empire recognizes transitional political institu-

[42] For an interpretation of this "right" see Alfred Cobban, *National Self-Determination*, pp. 105–109.

[43] The recent attitude of French colonial policy should be compared. "It aims now at cultural and economic rather than political assimilation. The legal system seeks to bring native personal law as far as possible into general conformity with French law. Education is almost everywhere in French rather than in vernacular. The aim is less that of wide popular education than the creation of an elite which will be bound to France by its participation in French civilization." Lord Haily, *Future of Colonial Peoples*, p. 41.

[44] McGuire, *Experiment in World Order*, p. 346. Mr. McGuire feels that the forces at work within the British system are no longer centrifugal—though not centripetal either. He thinks that authority and responsibility should be distributed and that a real increase of organic community, the only possible advance towards a world society, may then be seen. Possibly. The conduct of

tions as the technique of teaching popular rule over the course of time while breeding loyalty to the mother of parliaments: thus, some colonies have legislatures appointed by the Crown, others have partly appointed and partly elected law-making bodies, and others are fully self-governing. Through native authorities in African colonies, for example, an effort is made to utilize tribe, clan, or village customs.[45]

The United States, finally, seems destined to incorporate Hawaii and Alaska as equal partners, while it has already forged the independence of Cuba and the Philippine Islands, but the latter states are closely linked to the American republic by military bases and important economic considerations. In regard to the Latin-American states south of the Rio Grande River the powerful American republic has consciously pursued a "good neighbor" policy which might be called imperialism by persuasion rather than imperialism by intimidation.

With such evidence it does not seem too far from the truth to conclude that the concentration of power among a few states of the world has been accompanied by a clearer understanding of the values of noneconomic factors in the struggle for military-economic unity and that this realization is, in turn, a measure of progress toward the requisite features of a world government which would respect local diversity. But the blocs of power are neither homogeneous enough in their principles nor numerous enough for the effective balance of ambitions to ensure that balanced order and cooperation so essential to the peaceful adjustment of both economic and social frictions. The

---

Eire recently, the least "different" of the British communities, is not heartening. India and Pakistan have tenuous if not invisible, ties to the Commonwealth. South Africa wavers between its nationalist Boers and its military-economic dependence upon Britain.

[45] For a sidelight on British colonial policy and nationalism see Vernon McKay, "Nationalism in British West Africa," *Foreign Policy Reports*, XXIV (March 15, 1948), 2–11. West Africa contains 3,000 negroes to every white man; East Africa has about 300 to 1; the Union of South Africa roughly 4 to 1. These are inescapable ethnographic facts which place a heavy strain on any policy instituted by the minority.

world state will be, it seems, the product of the world community, the culmination of the good or evil within the several societies that compose the largest society. No man can construct this stupendous plan which surpasses centuries, but every man, if he is willing, can strive to open his own little society to the universal commandment—"Thou shalt love thy neighbor as thyself."

Part Three

JUSTICE, INTERNATIONAL LAW, AND
WORLD COMMUNITY

Chapter 7

He that has grown to wisdom hurries not,
  But thinks and weighs what Reason bids him do
And after thinking he retains his thought
  Until as he conceived the facts ensue.
Let no man to o'erweening pride be wrought,
  But count his state as Fortune's gift and due.
He is a fool who deems that none has sought
  The truth, save he alone, or knows it true.
Many strange birds are on the air abroad,
  Nor all are of one flight or of one force,
    But each after his kind dissimilar:
To each was portioned the breath of God,
  Who gave them divers instincts from one source.
    Then judge not thou thy fellows what they are.

Guido Guinicelli (thirteenth century),
translated by D. G. Rossetti

The Quest for Justice

THE UBIQUITY of power constrains society to heed the entreaties of a universal organization, but who will guarantee justice? In the whole iniquitous, putrid sewer of international relations, few actions have been taken without referring to justice, few declamations by politicians have omitted a passing comment on the righteousness of their own achievements or ambitions. Thus one leader has said, "I have, therefore, taken no step which violated the rights of others, but have only restored that justice which was violated twenty years ago," [1] and immediately plunged the world into a blood bath of war. Another self-anointed soul boasted that a gigantic Roman arch symbolized human determination "to realize peace on a great and truly indestructible basis of justice which reconciles its iron laws with that of light." [2] He thereupon stabbed his neighbor in the back.

Scarcely a day goes by in which some tremulous appeal to justice as the enduring foundation for a world commonwealth does not make its way into a sermon by theologians or a note by statesmen. Apparently if this awesome term "justice" could be satisfactorily defined, a long stride toward world government would be taken, for, indeed, the argument of the preced-

[1] Speech of Chancellor Adolf Hitler to the German Reichstag, April 28, 1939. Reprinted in *International Conciliation*, No. 361, June, 1939, published by the Carnegie Endowment for International Peace.
[2] Speech of Premier Benito Mussolini at Rome, April 30, 1939, advertising the "Olympiad of Civilization" exposition to be held in 1942. *Ibid.*

ing chapters might be sharply summarized as an effort to il-
luminate the stumbling blocks to a "just" government for the
universe, not the impossibility of one global dominion.

The identification of *ius*, the root of the word justice, with
both law and right in Latin is, of course, no semantic accident.
The Roman distinguished *ius* from *lex*, since the former term
implied a sense of morality, a sanction of custom, apart from the
mere enactment of legislation by the arbitrary will of a majority in the *comitia*. Within modern society, too, justice is
hardly requited by recourse to statutes, for positive law is
gravely limited by the faculty of legislatures to generalize and
translate the multitudinous demands of the state into single
commands. Where the political apparatus has not provided a
guide to the incessant frictions of life, custom and the interpretation of disinterested judges offer a rule. It would seem, nevertheless, that justice extends its pale fingers beyond both legal
enactments and customary decisions, for custom has been
tyrannous and statutes are fickle. Justice, indeed, has a first
cousin in the idea of equity.[3]

One author has wisely remarked that the starting point of
justice is an abstract principle of right from which appropriate
legal regulations may be created, while the starting point of
equity is a specific case to which a right rule may be applied.
Midway, therefore, justice and equity meet in their intentions.[4]
But in international law, while some spokesmen have affirmed

---

[3] "What creates the problem is that the equitable is just . . . not the legally
just, but a correction of legal justice. The reason is that all law is universal,
but about some things it is not possible to make a universal statement which
shall be correct . . . the law takes the usual case, though it is not ignorant
of the possibility of error . . . it is right then . . . to say what the legislator
himself would have said had he been present, and would have put into his
law if he had known. Hence the equitable is just, and better than one kind of
justice—not better than absolute justice, but better than error that arises from
the absoluteness of the statement."—Aristotle *Nichomachaen Ethics* Book V,
chap. x. For a thorough, academic analysis of the differences between *lex, ius*
and the *aequum et bonum* see Suarez, *On Laws and God the Lawgiver*, Book
1 chap. ii.

[4] Gustav Radbruch, "Justice and Equity in International Relations," in Bentwich et al., *Justice and Equity in the International Sphere*, p. 3.

from time to time a transcendental justice in the guise of "natural law," others have denied with equal fervor the existence of any useful rule not associated with either manifest custom or legislation through treaties. Furthermore, the application of equity to legal disputes between states of the world has been so carefully circumscribed as to enervate its historical function as an aid to existing law.[5] Thus, instead of a happy blending of right principles, commonly acknowledged, and right decisions, commonly enunciated, to bring about "justice under law," the nation-states persistently maintain a very personal and very relative view of their cause.

Is this because "natural law" is meaningless, and equity, therefore, impossible for the strenuous activities of the twentieth century? Clearly, without an agreeable index to the purposes of international life, the states of the world blink in befuddlement at their controversies and keep a rude hand upon their weapons. The growth of a universally just commonwealth would seem to depend upon a standard of right, but is one really definable? And how will it be transmitted to the souls of Americans, Germans, Russians, French, and Japanese?

Natural law is traced to Stoicism, but it should be recognized at the outset that what ancient philosophers deemed natural was also the perfect realization of the object. The ideal law, that is, the perfect, harmonious regulation of the universe, *was* the natural law, and this conception must be severed from the tortured efforts of modern philosophers to discover by empirical means "laws" of social conduct as inflexible as the physical formulae of Galileo, Kepler, Boyle, or Newton. The emphasis in the one case is upon an end toward which man strives by harmonizing his activities with ideal dic-

---

[5] Thus Article 38 of the Statute of the Permanent Court of International Justice states that the Court shall apply international conventions, custom, general principles of law recognized by civilized nations, judicial decisions, and the teachings of highly qualified publicists in determining the merits of a case. The Court *may* decide *ex aequo et bono* "if the parties agree thereto." The International Court of Justice, as part of the United Nations, retained these provisions *in toto*.

tates; the emphasis in the other case is upon the discovery of
an immanent order through the actual behavior of man.

The old postulate of an immutable law hovering above the
expedient arrangements of society, however, hinges upon sub-
jective interpretations. For example, the natural order was used
to justify individual rights outside of society, and with the same
facility it explained the sanctity of tradition within society.[6]
The proposition that some all-embracing norm claimed an allegiance superior to tribal law, local custom, or regal edicts
served on occasion as a rallying cry against the rigid exercise
of government, and in the name of natural law "serfdom was
destroyed, the foundations were laid of the freedom of property
from feudal burdens, the guilds were shattered, and the bonds
of commerce and industry were loosened." [7] By resort to this
same vague sphere of inviolable right, however, and as a rationalization of a familiar social order, natural law has been invoked
to justify the fixed status of the middle ages and the abuses of
laissez-faire economics in the nineteenth century.

Once the belief in the church as the interpreter of reason and
the curator of salvation had been destroyed, such a willowy
standard as natural law could not satisfy the perpetual search
of men for a star to guide their destiny. The pendulum swung
in the opposite direction to the scientific method of deducing
a principle from a series of empirical observations. History supplied a wealth of illustrations on the conduct of men in society
and was heralded as the criterion for all the rules of life. But
what the savants blithely denied was that "history" has no
meaning in itself, that all the items which comprise its study are
selected and evaluated by man. Certain experiences of the past
may be chosen as a reference for the present, but the future,
which will also be a part of "history," can only be created by
the determination of men to achieve such specific objectives as

[6] Compare, for example, Paine, *The Rights of Man*, and de Maistre, *Essay on
the Generative Principle of Political Constitutions*.
[7] Seagle, *The History of Law*, p. 208.

they consider worth while.[8] Ignoring the role of man's reaction to his experience and his ability to change direction, the logical necessity of history freed men from personal responsibility for the realization of justice in the present. The idea of right, however, could not be completely abandoned: Marxists writhed at capitalism and looked forward to the revolution as determinedly as the primitive Christian denounced sin and warned of judgment day. But in each case the reckoning of the future and the attainment of absolute justice is the rationale for current decisions, whatever their nature.

Thus, vacillating between an ethereal norm which could not be consistently translated into practical life and a doctrine of historical necessity which cut the bonds of personal obligation, men have thwarted their consciences for the pleasure of the moment or the glowing promise of the future. What occurred within nations could not fail to manifest itself in the conduct among nations. Without a sense of duty to something beyond temporal power and individual satisfaction, only force evoked obedience, while cooperation to realize a common good lagged.[9] The significant point, as Laurence Stapleton has ably expressed it, is that without some such conception as a universal idea of justice

there is nothing in . . . any man's philosophy to say why we should not sympathize with conquest or aggrandizement. And if the only sense of law is in the bosom of each tribe or nationality, force alone can be the arbiter of their disputes.[10]

[8] For a complete and pervasive attack upon the historical school by a "critical rationalist," see the masterly work of Popper, *The Open Society and Its Enemies*, Vol. II.

[9] For a more categorical and pessimistic view see Sorokin, *The Crisis of Our Age*, p. 319. "Coming on to the historical scene as a successor to, and as a substitute for, Christian ethics and law, the modern system of sensate ethics and law in its immanent development sowed the seeds of the degradation of man, as well as of the moral values themselves. Declaring the moral values to be mere conventions, it dragged them down to the level of utilitarian and hedonistic calculations . . . In the chaos of conflicting norms, moral values have been more and more ground to dust; they have progressively lost their binding power and given way to rude arbitrary coercion."

[10] Laurence Stapleton, *Justice and World Society*, p. 69.

But perhaps it should be further noted that even with a common acceptance of right principles, the use of coercion would not be obviated. Within the modern democratic state, an organization presumably founded on general agreement, the large standing police force, whose duty is to seize and punish murderers, robbers, rapists, and other felons, clearly indicates the willfulness of some individuals to be outside the law.[11] Those who expect a moral renaissance to usher in an age of harmony among nations should acknowledge the concomitant police force necessary to subdue the perennial recalcitrants to any kind of justice.

If in searching for justice one peers into the make-up of man instead of gaping at the large letters of the state, a premise about human nature is fundamental to any further reasoning. Whether the argument for justice be borne by Epicurus or Epictetus, Hume or Kant, the Utilitarians, the Stoics, or the latter-day historicists, the essential point is a postulate on the capacity of man and, therein, his potential achievement of the summum bonum.[12] Buffeted by psychologists, economic de-

[11] In the well-ordered city of London, for example, during 1947 the municipality maintained 15,000 policemen to check 125,000 crimes. It should be noted that the bureaucratization of the police was a late development of the modern state, considering the independence of the citizenry. In Greece the police function was incumbent upon every citizen. Not until 1792 in England and 1845 in America was a uniformed constabulary established. The chief function of the earlier continental police was political, a role that persists. All this should be compared to the endeavor of the United Nations to establish an international police force, but particularly with Article 51 of the Charter which enjoins the right of self-defense by states the moment the international authority begins to take the necessary action.

[12] "It is not possible to live pleasantly without living prudently and honorably and justly, nor again to live a life of prudence, honor and justice without living pleasantly."—Epicurus; "You can be invincible if you never enter on a contest where victory is not in your power . . . and if the reality of good lies in what is in our power, there is no room for envy or jealousy . . . and there is but one way to freedom, to despise what is not in our power."—Epictetus; "It is only experience which teaches us the nature and bounds of cause and effect, and enables us to infer the existence of one object from that of another. Such is the foundation of moral reasoning, which forms the greater part of human knowledge, and is the source of all human action and behavior."—David Hume; "Now, that in the sphere of human cognition, we have judgments which are necessary, and in the strictest sense

terminists, and racists, the individual has gradually shrunk in
recent years to a helpless pawn of his environment, or heredity,
his will ridiculed as an illusion, his prayers labeled a myth.
Under such circumstances justice can be nothing but a mock-
ery, for without *some* freedom of choice, right as against wrong
is meaningless. Merely to comprehend what nature has in store
for you and then attempt to coincide with that pattern in order
to avoid resistance involves a contradiction with the very definition of right and seems, for this analysis at any rate, sheer
hedonism.

Now freedom of choice must be related to ends, to wants,
and to desires which men hold in esteem. Among these wants
it would appear that free choice itself must be one, for without
an opportunity to select the hierarchy of needs man implicitly
admits sheer determinism in life. Indeed, for those who believe
(and this is the premise again) in some rational judgment of
man, the "social ideal," in the words of Stammler, is "a community of men willing freely . . . the final expression which
comprehends in unitary fashion all possible purposes of persons
united under the law." [13] To put it briefly, the consciously free-
willing individual may at different times put one need of life,
whether physical or psychical, ahead of another; but his paramount and perpetual want, it is suggested, would be free choice
itself. To the extent that the community by law recognizes and
encourages this aspiration, it tends toward justice.

The community of free-willing individuals, then, through
their political association, the state, can maintain their admittedly slim rationality only by insisting on the primacy of free
choice above all other social needs. The law which provided for
unlimited free choice would be absolutely just—and absolutely
impossible. Discretion must be curtailed as soon as more than
one individual or state covets the same thing, but the better

---

universal, consequently pure a priori, it will be an easy matter to show."—
Immanuel Kant.
[13] Stammler, *Theory of Justice,* tr. by Isaac Husik, p. 153.

the reconciliation made between all wills involved under the circumstances, the greater the inclination toward justice. This is the essence of a good compromise wherein each party feels contented by having secured the maximum expression of his choice in view of the countervailing desires of the other litigants.

Dean Pound has noted that at the end of the nineteenth century and the beginning of the twentieth

Jurists began to think in terms of human wants rather than human wills. They began to think that what they had to do was not simply to equalize or harmonize wills, but, if not to equalize, at least to harmonize the satisfaction of wants.[14]

But that still makes it necessary for someone to rank the importance of social wants. It is suggested here that the law which sets out to harmonize wills shall actually establish one social requirement, namely, the widest possible choice of activity, which should always receive first consideration. Perhaps it will be objected that this "justice" will be utterly perverted by the extravagant claims of one party in the name of free choice. But it should be remembered that he who maintains the principle of the widest possible freedom in selecting a way of life must, to be consistent, maintain it not only for himself but also for all the kindred beings of mankind who have the same frail faculty of reason and judgment.[15] And this would be the attitude of the state also if it should seek justice.

If an equitable world government must incorporate to perfection some such principle and standard of justice as outlined, the opportunities at the moment are dim. There is little evidence to support the sanguine hope that "in such an order there will be no room for submerged classes or individuals, for co-

[14] Pound, *Introduction to the Philosophy of Law*, p. 89.
[15] "The capacity, then, on the part of the individual of conceiving a good as the same for himself and others, and of being determined to action by that conception, is the foundation of rights; and rights are the condition of that capacity realized."—T. H. Green, "The Grounds of Political Obligation," in *Lectures on Principles of Political Obligation*.

lonial, or cultural, or racial, or class imperialisms." [16] This kind of thinking has the hollow ring of Utopia; in some ways it is not markedly different from such statements as:

This new culture of humanity that is united for the first time in human history, and has abolished all State boundaries, will, unlike capitalist culture, be based upon clear and transparent relationships. Hence it will bury forever all mysticism, religion, prejudice, and superstition, and will give a powerful impetus to the development of all-conquering scientific knowledge.[17]

Any argument for justice which does not grasp the realities of life as presented over a long period of time, the greed, corruption, lust, and insatiable ambition of men, is as useless a tool for prying open the door to world government as the blanket omission of man's tiny but important imaginative and free-willing faculty.

What is needed, it seems, are the rudimentary mechanisms which can alleviate, if not solve, the most impelling problems of states which threaten to erupt into violence, for violence, by its very nature, subverts the reasonable intellect and arouses intolerant passion, further eroding the miniscule sense of free choice in both the individual and the state. The mechanism of justice operates on a piecemeal basis, not a sublime formula, and it has a very genuine relationship to the pattern of power traceable in the world at any particular time. Reinhold Niebuhr has argued, for example, that all historic forms of justice or injustice are more the result of a configuration of power than rationalists or idealists would care to admit. He maintains that it is axiomatic that "great disproportions of power lead to injustice, whatever may be the efforts to mitigate them." [18] At the other extreme, equilibrium is only a principle of justice insofar as it prevents dominion and enslavement, but it may be a

---

[16] Ben Zion Bokser, " A Survey of Proposals for Postwar Reconstruction: a Jewish View" in F. Ernest Johnson, ed., *Religion and the World Order*, p. 91.
[17] Programme of the Communist International reprinted in Emile Burns, *Handbook of Marxism*.
[18] Niebuhr, *The Nature and Destiny of Man*, II, 262 *et seq.*

principle of anarchy if the unresolved tensions result in violence. Human society, therefore, requires an awareness and a conscious control of the many forces which interact to produce balances in order to avoid the frustration of one irreconcilable bloc by another.

Between 1907 and 1914 the six Great Powers of Europe became increasingly divided into hostile camps, the Triple Alliance and the Triple Entente. The opposition, however, was precariously poised on a purely negative (defensive) basis and, further handicapped by inadequate mechanisms for the adjustment of frictions, responded to the dynamic political, economic, and cultural situation with heavy-handed diplomacy. The decay of the Ottoman and Hapsburg empires left festering sores in the Balkans, never healed by the intense rivalry of the two alliances, and conflict broke out.[19] Similarly, in the mid-twentieth century, in a world shattered by six years of war, the polarization of power around the Soviet Union and the United States checks the arbitrary sway of either state over the world, but unless the underlying conflicts can be eased, such a rigid opposition of forces is an invitation to violence.

When Secretary of State Hull spoke of harmonizing the real interests of the United States, Russia, Britain, and China as the foundation for a reign of law and peace, he asserted that "agreement can be achieved only by trying to understand the other fellow's point of view and by going as far as possible to meet it." [20] This in essence is the hallmark of justice, for it recognizes that the highest service to the community is the encouragement of the widest possible free expression and free choice of its components. It is an old canon of liberalism which unfortunately got lost in its false identification with "rugged individualism," economic power, and a fixed social structure.

[19] Fay, *Origins of the First World War*, especially the concluding chapter of Vol. I.
[20] Radio address of April 9, 1944, on United States Foreign Policy reprinted in Leland M. Goodrich and Marie J. Carroll, *Documents on American Foreign Relations*, VI, 31.

The procedure of recognizing, discussing, compromising, and adjusting the several conflicts within a dynamic society, whether by arbitration or judicial decision, offers a long, delicate, tedious process of negotiation. For example, no statute of limitations exists in international law, and claims or disputes have sometimes dragged through the process of judgment. In the *Lord Nelson Case* a British application for redress of injury committed in 1812 was approved by an Anglo-American tribunal in 1914.[21] More recently the British government submitted a claim to the International Court of Justice against the Albanian government for the failure of that state "to fulfill its international obligations and to act in accordance with the dictates of humanity" by laying mines within its territorial waters without notifying friendly nations of their existence, thus causing the death of forty-four British seamen. The incident occurred on October 22, 1946; the Security Council of the United Nations recommended on April 9, 1947, that the two states involved refer the case to the World Court; on July 31, 1947, the President of the Court fixed time limits of October, 1947, and December 10, 1947, for the memorials of the applicant and the respondent, respectively; Albania filed an objection to the application of the United Kingdom; the Court then fixed a time limit of January 19, 1948, for observations on the preliminary objection; not until April 9, 1949, did the Court fix responsibility upon Albania, and on December 15, 1949, the Court gave a favorable judgment to Great Britain's claim for 843,947 pounds sterling. Even then Albania refused to accept the judgment of the Court. [22]

The arbitral or judicial procedure cannot give complete satisfaction to either party. It does not even purport to be "justice" at all times. Writing of the diligent approach of some statesmen and jurists to a spirit of continuous arbitration prior to the

---

[21] Hudson, *International Tribunals*, p. 85.
[22] For further details on this case see Hudson, "The 26th Year of the World Court," *The American Journal of International Law*, XLII (January, 1948), 1–19. See also *op. cit.*, XLIII (July, 1949), 558, and XLIV (July, 1950), 579.

First World War, Lassa Oppenheim commented: "Not iural, but peaceful settlements of disputes is the motto of these men; they do not desiderate justice in the sense of existing law, but equity such as contents both parties." [23] The time and patience required for such settlements, moreover, places a heavy strain on the self-control of states confronted by the economic exigencies of the day, the aroused temper of the multitude, and the military demands for national security; it is no wonder that countless times both small and great states have succumbed to the frenzy of the moment and brushed aside all suggestions of prolonged negotiation which might terminate in partial satisfaction.[24] In short, the process of compromising free wills is arduous, uncertain, a technique that is, in itself, the means and end of justice, and intimately dependent upon a felicitous disposition of power with an open-minded approach to mutual difficulties.

Norman Thomas, among others, has reiterated the need for a great positive unifying ideal which is widely held among the masses of the people and aptly notes that most schemes for world unity are based upon a rationalizatoin of fear, but he calmly walks into his own pitfall by attacking militarism and imperialism as the vicious enemies of peace.[25] A standard of justice has nothing to do with these excrescences of a faithless world; it concerns the kinds of negotiation which would minimize imperialism and militarism. Furthermore, to achieve world unity on the basis of a universal agreement on one end for the whole community may not be desirable. Such, indeed, is the unity of the totalitarian states or democratic nations under

[23] Oppenheim, *The Future of International Law*, p. 48.
[24] For further examples of long negotiations, tense situations, and the host of difficulties attendant on compromises between states see Cruttwell, *A History of Peaceful Change in the Modern World*, especially the prelude to the Webster-Ashburton Treaty of 1842, the Olney-Pauncefote communications on British Guiana, the Tacna-Arica dispute between Chile and Peru. The last quarrel involved only 35,000 inhabitants, 9,000 square miles of territory with negligible mineral wealth, yet it took fifty years of bitterness to settle it.
[25] See Thomas, *Appeal to the Nations*.

constitutional dictatorship in times of emergency, for the crucial problem of freedom is submerged in a wave of solid enthusiasm for a single cause. The peaceful democratic community, however, rests upon the multiplicity of interrelated interests in the groups which comprise the state: unions, churches, clubs, negroes, property owners, women, bureaucrats, farmers, and so forth. None of these categories of society, constantly overlapping each other, may agree on a particular economic or social system, but insofar as each of them is willing to compromise on some things, the widest opportunity for peaceful adjudication and freedom can be found.[26]

The international community, similarly, requires an enlargement of those spheres of interest in which members can gracefully yield. The aim of Lauterpacht's thesis on the function of law in the international community, for example, is to demolish the distinction between justiciable and nonjusticiable disputes between states by demonstrating a genuine continuity in the international legal system. It is not the nature of a dispute, he maintains, that makes it unfit for settlement by the application of law, but the unwillingness of a state to have it thus settled.[27] Indeed, to move toward justice under world government, there must arise an ever-increasing number of interests which states are habitually willing to submit to impartial decisions. But one should not be dismayed too readily by the sluggish response of the international community to this need or repulsed by the frictions of "national honor" or "vital interests" which stand as bars to arbitral or judicial procedures.[28] In a

[26] See Henry M. Magid, "Freedom and Political Unity" in *Ethics* (University of Chicago Press), XLI (January, 1941), 144–157.
[27] Lauterpacht, *The Function of Law in the International Community.*
[28] For example, out of 67 treaties of arbitration analyzed by the League of Nations as of 1927, 50 contained one or more reservations. Twenty-four excluded vital interests of third states. Previous disputes, territorial integrity, disputes arising from the First World War, internal legislation, national court jurisdiction, and constitutional questions were other, though less prevalent, types of controversies excluded from arbitration. See *Arbitration and Security*, prepared by the Legal Section of the Secretariat of the League of Nations pursuant to the Council's Resolution of Dec. 12, 1925.

world of enormous discrepancies in wealth, culture, and morality, without a legislative organ to effect changes in policy, such
restrictions answer a heartfelt need of the community, a feeling
which can neither be ignored nor destroyed by invectives.
Finally, it may be recalled that fifty-seven years elapsed under
the United States Constitution before the Supreme Court ven-
tured to pronounce judgment upon an interstate dispute, a
controversy between Massachusetts and Rhode Island over a
boundary line. Since that time the Court has been more assured
in extending its jurisdiction, but even today "we find in substance that the Court recognizes the well-established distinction
between political and legal disputes." [29]

Perhaps nothing is more illustrative of the inadequacy of
international tribunals than the fact that they are so seldom
used. Beginning with the Pious Fund Case in 1903, twenty-one
suits have been referred to the Permanent Court of Arbitration
established by the Hague Conference of 1899. Of these controversies, however, seventeen were judged before 1914 and
only four since the First World War.[30] Part of this decline, of
course, is explained by the creation of the Permanent Court
of International Justice through the Peace of Versailles, but
between 1922 and 1940 a mere thirty-two judgments were
rendered by that judicial organization, with twenty-six other
advisory opinions. To condemn states for their failure to sub-

[29] Herbert A. Smith, "Interstate Disputes in the American Supreme Court,"
in Norman Bentwich and others, *Justice and Equity in the International
Spehre*, p. 23. *Rhode Island vs. Massachusetts* concerned a boundary dispute
dating from the colonial period. Proceedings began in 1833 and over the
vigorous protests of Massachusetts, the court declared itself competent to
judge, five years later. In 1900, however, under the police power, Texas imposed quarantine upon goods shipped from New Orleans, presumably to
protect health, but allegedly to divert trade from the Louisiana port to Gal-
veston. For technical reasons, the Court denied its own jurisdiction, although
the political nature of the embargo was an obvious cause. The problem of enforcement is the dilemma—and courts alone are incompetent on this political
aspect of controversies. In the amorphous community of the world, then, it
should not occasion surprise that tribunals are so limited in their function.
[30] The United States and Norway on shipping claims; the United States and
the Netherlands on the Palmas Islands; the United States and Sweden on
shipping claims; Great Britain and France in the Chevreau case.

mit disputes to judicial settlement, however, is a rather tenuous indictment, for the machinery of national administration fully demonstrates the symbiotic relationship of the courts and the political branches of government and suggests that the problem of securing justice must be regarded as a manifestation of power as well as a juridical decision.

The brilliant lessons of Sir Henry Sumner Maine, for example, that law has been brought into harmony with society through legal fictions, equity, and legislation, in that chronological order,[31] may induce theorists to suppose that prolific court action can spawn a new universal order presently evolving into a rational agreement upon world government. Indeed, early societies show little or no differentiation between the legislative and the judicial functions: the ecclesia of the Greeks gave decisions rather than formulated laws; the history of the centralization of England, especially between the reigns of Henry the First and Henry the Third, is the gradual domination of the royal tribunal over local courts.[32] The Norwegian democratic assemblies of the ninth century, such as the Eidsivathinglaw, the Gulathinglaw, and the Frostathinglaw, had as their first important business the appointment of a committee called the logretta or law court to dispense justice to the farmers;[33] the French courts of the *ancien régime* were known as parlements; and the State Legislature of Massachusetts is still known as the General Court.

But if modern legislatures indicate a relatively advanced

[31] Sir Henry Sumner Maine, *Ancient Law*, 10th ed., with introduction and notes by Sir Frederick Pollock. "Legislation, the enactments of a legislature, which, whether it takes the form of an autocratic prince or of a parliamentary assembly, is the assumed organ of the entire society, is the last of the ameliorating instrumentalities. . . . Its obligatory force is independent of its principles. The legislature, whatever be the actual restraints imposed upon it by public opinion, is in theory empowered to impose what obligations it pleases on the members of the community."

[32] See Allen, *Law in the Making*, p. 120. A more complete account of the hegemony of the royal court over local tribunals may be found in Jenks, *Law and Politics in the Middle Ages*, chap. iv, "Administration of Justice."

[33] For a complete history of the early Norse "things" or assemblies see Larson, *The Earliest Norwegian Laws*.

technique of government, that is, a better method of crystalliz-
ing opinion and providing direct public remedies for the wants
of the community, their functions have been drawn from kings
as well as courts. Neither Roman praetors nor the English
Bractons, Smiths, or Cokes were the whole of the legal fabric,
which ultimately depended upon the internal order and external security of the realm. Similarly, for world government,
the quick reaction to opinion and the explicit direction of the
community in new situations would be a political matter,[34]
and if world legislation is ever to develop from a rudimentary
organ, it will, like national parliaments, be a division or modification of the executive power. International policy today, however, is effected by several executive powers, the individual
nation-states, and clearly the area of agreement among these
entities is still too narrow to permit a compromise upon a lawgiver. Thus, though treaties and multipartite agreements fail
to meet the standards of domestic law-making for want of a
single administration, they are in a real sense "international
legislation" and the main channel through which the peaceful
establishment of world government can flow.[35] An approach
toward justice on this level of negotiation is vital.

John Foster Dulles correctly gauged the issue of diplomatic
justice.

We need to develop in world affairs a feeling that change is not
per se abnormal and strange and to be avoided except as a matter
of dire necessity. . . . This would become possible if we could
develop in international affairs a viewpoint corresponding to that
which is epitomized by the common law.[36]

[34] In 1943, for example, a committee of the American Bar Association admitted
"that the relation to be borne by the (international) Court to such central international organization as may ultimately emerge cannot now be determined"; but the committee stressed "the importance of separating the judicial
from the policy-making function." Report of the Committee of the American
Bar Association, *Postwar International Judicial Organization*, March 29, 1943.
[35] The term "international legislation" has been popularized by Manly O.
Hudson, notably through his collections of multipartite international agreements. See *International Legislation*.
[36] Dulles, *War, Peace, and Change*, p. 156.

Explicit recognition of changing circumstances which might render old treaties inapplicable was given by the League of Nations in providing that the Assembly might "advise" the reconsideration of such agreements by Members, but the article was a dead letter.[37] The United Nations, perhaps with the same intent, but less specifically, provides the General Assembly with the right to recommend measures for the peaceful adjustment of any situation.[38] Now to overlook the absolute rise and fall of power within states or to resist with dogmatism every impact of these undulations on the international scene is extremely dangerous. Empires seem to wax and wane; populations multiply or diminish; industries flourish or decline; first one people then another is favored by nature. The military greatness of Spain, Austria, Turkey, and France has faded with time. Perhaps an Age of Contending States is drawing to a close and a Cosmopolis confronts the world. Still this does not justify the total pessimism of Spengler.[39] An American or Russian century may go the same way. It rather indicates the necessity of accommodating the inherent changes of society in such a manner that the frictions do not set the world on fire

[37] Two attempts were made to use the Article: In 1920 Bolivia requested a modification of a treaty concluded with Chile in 1904. Needless to say, the League showed no inclination to back with force any change. In 1929 China suggested a committee to investigate means for giving effect to the Article, but the *status quo* forces vitiated the clause at every turn by insisting upon the need for unanimity—including the disputants—on any revision. See Schwarzenberger, *Power Politics*, p. 237. There were some "revisions" of the Versailles Treaty, of course, through the Dawes Plan, the Young Plan, and the Lausanne Agreement between 1924 and 1932, but the emergency nature, the gross political expendiency, and, indeed, the scant regard for legality, of these adjustments hardly serve as paragons of justice. See Stephens, *Revisions of the Treaty of Versailles.*
[38] Article 14, *The United Nations.*
[39] "Once the Imperial Age has arrived, there are no more political problems. People manage with the situation as it is and the powers that be. In the period of Contending States, torrents of blood had reddened the pavements of all World Cities, so that the great truths of Democracy might be turned into actualities, and for the winning of right without which life seemed not worth the living. Now these rights are won, but the grandchildren cannot be moved, even by punishment, to make use of them. A hundred years more, and even the historians will no longer understand the old controversies." Spengler, *The Decline of the West*, tr. by C. F. Atkinson, p. 432.

and thereby destroy the fragile stilts of morality which have raised mankind above the bestial herd.[40] A world government looking toward justice would have to provide such a mechanism for change. In a universe now governed by a multi-headed executive which actually makes and administers such rules, compromise and concession on the issues at stake are therefore fundamental. If nothing but sheer power will convince recalcitrant negotiators, the idea of justice is meaningless, for it is then, in the blunt words of Thrasymachus, "always in the interest of the stronger."

The Soviet Union's conduct is illustrative of the difficulties confronting any universal standard of right on the international scene. In their weakness, the Socialist Republics of 1919 accepted the offer of the Allied Powers to mediate between the Reds and the Whites; again in 1926, Russia acknowledged the process of mediation by France between the Soviets and the Swiss federation; but Soviet Russia has never resorted to a fact-finding commission, such as recommended by the Hague Conferences, nor has arbitration ever gone beyond technical disputes or controversies involving private rights.[41] A bold pronouncement upon international law by a Soviet spokesman maintains that representatives of the USSR have always and everywhere been the foremost champions of "democracy and international justice" and adds significantly,

The principles of a new and broader democracy going farther than parliamentary forms and election ballots, yet directly expressing the will and the heroic ardor of the popular masses are entering the international arena as well.[42]

[40] Morris Ginsberg has presented some convincing arguments for moral progress, infinitely tedious as the process may be. He maintains that (1) the range of persons to whom moral judgments are applied has been extended; (2) that there has been an "internalization and individualization" of conscience, free of external sanctions; and (3) there has been a growing rationalization of moral judgment, a distinction between ritual rules and moral values. *Reason and Unreason in Society.*
[41] Taracouzio, *The Soviet Union and International Law*, pp. 293 *et seq.*
[42] Korovin, "The Second World War and International Law," *The American Journal of International Law*, XL (October, 1946), 742–755.

The parliamentary forms, however, though somewhat linked to class interests as argued by Marxists, nevertheless signify a rostrum for discussion and a willingness to abstain from an absolute arbitrary rule of the stronger forces. The young Soviet citizen, on the other hand, is exhorted to be brave, courageous, honest, steadfast, and disciplined. "They must hate their enemies, fear no difficulties, and overcome all obstacles. Such is the moral force of the new man, of the man of the new society." [43]

Carrying these attitudes to the world councils, the negotiators of Russia have fixed their standard of justice upon the success of one economic-social pattern, whereas "right" is only intrinsic to the methods of securing any particular order of society. Other national statesmen who adhere to their familiar way of distributing the rewards of cooperative undertakings, whether monetary gains or social distinctions, as an immutably just way of life, are prone to the same fallacy. In brief, no one can really demonstrate in a dynamic society that "justice" will be guaranteed by a specific allocation of resources, but man, in his half-blind, stumbling way can have some assurance of inching along the eternal, circuitous route toward justice so long as his choice receives a hearing on some merit other than the clenched fist behind it. If a mechanism for change within world government must seek its forebears, the present-day disputations of diplomats in their treaty formulations, their concerts, leagues, and charters are the proper field of investigation.

Imagine a long string of pacific negotiations among the states of the world. Contemplate the recurrent use of arbitrators, courts, and diplomatic conferences tirelessly, phlegmatically at work to create temporary settlements for the rumblings of an interacting, interdependent world society. The underpinnings of a magnanimous world government might protrude through

[43] *I Want to Be Like Stalin,* from the Russian text on Pedagogy by Yesipov and Goncharov, tr. by George S. Counts and Nucia P. Lodge, p. 142.

the muck of despair and support an edifice of universal administration fit to cope with the savage pressures of economic
and social inequality. How does the international scene square
with this vision? Obviously it does not.

Some theorists even maintain that since the rise of the modern
nation there has been a constant gnawing at the thin ropes of
self-restraint which once limited the utterly selfish actions of
states and at least held negotiations and the observance of pacts
within a loosely defined moral sphere. Thus, E. H. Carr speaks
of the seventeenth and eighteenth centuries as the most "international" period of history in view of the flesh-and-blood sovereigns of the day who spoke the same language, owned a common tradition, and were conscious of a common interest in
maintaining their royal and despotic institutions. "A sense of
obligation deriving from the unity of Christendom and the
validity of natural law . . . survived in the secular trappings
of the Enlightenment." [44]

Many of the encomiums showered upon the "Christian community" of the centuries before the French Revolution are difficult to swallow. The Truce of God, for example, testifies rather
to the utter anarchy of the early medieval period than the efficacy of moral restraint, and the establishment of the "king's
peace" by a few strong dynasties within their realms was much
more successful.[45] Furthermore, the degrading struggle for
power between the Pope and the Emperor in the fourteenth and

[44] Carr, *Nationalism and After*, p. 4.
[45] About 990 the church attempted to get the fighting gentry to take oaths not
to attack and destroy everything with complete ruthlessness—churches, farms,
cattle, women, crops, and to respect the "peace of God." In 1025 the idea of a
truce in fighting during the Sabbath was extended to special days and seasons,
especially with an eye to harvest. "But anathemas and fines were not enough;
an armed force was needed, capable of making its decrees and penalties respected." Certain diocese associations were formed, known as "peace jurors"
or "peace communes," by clergy and high-minded nobles to end the anarchy.
These had some effect in France, Italy, and Germany, but never penetrated
England, where the Norman kings were capable of a better "peace." See
Bemont and Monod, *Mediaeval Europe from 395 A.D. to 1270 A.D.*, tr. by
Mary Swan, pp. 265–266; also Baldwin, *The Mediaeval Papacy in Action*,
p. 92; also Ault, *Europe in the Middle Ages*, pp. 280–281.

fifteenth centuries, the vicious corruption of the Holy See itself, certainly nullified all practical force in the medieval conception of a great World Church long before the schism. Indeed, there was a constant exhortation addressed to princes by moralists who sought good conduct, honor, and justice in the name of the true religion; Peter Damien, John of Salisbury, Thomas Aquinas, and Desiderius Erasmus,[46] all wrote such tracts, and this literature gives a distinctive merit to the age; but Machiavelli's infamous essay corresponded more accurately with the politics of the ruling families. Next, it should not be forgotten that modern international law stems from a sincere protest against the barbarity of warfare in the sixteenth and seventeenth centuries. The heart of Grotius' thought is that law is not founded on expediency alone and that "there is a common law among nations which is valid alike for war and in war." [47] This Dutch virtuoso was familiar with the Spanish pacification of Holland, wherein Haarlem was smashed to bits and two thousand of its inhabitants murdered in cold blood, and Antwerp, the richest ornament of sixteenth-century Europe, was gutted, while eight thousand of its men, women, and children were deliberately slaughtered.[48] Moreover, the Thirty Years' War, which raged for twenty-seven years of the jurist's life, was unsurpassed in fiendishness.[49]

[46] See Born, *The Political Theories of Erasmus*. In a letter to Anthony Bergen, Abbot of St. Bertin, March, 1514, Erasmus shows that he was well aware of contemporary Machiavellian policy: "But you will say, that the rights of sovereigns must be maintained. It is not for me to speak inadvisedly about the acts of princes. I only know this, that *summum ius* is often *summa inuria;* there are princes who first decide what they want and then look out for a title with which to cloak their proceedings."
[47] In the Prolegomena to *De jure belli ac pacis,* tr. by F. W. Kelsey and others.
[48] See A. H. Johnson, *Europe in the Sixteenth Century.*
[49] "Every war produces its characteristic horrors, but in no other instances of modern warfare did the civilian population suffer so much as this. It mattered little whether the army over-running a province was friendly or not; whether it was Swedish, French, or Spanish, it had to be supported at the expense of the inhabitants. . . . Reprisal provoked more bitter reprisals; human beings murdered and maimed with a ferocity to be found only in men who know that it may well be their turn next; a dreadful fatalism and cynicism in wickedness seems to deepen as the war drags its interminable length . . . hundreds

The Peace of Westphalia confirmed the bankruptcy of the empire and papacy and admitted the secular state, potentially hostile to its neighbors, restrained only by commercial interdependence. Louis XIV, who dominates the latter half of the seventeenth century, considered himself responsible to God alone and not to be bound by human contrivances such as treaties. His assertion that it was for the king to decide when a treaty no longer suited a change in circumstances is a view which has found favor among modern "sovereigns" too. Of the eighteenth century, one historian writes:

Diplomacy was corrupt and international immorality was universal. . . . The invasion of Silesia, the partition of Poland, and attempted dismemberment of Prussia, are well-known illustrations of contempt for established rights. . . . Anarchic principles were abroad, morality and religion were at a low ebb, treaties were lightly broken, most European states were at the time of the French Revolution either ruined or worn out . . . the secret diplomacy of the middle of the Eighteenth Century marks the lowest depths arrived at in the history of the relations of European states to each other.[50]

It is true that "enlightened monarchs" disregarded nationality as a criterion of right, that the Prussian Frederick and the Russian Catherine cultivated French literature and philosophy, that Joseph II of Austria sought to merge the diverse and heterogeneous elements of his dominions into an orderly, united empire, that statesmen, soldiers, and citizens could still pass from one government to another without prejudice, that there was a kind of class solidarity among the princes in holding the masses of the people in their subordinate roles, and that all the representative writings of the age were permeated by a consciousness of the unity of mankind. But there is no indication that this

---

of villages were left without a single inhabitant . . . dead men were found with grass in their mouths . . . cannibalism broke out in several parts of Germany . . . tortures inflicted on defenceless inhabitants . . . and great trees weighed down by the suspended bodies of peasants."—Ogg, *Europe in the Seventeenth Century*, 4th ed., p. 167.

[50] Hassall, *The Balance of Power*, Chapter One.

"internationalism" raised a standard of justice which secured even cursory regard in foreign affairs.[51]

More significant for the eighteenth century, however, as a limitation of political excesses was the expansion of commerce —producing both the beginnings of a bourgeoisie with reciprocal interests and the emergence of a strong naval power, Great Britain, to keep the expanding channels of trade open.[52] This order was the realization of the nineteenth century and accounted in large measure for the phenomenal growth of international agencies between 1815 and 1914, in which such high hope for a "functional" international organization and "progressive arbitration" were entertained. Protestantism and the cult of reason, meanwhile, had tipped the scales toward democracy in a number of states; the industrial revolution, by concentrating production and workers, reshuffling the wealth of kingdoms, and opening communications to the masses, ushered in the era of the plebian state. The highest obligations of the nation were gradually shifted from an ambitious, and usually unprincipled, personal sovereign to the legal sovereignty of the amorphous "people." How this transition has affected the quest for justice is a fundamental problem of world government.

[51] Writing of the effect of the Enlightenment upon Prussia, for example, Hans Kohn notes, "Thus, enlightened rationalism in the service of power—not power in the service of reason, ethical goals, or human happiness became the distinct character of (Prussia). . . . Religion was only tolerated insofar as it was useful to the state. Peace among the different religions and creeds became a governmental policy because it was a condition for the economic progress and the military strength of the country." *The Idea of Nationalism*, p. 358.

[52] Prussian and Austrian commerce was virtually unchanged between 1500 and 1700. With the eighteenth century, the governments perceived the political advantages of a strong national industry and trade; the worst abuses of the die-hard guilds were overcome; manufactures were fostered by direct subsidies and protective tariffs; some feudal highway and waterway tolls were abolished. Between 1716 and 1787 French trade with Europe multiplied almost four times, with Africa and Asia almost five times, and with America ten times. During the eighteenth century the foreign trade of England increased five to six times its 1700 level. For example, raw cotton imports jumped from 4,000 bales in 1741 to 28,000 bales in 1744. It was estimated, unfortunately, that British vessels also carried some 20,000 slaves a year and that Liverpool employed as many as 190 slave ships in 1771. See Day, *A History of Commerce*, chaps. xxi, xxii, xxiv, xxvi.

"What is not so clear," Carr states, "is why the rugged individualism of nations should have been regarded as less self-assertive and menacing to peace than the rugged individualism of monarchs, why nations should not have been expected to display the princely qualities of aggressiveness and greed." [53] Indeed, not only did governments become the agents of the "general will," but the later advent of the "social service" state thoroughly committed them to the active assistance of their national citizens in every way. Having bent its energies so deeply inward, the state government now justifies foreign policy more glibly by the satisfaction of its own "people" rather than by a religious dogma or a supra-national class interest. The implications are totally secular and parochial, a standard of right guided by a national interest instead of universal reason. Yet considering the paltry response to the old admonitions in politics, it seems utterly naïve to fulminate at the new selfishness of the modern state. To be sure, its cultural intolerance has been incomparable, but certainly the religious fanaticism of the past or the despotism of autocrats is scarcely preferable.

Christianity, economic interdependence, and Marxism have each exercised some restraints upon the egocentrism of the nation-state and offered a means of acquiring a universal order; but each has been warped through narrow application by a class or élite, and each has succumbed to the postulates of justice advertised by those who control the state. Thus, churches, cartels, and internationales have been seduced by the Great Leviathan. With the wane of Christian strength, material and moral, and the rise of the demigod nationalism, the churches have either acquiesced or are forced to accept whatever state policy preserves their limited influence; [54] international capitalism has long been subjugated by the interests of the new socialized or

[53] Carr, *Nationalism and After*, p. 9.
[54] For an interesting chapter on how religion has throughout history assisted national unity for its purposes and, in turn, how nationalism has molded religion, quite sincerely, to its needs see "Religion and Nationality" by Hertz, *Nationality and Politics*, pp. 98–145.

semi-socialized state, as the Second World War, in its totalitarian character, fully confirmed; nor is the Cominform a spon-
taneous, universal growth among the laboring peoples of the
world dedicated to a policy of peaceful conversion.

Only public conscience itself, working through the strongest
institution, the state, now fixed upon the stage of history, seems
to remain as an antidote to wicked public international policy,
and the final resort for a standard of justice. Yet here two difficulties begin.

The expectation so frequently entertained by the people of one
country when they feel morally outraged by the policy of another
government, that the subjects of that government will themselves
feel equally outraged is doomed to disappointment. For in all countries the subjects are exposed to very much the same influence as
the rulers, and the canons of morality which are accepted by both
ruled and rulers in one State are likely to be rejected by both in
another.[55]

This contradiction is even more serious where the basic philosophy of life is markedly different—as the clash between Western
liberal democracy and fascism or communism aptly illustrates.
For good reason the seventeenth-century international law
writers were greatly concerned over the same problem of finding a moral basis of agreement among peoples of different
faiths.[56] It cannot be overlooked that it was Christian Europe,
and more particularly the Europe which had preserved most
fully the Stoic-Roman natural law tradition, in which the
threads of state policy were woven into the mantle of an international law which, in the last analysis, was based upon individ-

[55] The Royal Institute of International Affairs, *Nationalism*, p. 319.
[56] The seventeenth century, of course, was thinking of the Moslem Turk and
the "Asiatic" Russian who impinged upon the Western Christian society.
Alberico Gentilis, for example, maintains that war should not be made *because*
of religion; nor is commerce among strange faiths forbidden. "We are here
inquiring about a treaty, a special union, and what has been said above does
not convince me that this is lawfully contracted with men of a different religion." *De iure belli*, p. 401. Men like Emeric Crucé or Grotius, whose chief
works incidentally were published within one year of each other, took a
contrary view.

ual conscience and which recognized obligations to mankind under the universal commands of nature. Clearly, the extension of such a standard to communities which have had no individual experience with conscience nor regard for universal brotherhood has met with unhappy results.

If a standard of justice for world government revolves around compromise, there would need to be instilled in the hearts of the masses a sentiment untarnished by bigotry or provincialism, and if one presumes that all men have the precious faculty of reason and will, whether it be called the inspiration of God, a life force, or the strange kinks of the human brain, it may be induced that free communication is the best stimulus to an apprehension of the good of arbitration and compromise. But because this peculiar talent of organization and judgment provides only a fragment of the human personality, the road to justice is forever scarred by pot-holes which break the wheels of tolerance. At the same time, free communication is the hardest won and the most dangerously maintained of all rights, and in every epoch it rests upon a possible antithesis of naked power.

Recently Arnold Toynbee has described the United Nations as "a political machine for putting into effect the maximum possible amount of cooperation between the United States and the Soviet Union." [57] Indeed, the United Nations, like the League, is pretty much of a talking shop, but for just that reason it is worth not a little on the international plane. Similarly, within the emerging empire-states of the world, upon which the foundations of order must be based, an internal balancing of force which can demand the exchange of information among its own citizens at least offers the possibility of influencing policy by argument from every source, including transnational reflections. Domestically such counsel may lead to hesitancy and moderation, perhaps less purposeful and efficient

[57] Toynbee, "The International Outlook," in *International Affairs* (London), XXIII (October, 1947), 463–476.

action, but clearly from the standpoint of universal right, it reveals slightly more informed and more objective guides to conduct.

To obtain such intercourse among nations is an essential task of any world organization if public conscience is ever to have a chance of controlling the intemperance of public policy, but it must be confessed that the invasion of national governments into the propaganda field has perverted free communication into another instrument of state policy rather than assisted the slow process of international understanding. Harold Nicolson points out that until the war of 1914 "it was still considered unfitting and unwise for a statesman to make public pronouncements to his own people which public opinion in other countries would know to be totally untrue." [58] Again, the problem of world government dwells within the nation-state itself. To find a universal standard of justice, the beginnings must be made inside the familiar political frames of the peoples concerned, yet considering the lack of experience with free communication everywhere as well as the constant harassing of this singular index to free choice, moderation, and compromise, no justice-seeking world government can avoid a long period of gestation.

[58] Nicolson, *Diplomacy*, p. 87.

Chapter 8

The Rhine was red with human blood,
The Danube roll'd a purple tide,
    On the Euphrates Satan stood,
And over Asia stretch'd his pride.

    He wither'd up sweet Zion's Hill
From every Nation of the Earth
    He wither'd up Jerusalem's Gates
And in a dark Land gave her birth.

    He wither'd up the Human Form
By laws of sacrifice for sin,
    Till it became a Mortal Worm,
But O! translucent all within.

    Is this thy soft Family-Love,
Thy cruel Patriarchal pride,
    Planting thy Family alone,
Destroying all the World beside?

    A man's worst enemies are those
Of his own house and family;
    And he who makes his law a curse,
By his own law shall surely die.

    In my Exchanges every Land
Shall walk, and mine in every Land,
    Mutual shall build Jerusalem,
Both heart in heart and hand in hand.

                                William Blake

The Practice of
International Law

DESPITE ALL THE VICISSITUDES of world politics, people continue to write constitutions for a world government. One of
the most commendable efforts of recent years, especially among
a spate of nonsensical diagrams, has been the document produced by several savants of Chicago and elsewhere entitled a
"Preliminary Draft for a World Constitution." [1] Its value lies
partly in the humility of the authors, for they recognize that
the conceivable circumstances for the implementation of the
articles are not at hand; but most of its worth is due to its intelligent delineation of the essential grants of power and terms of
law necessary to make an Anglo-American kind of world government viable. The draft constitution with its ten grants of
power to the world government, including the maintenance of
armed forces, tax and fiscal controls, commerce and immigra-
tion between states, boundaries, and so forth, leaves little doubt
as to the inescapable omnipotence of the world law. Unfortunately, the peoples of the world do not have the remotest
prospect of such a *de novo* creation, but at the moment are still
fumbling along with the shambles of traditional international
law.

[1] Hutchins and others, "Preliminary Draft for a World Constitution," *Common Cause*, Vol. I (No. 9, March, 1948).

It is, therefore, to a rejuvenation of international law, or as Mr. Jessup has phrased it, "a modern law of nations," that many advocates of a new world order turn, in the expectation that the framework of legal international relations which has been erected over the course of centuries can be strengthened rather than dismantled, its foundations buttressed and its structural defects eliminated so as to provide more tenable rules for the world community:

. . . some minds seek a complete change through the immediate creation of a world government. Others would prefer to build more slowly. . . . One point of agreement may be found in all plans and proposals . . . the necessity for adequate international law.[2]

Prior to the First World War there was an especially strong tide of opinion, led by such men as William Howard Taft, which sought a more consistent and more comprehensive international law as the cornerstone of any future world organization. Indeed, the experience of the two Hague Peace Conferences with their imposing declarations of international law attended by the establishment of a permanent panel of judges to assist in the increasing number of interstate controversies being submitted to arbitration gave ready evidence of the need for a world court. James Brown Scott, a tireless worker for the establishment of an International Court of Justice, wrote that "there is a law of evolution in the judicial as in the animate world and that law is from self-redress through arbitration to judicial proceedings in a permanent judiciary," and he gave scholarly illustrations of arbitrations under the American Articles of Confederation, as well as the Swiss Confederation, leading up to the agreement upon a permanent federal tribunal within those confederations. Yet in the same breath he denied that the establishment of such a court either presupposed or required a federation of the world.[3] So far as sanctions for the

---

[2] Jessup, *A Modern Law of Nations*, p. 1.
[3] Scott, *An International Court of Justice*, pp. 45–51. He vehemently rejected a federation of the world for all purposes as not only a calamity, but "as destructive of international law."

legal judgments of the International Court of Justice is concerned, the pitiless light of publicity and public opinion was deemed an adequate deterrent to outrageous disobedience of the law by any state.[4] As long as states entered the court, it was believed, international law could grow, adapt itself to new contingencies, and gradually secure the allegiance and respect necessary for a peaceful society.

The attitude of the early twentieth century American Society for the Judicial Settlement of International Disputes went as far back as William Ladd for its rationale—that no state could justify its war policy to the nation "if there were an impartial tribunal to judge its case"; [5] but the root of the thought lay with the English Utilitarians Jeremy Bentham and James Mill, with their utter confidence in an educated public opinion. Confident of the ability of men to choose right, if the situation were presented in lucid, sober terms, the Utilitarians maintained that the solemn decree of the court would be a sufficient sanction for the law, provided a free press were guaranteed in each state.[6]

After two world wars and the indubitable tendency toward omnipotent government in all states, few publicists would be so sanguine about the prospects of international adjudication, enforced by public opinion, particularly as a stepping block to world government, and it would be virtually impossible to discover in contemporary literature any opinion in the tone of Hall's famous lines:

[4] Taft, *The United States and Peace,* pp. 179–180: "But the query is made: How will the judgments of such a Court be enforced; what will be the sanction for their execution? I am very little concerned about that. After we have gotten the cases into court and decided and the judgments embodied in a solemn declaration . . . few nations will care to face the condemnation of public opinion and disobey the judgment."
[5] See James Tryon, "Proposals for an International Court," in American Society for the Judicial Settlement of International Disputes, *Proceedings of the 4th National Conference, Dec. 4–6, 1913.*
[6] See *Benthamania,* select extracts from the work of Jeremy Bentham, ed. by John Hill Burton, p. 421, for a summation of Bentham's contribution to international law. Also, for a more complete Utilitarian view see James Mill, *Law of Nations,* Doubleday Doran Series in Philosophy, pp. 281 *et seq.*

. . . we see international law at the close of each fifty years in a more solid position . . . it has taken firmer hold, it has extended its sphere of operations, it has ceased to trouble itself about trivial formalities, it has more and more dared to grapple in detail with the fundamental facts in the relations of states.[7]

Instead, a consensus of students today would readily endorse Quincy Wright's admonition that international law and international organization, with their adjuncts of democracy and liberty, have receded before the assaults of new despotisms intent on organizing the world in an imperial, hierarchical way, and that if a world federation permitting Western democratic liberties is to remain feasible, "a more perfect international law must be developed to sustain it." [8]

In the phrases "a more perfect international law" and "a modern law of nations," however, there seems to be an unnecessary disguise, for the actual problem is to extend the kind of society which nurtured international law itself, not the perfunctory modification of the written rules about minorities, contracts, or courts. The failure to expand the Western European community is the reef which tears out the bottom of international law and leaves its postulates, principles, and proposals drifting as wreckage upon the heaving political seas.

At the opening of his chapter on the history of international law, T. J. Lawrence wrote in 1910:

International law, as we know it, is a system of rules for the guidance of civilized powers. It sprang up originally in Europe, and extended its authority to states outside European countries as they adapted themselves to European civilization.[9]

[7] Hall, Preface to 3d ed., *A Treatise on International Law*, p. ix. In fairness to Hall, these words are followed by the keen observation that another war would (as it did) impose serious difficulties upon international law. He writes, "It would be idle also to pretend that Europe is not now in great likelihood moving towards a time at which the strength of international law will be too hardly tried." Yet he concludes on an optimistic note that although war may shatter the old rules, new and better ones will arise ten years later.
[8] Quincy Wright, "International Law and the World Order," in Laves, ed., *The Foundations of a More Stable World Order*, pp. 133–134.
[9] Lawrence, *The Principles of International Law*, 4th ed., p. 17.

Certainly it is not pure cynicism which leads one to inquire whether in the decade before the First World War the enthusiasts had thoroughly examined their premise that states outside the European boundaries had really adapted themselves to European civilization. And if foreign states had not assimilated the culture to which Mr. Lawrence referred, could they accept the authority of international law? In a schismatic world, could a common virtue prevail, and how would the divisions of society be joined in a cooperative family of stalwart brother nations?

From the most ancient times there have been agreements between different political entities—between river cities of Mesopotamia, between the Greek *polei*, between Rome and the tribes of the Italic peninsula during the ascendancy of the republic. While it is reasonable to ascribe the incentive of modern international law to the flourishing independent communes in the Piedmont, Lombardy, Tuscany, and Venice, there may be some value in first exploring the authority of ancient compacts for analogies with modern times.

The antagonism, indeed, the scorn, for foreigners outside the racial-religious pale is a recurrent phenomenon of the old world. In China, as well as in Greece, there was a feeling of community among several rival states, which did not extend to "barbarians." For example, the Tartars of the northwest were regarded by the Chinese with as much disdain and hostility as was expressed in Aristotle's famous dictum on the inferior relationship of barbarians to Hellenes. Throughout the ancient world, of course, religion was indistinguishable from public conduct, and the sanctions of a common faith, whether in one state or between states, tempered relationships by providing a mutual obligation beyond the whims of pure force. Indeed, the earliest known treaty in history, between Lagash and Umma, about 3100 B.C., in Mesopotamia, is affirmed by an oath to six or seven Sumerian gods whom both states commonly acknowledged.[10]

[10] See Nussbaum, *A Concise History of the Law of Nations,* p. 8.

The extensive Greek international law indicated by the manifold treaties and practices between the Hellenic communities
was coterminous with the municipal-religious law.[11] Similarly,
the Romans depended upon sacred formulae as an indispensable
guide to all legal relationships—whether local or international
—and, especially in the early years of their history, prided
themselves on a genuine attachment to good faith, while con-
demning the infidelity of other peoples.

"Punica fides," "Graeca fides," and the like became proverbial expressions of reproach. "Bona fides" was closely allied to religious-
ness, piety, and respect for the gods.[12]

From this close relationship between formal religion and law,
however, it need not be inferred that there was an utter absence
of human compassion, for there are many illustrations of un-
selfish assistance to fellowmen, especially foreigners, across the
divisions of race or dogma. Thus, when the Delphic temple was
accidentally burned down in 648 B.C., the Delphians went from
country to country begging for funds to rebuild, and King
Amasis of Egypt gave them an exceedingly generous donation
of a thousand talents of alum.[13] And when in 244 B.C. a great
earthquake tumbled the Colossus, with the walls and dockyards
of Rhodes, magnificent presents from dozens of foreign princes
were showered upon the city: silver, corn, ship timber, bronze,
sailcloth, artisans, and workers, and so many other gifts that
Rhodes actually profited from its misfortune.[14] Furthermore,
there is an abundance of evidence of hospitality to strangers

---

[11] "The people of antiquity who came closest to a 'system' of international law
were the Greeks. . . . In view, however, of the fact that the Greek cities
were so often united in leagues or confederacies, this law is perhaps more
properly to be regarded as federal or inter-municipal rather than international
law. . . . Indeed, the Greek cities, like the Chinese and Hindu states as well
as the Phoenician cities, probably illustrate a valid generalization that archaic
international law flourishes only among related peoples who consider themselves the possessors of a common culture." Seagle, *The Quest for Law*, p. 352.
[12] Phillipson, *The International Law and Custom of Ancient Greece and
Rome*, 68.
[13] Herodotus ii. 80.
[14] Polybius v. 88–90.

accidentally stranded in Egypt,[15] in Carthage, and elsewhere, while the liberal Periclean policy toward foreigners in Athens is in marked contrast with Sparta's hostility.

But it would still seem that the articulation of positive agreements between peoples depended upon religious sanctions to support the legal fabric during these centuries and that any compact, going beyond the exigencies of force, relied very heavily upon pledges to the deities and a sense of personal responsibility to the protecting gods.[16] While it would be naïve to expect the subjugation of ambition and covetousness by the scrupulous observance of treaties in that early epoch, nevertheless, "the simplicity of ancient manners and the religious character attributed to international obligations seem to have contributed materially to that purpose." [17]

International law within a single strong empire is meaningless. So was it meaningless for Rome. With the revival of commerce among the towns of northern Italy within the shattered empire after the twelfth century, however, a number of inter-city treaties came into force: reciprocal trade pacts, guarantees to communications, agreements for the protection of merchants, free river navigation clauses, and promises of extradition for crime and debt. Furthermore, there were many traditional rules recognized as binding, such as a minimum standard of treatment for foreigners, and faith and credit extended to the laws and decisions of other towns in respect to wills, contracts, etc.

[15] Herodotus (ii. 114–115) tells the story of Alexander, who had seduced Helen from her husband, Menelaus, in Sparta, being driven by an Aegean gale to the shores of Egypt. The King at Memphis summoned Alexander to appear at the Court and gave him a tongue-lashing for his wicked deed—not only stealing the wife of his host, but plundering his house. "Did I not regard it as a matter of utmost consequence that no stranger driven to my country by adverse winds should ever be put to death, I would certainly have avenged the Greek by slaying thee . . . I command thee to be gone . . . within three days . . . otherwise at the end of that time you will be treated as enemies."
[16] See Polybius iii. 25, for the religious sanctions to the treaties between Rome and Carthage.
[17] Hosack, *Rise and Growth of the Law of Nations*, p. 5.

These rules, which were in substance based upon the principles of Roman law adapted to new times, originally constituted the common law of Italy, or more exactly, the common law of the Italian portion of the Holy Roman Empire. Therefore, this law was not, in its inception, international law: that is, a law in force among independent entities, but municipal law of the empire which cities had to apply . . .[18]

The actual authority of the Emperor, especially after Frederick Barbarossa's defeat by the Lombard League in 1176, had given way to a nominal vassalage among the communes, but although the imperial sway virtually disappeared the prestige of the Roman law with its long tradition and its adaptability to the needs of the emerging city-states was not diminished. Medieval theorists, such as Bartolus and Dante, still revered the Emperor, not so much as a direct governor of the Italian communes (which had clearly established their independence by this time), but as a universal authority who should coordinate the separate and conflicting states within the Christian community. It was in this sense that pre-Reformation spokesmen recognized unity, a Roman universalism which never was achieved. The sprouting of interstate rules and procedures during the fourteenth and fifteenth centuries in Italy, therefore, appears as a phenomenon of independent political entities within a larger framework of the religious-legal homogeneity nurtured by the Holy Roman Empire, and this occurrence seems to have a rough resemblance to the inter-state practices within the ancient Mediterranean and Indian and Chinese worlds.

Long ago Henry Maine pointed out that a great part of eighteenth- and nineteenth-century international law was Roman law—especially the branch of it subsumed under *ius gentium*—which had permeated every legal system of Europe. Despite the fragmentation of the Continent, the local customs of the new states showed strong resemblances to Roman legal practices, for in some countries the Roman law never ceased to be observed, although corrupted by barbarian usages, whereas

[18] Sereni, *The Italian Conception of International Law*, p. 14.

in other communities the skeleton of tribal law, Norse, Frank, Gothic, and so forth, was rapidly filled out by the solid substance of the Roman system.[19] Moreover, J. B. Scott has categorically traced the intimate connection between the Roman Catholic Victoria as the expounder of international law and the Protestant Grotius as the systematizer of international law.

For if Grotius was not a Spaniard by blood, he was Spanish in his conception of international law, and so far as the basic principles of his system are concerned, he was indubitably a member of the Spanish school.[20]

In truth, the line of reasoning is clear from Aristotle through St. Thomas to Victoria that a natural law for mankind does exist, and does exist even outside Christian divine law; but the Spaniard has added that international law obtains more than the force of a pact or agreement between men, since in effect the world is like a single state and may thus create just laws by consent or common usage. "They who violate these international rules . . . commit a mortal sin." [21] In other words, the flexibility of custom is attached to the abstract conception of the immanent natural order which pervades international affairs. This, of course, is the old reconciliation of *ius naturale* as a philosophic expression and *ius gentium* as the practice of peoples, now being applied to a sixteenth-century continent.

It is correctly argued, too, that Grotius' achievement is best reflected by the extent to which he secularized international law: that is, buttressing his postulate that a common law exists among nations in peace and in war with evidence from Euripides, Philo, Thucydides, Chrysostum, Cicero, Seneca, and a host of other pre-Christian, nontheological authors. But the continuity of the central theme of a supra-national law binding

[19] Maine, *International Law*, pp. 18 *et seq.* Maine gives the interesting analogy of the sketchy Indian law which was filled out with British practice during the nineteenth century.
[20] Scott, *The Spanish Conception of International Law and of Sanctions*, p. 51.
[21] Francisco de Victoria, "Lecture concerning Civil Power," Chapter 21, translated by G. L. Williams in *Francisco de Victoria and His Law of Nations*, ed. by J. B. Scott.

upon all men and discernible through reason, and the continuity of the thesis that "by mutual consent it has become possible that certain laws should originate as between all states, or a great many states" [22] is evident. With the Reformation and the religious wars, however, the authority of the church had been challenged, the pope had become a partisan, and the international law of the Roman Catholic doctors had become suspect. New sanctions were sought for the old law so that it might still span the fractured community—and this was the task of the great international jurists of the seventeenth and eighteenth centuries, who were virtually all Protestants! [23] Oppenheim has summarized splendidly various important factors which prepared the ground for the growth of the present international law, but none throws more light on the proposition of new sanctions for the old law than this comment.

The Renaissance of science and art in the 15th Century, together with the resurrection of the knowledge of antiquity, revived the philosophical and aesthetical ideals of Greek life; and transferred them to modern life. Through their influence the spirit of the Christian religion took precedence of its letter . . . that the principles of Christianity ought to unite Christians more than they had done hitherto . . .[24]

In brief, there was a sound basis for describing international law as "European" international law; but the adjective was geographic incidentally, for the qualification pertained to a peculiar religious-cultural heritage from Roman and Christian

[22] Grotius, *De iure belli ac pacis*, Prolegomena, tr. by F. W. Kelsey, ed. by J. B. Scott, "Classics of International Law," p. 15.
[23] For example, Gentili, Grotius, Bynkershoek, Pufendorf, Rachel, Zouche, Wolff, and Vattel. It is also interesting to note the close connection of most of these men with theology. Vattel was the son of a minister; Wolff fell into difficulties with the Protestant orthodoxy in Prussia; Bynkershoek originally studied theology, though his legal work is devoid of religious references; Rachel was the son of a Lutheran minister as was Pufendorf; Gentili was a refugee of the Italian Inquisition, and Grotius, of course, was a famous theologian.
[24] Oppenheim, *International Law*, Vol. I, 3d ed., ed. by R. F. Roxburgh, pp. 60–61. See also G. A. Finch, *The Sources of Modern International Law*.

civilization invigorated by humanism of the Renaissance and the piety of the Reformation.

The spread of European international law resulted from the extension of European rule across the seas. In the New World there was a continuation of the Christian tradition and a sense of community both with the parent lands of the Continent and among the newly formed states. The official papers of Jefferson, as Secretary of State, for example, resound with frequent invocations of the traditional law of nations.[25] And President John Quincy Adams, in response to a cordial invitation to send delegates to the Congress of Panama in 1826, the first attempt to establish a permanent inter-American organization, said that the South American states have "political principles and systems of government, congenial with our own." [26] Simultaneously, the great liberator Simon Bolivar closed his circular invitation to the former Spanish colonies with this flourish:

When after a hundred centuries, posterity shall search for the origin of our public law, and shall remember the compacts that solidified its destiny, they will finger with respect the protocols of the Isthmus. In them they will find the plan of the first alliance that shall sketch the mark of our relations with the universe. What, then, shall be the Isthmus of Corinth compared with that of Panama? [27]

To behave as sovereign nations, with both a high consciousness of the privileges granted by traditional international law and some acknowledgment of its obligations, was the indoctrination of the New World by the Old, despite recriminations and outright revolution. Canada, New Zealand, Australia, and the Cape Colony, of course, never left the actual framework of British international law. But the industrial-political hegemony of Europeans over the rest of the universe, the out-

[25] See, in particular, the correspondence of Jefferson with Citizen Genêt, Minister Plenipotentiary of France, in *State Papers and Publick Documents of the United States, 1789–1796*, pp. 57, 67, 74 *et passim*.
[26] Quoted from Scott, *The International Conferences of the American States, 1889–1928*, Introduction.
[27] Text of the document is quoted in *ibid.*, pp. xix–xx.

standing phenomenon of world politics prior to the First World War, was not accompanied by an actual colonization of the subdued areas—Africa, the Turkish Empire, Southeastern Asia, China—nor the slightest penetration of that huge subcontinent, Russia, which had remained outside all the liberating struggles between pope and emperor, outside the beneficent revival of Greek humanism, and outside the unrelenting challenge to the absolutism of the Holy Church itself.

It is a familiar story how Turkey, in 1856, for example, was "admitted to participate in the advantages of the Public Law and Concert of Europe" and how Europe guaranteed "to respect the independence and territorial integrity of the Ottoman Empire." [28] Presumably, then, a revision of the system of capitulations would have been due, for the advantage of entering the community of Western nations would be meaningless without the concomitant right of territorial sovereignty as enjoyed by Christian states. But no Great Power contemplated an abrogation of its special consular and commercial privileges within the empire, and, therefore, they provided that "treaties which existed before the war between the belligerent powers should continue in force until renewed or replaced." [29] In many subsequent agreements between the Sublime Porte and the Western states there was to be found a solemn declaration in the opening articles assuring the perpetuation of all rights, privileges, and immunities which Turkey had previously conferred upon Europeans or Americans.[30] The point is that for Turkey, a sprawling, decaying empire of diverse peoples, international law was neither an indigenous growth nor a natural application of universal rules to a brotherly state; indeed, the techniques of modern international law, the fol-de-rol of plenipotentiaries, protocols, and palaver, were applied to Turkey as expedients of

[28] Article VII, General Treaty of Peace between Great Britain, Austria, France, Prussia, Russia, Sardinia, and Turkey, Paris, 30 March 1856. For complete text see Edward Hertslet, *Map of Europe by Treaty*, II, 1250 *et seq.*
[29] Article XXXII, *ibid.*
[30] See Sousa, *The Capitulatory Regime of Turkey*, for illustrations.

the Great Powers in their Near Eastern imperial policies, but the fundamental community of Christian peoples under the strictures of Roman law was not thereby automatically extended.[31]

In another instance, China was rejected by the West as a partner in the law of nations in the nineteenth century, and reciprocally China scorned the conception of European states as independent and equal with herself. George Keeton has gone so far as to declare that China, being unable to sustain either rights or obligations, was in the position "of a peregrinus from the standpoint of the *ius civile*—totally extraterritorial in fact" and that it was therefore necessary for the West to elaborate a set of rules modeled on international law, but "with certain necessary modifications, applicable to China." [32] This jejune equivocation seemed to mean: China cannot be considered a state under international law, but China has to be put under international law so that Europe can use legal forms to extort commercial concessions. Stripped of jargon, the facts of the case for Chinese extraterritoriality rested upon the complete dissimilarity between Chinese domestic law and European procedures, standards of right, and so forth. Until the overthrow of the Manchus in 1911, for example, China had no judges in the Western sense at all, since appointments to the magistracies

[31] Of course, there were other "agreements" between Turkey and the European states prior to this famous date, mostly treaties of alliance or peace terms with Venice, the Hapsburgs, France, Russia, and others in the sixteenth, seventeenth, and eighteenth centuries. With the wane of Turkish power, the permission granted to Europeans either to care for their religious minorities or pursue trade, became virtual prerogatives. In 1825 England declared her neutrality in the war between Greece and Turkey, saying "great numbers of His Majesty's loyal subjects reside and carry on a beneficial commerce, and possess establishment and enjoy privileges within the Dominions of the Ottoman Porte, protected by the faith of treaties between His Majesty and that Power." And Turkey joined Britain, France, and Russia, in a definitive settlement of the Greek boundaries in 1832. If Turkey was admitted to the "advantages of the Public Law and Concert of Europe," it was scarcely more than a fatuous legalism designed to strengthen the British-French position against Russia.
[32] Keeton, *The Development of Extraterritoriality in China*, Vol. I, especially pp. 11 *et seq.*

simply hinged upon a perfunctory proficiency in the classics, regardless of legal training or experienced public service. Moreover, the judicial function was not separated from the legislative or administrative functions, nor was it limited by codes or standard procedures, or restrained by some of the basic individual rights of Western civilization. The use of torture to wring out confessions, severe corporal punishment for misdemeanors, and prisons which lagged from fifty to one hundred years behind contemporary reforms in Europe all served to mark off China from the Western community.[33] If China became a subject of international law, it was because of coercion; for the right of equal association among nations, the right to trade, the right of nationals to emigrate, the right of free communication between citizens and aliens, the right of peaceful transit through national territories, to name but a few achievements of Western society in the nineteenth century, were never regarded as "rights" in any way by China or, least of all, considered part of an inviolable law of nations.

But if Eastern peoples never acquiesced in European international practices because their domestic law was foreign to traditional Western procedures, there was also a jagged gash ripped through the flimsy fabric of international law by the iron hand of the totalitarian state in twentieth-century Europe itself. Certainly the regime of a totalitarian state is philosophically incompatible with the traditional law of nations, for to make the glorification and the extension of the state, as an organic entity, the paramount objective of public policy is to

[33] For instances of the arbitrary or chaotic administration of justice in China see United States, Commission on Extraterritoriality in China, *Report*, especially for examples of the interference of the military, the lack of universal application, and the structure of the judicial system, pp. 89–104. Arbitrary execution without trial was common, the granting of bail uncommon; torture was still practiced in several places by the military, the police, the magistrates. There were (in 1925) only ninety-one courts of first instance in the land, and most of the cases came before trial magistrates who combined administrative, legislative, and judicial functions. According to Western jurisprudence, moreover, the most flagrant abuses of even this scant machinery of justice prevailed.

destroy the whole conception of a coordinate brotherhood of nations promoting Christian values in the individual. In turn, values became little more than pragmatic, tested for truth or reality by the immediate demands of the state, or, moving back one step farther, the self-selected clique which controls the government of the state.

National Socialist Germany, for example, maintained that law could be nothing but a reflection of reality, since the actual relationships of society must determine the character of the law. For the Nazis, however, retraversing the grounds of Fichte, Herder, Gobineau, and Chamberlain, reality comprised the divisions of the world into races and nations. The "natural law" of this world had no connection with individual reason coupled to an abstract ethical norm, but rather was indicated by the ingrained blood ties and spiritual attributes of the nation. Each nation, therefore, had its own normative structure. "National self-determination" became the appreciation and implementation of a singular historical role of the nation rather than the claim of the equal right for all national groups to independence in their domestic affairs. Descending to practical matters by such tortuous reasoning, the Nazis found that the mission of Germany, as the purest and strongest race, was to establish and lead a New Order for Europe.[34] Indeed, Nazism completely rejected the heritage of the West, especially the elements of Western civilization that had been created by the accumulation of Greek, Roman, Hebrew, and Christian thought and practices, the very mortar of international law.[35]

Nothing could incriminate the unscrupulous doctrines of the Hitlerite superman more fully than the florid testament of one of their key spokesmen.

When I am told that justice is eternal, that everything could crumble, but not justice—then I can only say that justice changes daily

[34] See Virginia L. Gott, "The National Socialist Theory of International Law," *The American Journal of International Law*, XXXII (October, 1938), 704–718.
[35] Ebenstein, *The Nazi State*, p. 312.

. . . but the feeling of right, that remains eternal. . . . It grows from father into son and is therefore born of the blood of a nation. . . . Nations are primary and carry their laws unwritten as the holiest possession in their breast.[36]

Such mystical blatherings wound the very heart of international agreements, which must find their binding force in something less occult and certainly less whimsical than a racial-national conscience.

In respect to the rules of international law which evolved in an era of private-enterprise economy and negative government, the totalitarian state has shattered many time-honored concepts. For example, immunity to the action of foreign courts in many spheres was granted to states on the assumption that communications and commerce of an interstate nature would be the business of individuals subject to the normal processes of civil liability. The nationalization of industries, however, government ownership of merchant fleets, the growth of public corporations, and so forth, demand a new approach to this custom. Furthermore, the hoary dictum of neutrality is intolerable to a totalitarian state which might find other nations (through private enterprise) assisting one or both belligerents while state-controlled industry was forbidden to deliver its wares to either contending force under traditional international laws.[37]

Those are matters of some consequence to the distortion of international law. But it is more significant that any state aspiring to world or regional hegemony must pervert international law, for rabid imperialism and its practices are contradictory to the most fundamental tenets of the law of nations. Fascism

[36] Blood-Ryan, *The Political Testament of Hermann Göring*, pp. 118–119, "Speech to the German Academy of Justice," November 13, 1934.
[37] W. Friedmann gives an excellent summation of this topic in his article "The Growth of State Control over the Individual, and Its Effects upon the Rules of International State Responsibility," in the *British Yearbook of International Law*, written in 1938, on the eve of the Second World War, pp. 118 *et seq.* See also Kuhn, "The Extension of Sovereign Immunity to Government Owned Commercial Corporations," *American Journal of International Law*, October 1945, pp. 772 *et seq.*

blatantly asserted its superior claims over inferior peoples—yet, as has been indicated before, even the Western liberal powers failed to extend their interstate privileges to Asia and Africa. In this connection the main point of interest, however, is that Italy, with its deep attachment to the Roman past, frequently violated "the spirit and purpose of international law while formally complying with the letter." [38] For instance, the bombing and occupation of Corfu in 1923 was labeled a reprisal. Self-defense was the excuse for the war in Ethopia. Entire divisions of the Italian army which assisted Franco were hailed as "volunteers" as they helped destroy the *de iure* Spanish government. And before June, 1940, Italy raucously asserted her "nonbelligerency," a term without legal significance, thus claiming the privileges, but not the obligations, of a neutral—though demonstrating an obvious partiality toward Germany.

The danger for those who scan the billowing clouds for a sign that international law is making its way throughout the universe—like a Baptist announcing the Messiah of world government—is the danger of accepting token forms for the heartfelt reality, of adding up the sum of agreements, protocols, and international organizations established by diplomatic fanfare without reckoning the profundity of sentiment, the conscience, the virtue and the philosophy which accompanies the international bargain. When Eugene A. Korovin, professor of international law at Moscow and contemporary (1946) apostle of the Soviet Union on international jurisprudence, neatly defines the specific nature of international law in the coming period of history as "the sum total of legal norms guaranteeing international protection of the democratic minimum," perhaps one should not be remiss in inquiring about the meaning of "democratic minimum," especially since he immediately asserts that anti-democratic trends still exist in international law and that the struggle of the progressive elements of mankind must be

[38] Angelo Sereni, *The Italian Conception of Internation Law*, p. 352.

directed toward abolishing them.[39] Perhaps it is forgotten that Korovin also remarked some years ago that the Soviet Union "considers the organized proletarian masses, scattered throughout the noncommunist states, as distinct persons in international law"! [40]

The mere participation in international agencies cannot be construed as an indication of the growth of law, for much depends upon the nature of the agencies and the objectives of the participants. The Soviet Union participated in the 4th Preparatory Commission for the Disarmament Conference and the International Economic Conference as early as 1927; she adhered to the Briand-Kellogg Peace Pact; she joined in the International Convention for the Suppression of Counterfeit Money; she concluded numerous treaties with other countries on patents, trademarks, and copyrights and cooperated with the International Hydrographic Bureau, the Office for the Control of the Liquor Traffic in Africa, and the Nansen Office for Refugees, while acceding to the Baltic Geodetic and the Universal Postal Union conventions; she solicited the cooperation of the Health Organization of the League and joined the International Labor Organization.[41] But the chief agency for peace and world order, the League of Nations, was subjected to utter vituperation by the Soviets, until it appeared that Japan and Germany were becoming dangerous to the Russian national interest, and it was then, in 1934, that the Soviet Union joined the organization, only to be expelled in 1939 for aggression against Finland. Both the Permanent Court of Arbitration and the Permanent Court of International Justice were definitely avoided.[42] Certainly an attachment to socio-economic agencies

[39] Eugene A. Korovin, "The Second World War and International Law," *The American Journal of International Law*, XL (October, 1946), 743.
[40] Quoted by Taracouzio, *The Soviet Union and International Law*, p. 16. Korovin has publicly retracted this statement.
[41] See Price, "The USSR and International Organization," *The American Journal of International Law*, XXXVI (July, 1942), 425.
[42] The Soviet Union is now a member of the International Court of Justice by virtue of its membership in the United Nations (Article 93). As yet, it has

which are useful to all states with no derogation of power to any or a connivance to exploit such international organizations as the national interest may sporadically dictate would not seem to engender the progressive development of international law based upon an ever-widening Roman-Christian community and leading, thereby, to constitutional world government.

International law is not without flexibility. It has shown, from time to time, a tendency to adjust to new moral standards and improved modes of transportation-communication: the antislave trade conventions, the suppression of obscene publications, and the rules of warfare are outcroppings of the human urge to crystallize by law, impersonal and universal, an almost imperceptible advance of international ethics. More recently it has been maintained at the Nüremberg trials that aggressive war is now an international crime, although international law is not created by a sovereign body or laid down in statutes. "It grows and develops as the consciousness of nations grows and widens and deepens. That is how international law became law, and there must come a point when some authority for the first time says: This is now the law." [43] Yet the harassing jibes of critics who questioned the legal aspects of the war crime trials might seem to indicate that the test for international law, as for all law, must ultimately rely upon practice, despite the apologists who have blandly approved the evidence and conduct of the cases. The unique declaration of international law by a victorious coalition, valuable as it may prove as a precedent, right as it may appear to momentary feelings, can only find its final justification in a series of such accusations, trials, and judgments by the whole community over the future course

referred no case to the Court. Perhaps it is noteworthy that Korovin devotes three sentences in a thirteen-page article to the function of the Court. One of the sentences, moreover, reads: "Execution of the decisions of the tribunal are guaranteed by the Security Council with all the means at its disposal." A single Great Power veto can virtually nullify any decision.

[43] Justice Birkett, "International Legal Theories Evolved at Nüremberg, *International Affairs*, XXIII (July, 1947), 317.

of history. Herein lies the basic problems of paralleling ethics with enforceable law, of making general rules which will be continuously applied to the whole community, and of drawing up a legal guide to world order.

J. W. Brierly, pursuing a provocative thought of E. H. Carr,[44] has neatly shaped the argument that a rule of law is necessarily expressed in general terms, for it aims at an impersonal and universal application. To the extent that the citizens of a national community can be regarded as "social types," roughly alike in their individual needs, physical strength, and moral imperatives, the attainment of the impersonal and universal exercise of the sanctions of the community is so much easier, even discounting the veiled monopoly of force which the nation-state has achieved and which is admittedly part of the legal process. But the states of the world, which are the main subjects of international law, can by no excitement of the imagination be regarded as "persons" of approximately the same dispositions and therefore are not inclined to yield to some one universal standard of right, applied to themselves and others without distinction. Indeed, the barbs of the revisionist of the law of nations are darted against the dusty, dog-eared textbooks, especially pricking those pages which solemnly assert that "sovereign states are the subjects of international law," for to accept such a fiction is to deny implicitly the legal creation of a world government. Why? Either one must expect a millennium under such circumstances, when all states will actually come to resemble each other as genuine persons of international law, amenable to a single rule of law, or else admit the stagnation of a world society which cannot extend its order beyond opportunistic political divisions of the universe.

So far have the realistic criticisms of international law gone, in a world trembling before its own shadow of chaos, that to-

[44] Brierly, "International Law: Some Conditions of Its Progress," *International Affairs*, XXII (July, 1946), 352. Cf. Carr, *The Twenty Years Crisis, 1919–1939*, p. 228,

day at least one analyst finds little but sham and obfuscation in the reiterated jargon on the subject.

Certainly if the specialists in "international law" would recognize these rules for what they are—a code of diplomatic etiquette, a set of practical expedients subject to practical limitations—and would content themselves with expounding them unpretentiously, they would spare themselves a lot of frustration and the world a good deal of confusion.[45]

This dash of cold water for pedantry is needed. Yet too frequently the affirmation that international law is merely a convenience or an etiquette, and therefore a fishy kind of law, is passed unchallenged. Is it not contravened by the illustration that most law is an expedient, a convenience, or an etiquette, rules which each individual feels are suitable to his particular interest—like the guarantee of a single coinage system, or the free exercise of religion, or driving on one side of the road only—and also suitable to the general interest? To be sure, as governments become less democratic the identification of a particular interest and a hierarchy of command becomes sharper, yet in this respect, too, there are limitations upon ignoring the mores, the habits, the sentiments, and the etiquette of society in the most dictatorial organization. Now it is plain that the distinction Sir Alfred wished to draw was between etiquette which carries no strong mandate for its performance and law which ultimately rests upon physical coercion. But a community substantially agreed upon premises of right and wrong depends much less upon the policeman, for the more homogeneous the society, the less the need for gross coercion. No people can realistically be considered under a rule of law unless the power of government to repress law-breakers is manifest; nevertheless, in a world of peoples unreconciled on the psychology of man, on the divisions of the social power, on the purposes of life itself, "diplomatic etiquette and practical

[45] Zimmern, "World Peace Authority," *The Saturday Review of Literature,* XXXI (July 10, 1948), 6.

expedients" at least serve to bridge some of the harrowing crevices between the spiritually bellicose states. Moreover, by the very narrowness of their span such rules indicate the mighty and tyrannous engines necessary to close the deep fissures of this world.

The dilemma for a world government which seeks to follow international law is that common sentiment and recognized kinship has not only failed to extend itself throughout the world, but also that social upheavals engendered by the industrial revolution have been cracking the thin crust of custom and acknowledged obligations to humanity even within the Western sphere of Roman-Christian jurisprudence. To paraphrase James T. Shotwell, from a book written in the midst of the Second World War, a historical background is absolutely vital to the comprehension of international law, in its promises and its performance, for "it is a philosophy as well as a practice." [46] And it would not be too much to say that states such as Italy, Japan, Germany, and Russia withdrew from the Western community and its verbose, inflated code of international morality, not merely because the way of life within these totalitarian nations could no longer be harmonized with fundamental Western tenets but also, to speak honestly, because there were glaring contradictions between the word and the act of international law in its own cradle.

The decline in international standards does not seem absolute no matter how constantly this yarn is spun in periodical literature today, for the suspiciously re-echoing plaints of those who find the nineteenth century the age of liberal democracy which envisaged a decent and tolerable existence among the states of the world seem to ignore the antidemocratic Holy

---

[46] Shotwell, *The Great Decision*, p. 112. "The law of nature which recognized the fundamental similarities in all mankind is the philosophic principle upon which it is based; but the practical questions with which it has to deal are rather those of the differences between nations than their common interests."

Alliance in one period and the sordid politics in Turkey, Persia, and China, the plunder of Africa, and the abuses of Latin America in another. Still, this evidence need not be tossed about to prove a contrary assertion—that the activities of the Japanese in Manchuria, of the Italians in Ethiopia, of the Germans, the French, and the British in Czechoslovakia, or of the Russians in Finland are less heinous offenses against international ethics. What it may illustrate is the further imperfect widening of the European sodality, the increased impression of danger from a mechanized, atomic bomb age, and a heightened criticism of the breaches of good faith which can be more widely advertised through mass communication.

In earnest, how can it be shown that the sanctimonious spirit of international law prior to the First World War nurtured a "better" organization in the League of Nations than the United Nations which was spawned during the supposed decadence of the pre-1945 years? Both organizations were products of a victorious alliance—with many of the same virtues and errors—and if they collapse the observer who frankly admits the wobbly foundations upon which such legalistic organizations rest need not be stunned. A halt is required to the atomization of cultures and philosophies which continue to disintegrate international law, for, as Payson S. Wild has studiously maintained, law cannot fill the gaps of social divisions, and international law is virtually confronted with religious cleavages.

. . . there is no point in pretending that international law is of vast extent when the world community of interests hardly goes beyond such prosaic items as weights and measures, bubonic plagues, and the rights of diplomats . . . if world society is to be divided into different fighting faiths, virtually all first principles may crumble, for what mutual interests and oughts exist between a fascist and communist except the desire for one another's extermination . . .[47]

[47] Wild, "What Is the Trouble with International Law?" *The American Political Science Review*, XXXII (June, 1938), 478.

International law has groped for a way to accommodate a collection of willful states, to mitigate in some way the blind, arbitrary decisions of the strong by offering certain conveniences for all states over the course of time and despite the vicissitudes of shifting politics. Growing out of a partly homogeneous clique of precapitalistic states, international law at first haphazardly accompanied its original theology and then quickly outstripped it under the excitements of the teeming universe. Could the many valuable guides to legal analysis developed by classic international law and its wealth of historical experience be reshaped to the new fundamentals of social psychology and organization, the burden of creating a world government would be enormously lightened. But the fundamentals themselves are in dispute.

Finally, "no chronological order of priority," wrote John Westlake thirty-five years ago, "[exists] between society, law, and rights and wrongs. They must have arisen together at the earliest times." [48] It would seem that a world law might learn something from the concepts and procedures of international law, as international law profited from Roman law and Christian ethics, but that it must nevertheless be indistinguishable from the world society in which it arises, part of the very fiber which holds the community together, not a superstructure of rules and regulations born from the mind of the most ardent lover of law. All modern societies, however, seemed to have been fused within a vise of power, a conquest, a coercion, or an original military effort. Should such a clamp of power press upon the world (as the overwhelming combined might of the United States, Britain, and the Soviet Union actually did at the very end of the Second World War) the possibilities for a constitutional world government could only be measured by the strength of the psychological-cultural integration of the peoples involved. This gauge seems not only a painfully true one now,

[48] Westlake, *Collected Papers*, ed. by L. Oppenheim.

but a reasonable meter for the future, so that some concluding remarks on the cultivation of universal mores would be highly pertinent to a study of world government.

Chapter 9

Must hapless man, in ignorance sedate,
Roll darkling down the torrent of his fate?
Must no dislike alarm, no wishes rise,
No cries invoke the mercies of the skies?
Inquirer, cease: petitions yet remain,
Which Heaven may hear: not deem religion vain.
Still raise for good the supplicating voice,
But leave to Heaven the measure and the choice.
Safe in his power, whose eyes discern afar
The secret ambush of a specious prayer,
Implore his aid, in his decisions rest,
Secure, whate'er he gives, he gives the best.
Yet when the sense of sacred presence fires,
And strong devotion to the skies aspires,
Pour forth thy fervors for a healthful mind,
Obedient passions, and a will resigned;
For love, which scarce collective man can fill;
For patience, sovereign o'er transmuted ill;
For faith, that, panting for a happier seat,
Counts death kind Nature's signal of retreat.
These goods for man the laws of Heaven ordain,
These goods he grants, who grants the power to gain;
With these celestial Wisdom calms the mind,
And makes the happiness she does not find.

Decimus Junius Juvenalis,
translated by Samuel Johnson

World Culture and
World Community

WHAT ARE THE POSSIBILITIES of extending social cohesiveness on a democratic plane of activity? That is the question which plagues the mind. A democratic world government is unthinkable except in terms of a democratic community constantly nourished by a vigorous belief in the freedom of individual choice, the toleration of minorities, and devices which permit critical opposition in government. On the presumption that rough equivalents to this kind of thinking presently exist among groups of men, how is such a culture of life to be diffused universally? Can it be transmitted? Or will the very process of transfusion in an age of unparalleled technology require such ruthless methods that democratic values themselves will be destroyed in the act?

Perhaps one of the most interesting phenomena of recent world politics is the growth of cultural imperialism, and it is at least one point of departure in analyzing the spread of kindred communities, for by widely advertising the virtues of its own society through press releases, radio broadcasts, good will tours, exchanges of students, and other educational-religious-philanthropic contributions, the modern nation-state now accepts the psychology of making foreign friends and influencing foreign peoples. Until recently no state had been more adept at this program than France.[1] Up to the close of the last century the French Ministry of Foreign Affairs had poured more than 20,000,000 francs into religious missions, schools, and hospitals in the Near and Far East to maintain French moral influences over these areas. From 1900 onwards an ever-increasing sum of francs was devoted by the French government to "Œuvres français à l'étranger": credits were given to schools in the East, in Europe, North and South America to encourage the study of French culture. French books, films, lecturers, and glowing brochures of Gallic life were exported; university chairs were endowed, students were exchanged, and every effort was made to cultivate an interest in French civilization.

Other states were not laggard in recognizing this kind of propaganda as an invaluable aid to foreign policy. In 1901 the German Secretary of State of the Foreign Office admitted sub-sidizing private German schools in the Orient and the Trans-vaal, while noting that in Brazil alone some twenty-eight schools were receiving financial aid from the Reich. During the Weimar Republic, German statesmen frequently empha-sized the fact that Germany's political weakness required a determined promotion of German culture abroad—both to retain the loyalty and affection of expatriates and to gain the esteem of foreigners. As early as May 31, 1931, the National Socialist Party had established a Foreign Division at Hamburg, and by the close of the year Nazi propaganda began to sprout in the fertile ground of the German schools and communities abroad. The program of the National Socialists after 1933 was the apogee of cultural imperialism, for the Hitlerian con-cept of the great German community of blood, with its in-struments of party discipline and global warfare, marshaled

[1] For the following account of the growth of cultural relations programs I am indebted to Ruth Emily McMurray and Muna Lee, *The Cultural Ap-proach—Another Way in International Relations*, especially chaps. ii, iii, vi, viii. In this volume an excellent survey of the propaganda practices of some twenty-nine governments are described with official documentation by re-ports, laws, decrees, debates, and so forth.

every facet of Germanism both within and outside the Third Reich.[2]

The British and the Americans were the last Great Powers to join the movement toward cultural propaganda. Japan had already created the Association of Great Asia by 1934, to promote "friendship, mutual knowledge, and cooperation" between the Empire of the Rising Sun and the other countries of Asia, and this was effected by extensive student exchanges, tourist programs, and the distribution of subsidized magazines, movies, and radio broadcasts. It was not until 1935 that Britain established the Council for Relations with Other Countries, and not until 1938 that the United States launched both the Interdepartmental Committee on Scientific and Cultural Cooperation, primarily for Latin America, and the Division of Cultural Relations in the State Department itself. Within a few years the Colossus of the North became an especially good neighbor to the central and southern hemisphere republics by appointing a number of cultural relations officers to American embassies, lending or giving American transcriptions, books, and moving pictures, subsidizing libraries, and establishing cultural institutes to teach English.[3] During the Second World War the United States virtually blanketed the earth with its excellent propaganda from both the Committee for Inter-American Affairs and the Office of War Information, all as part of a vast psychological warfare apparatus. But three years after the Armistice the Voice of America was broadcasting to the world in fourteen languages, while the United States Information and Education Exchange services supplied some 130 posts in

[2] Samuel Guy Inman tells of one raid in Argentina upon a division of the German Embassy during the Second World War in which 100,000 individual cards were discovered. Each of the cards described one German in Argentina, his history, photograph, occupation, salary, and contribution to the Embassy. See Beals and others, *What the South Americans Think of Us*.
[3] For a complete description of the cultural-cooperation program of the United States from its inception in 1938 to 1943, see *Report on the Cultural-Cooperation Program* prepared by Haldore Hanson for the Department of State.

82 countries with American films, press news, books, exhibits, and so forth.[4]

In each instance the cultural relations program was, and is, guided by the national interest and may be fairly viewed as a tool of diplomacy. Regarded in this light, there is nothing more insidious about spreading friendly information about one's country than other useful pressures of negotiation between foreign offices. But it would be an error to assume that since modern communication makes it incumbent upon national powers to employ mass propaganda,[5] for both domestic and foreign consumption, a free market of ideas is being fostered and that, like some magic economic mechanism, the people of the world will select the most democratic. Indeed, the acceleration of cultural imperialism and the paramount importance of indoctrination in a world of states which for the first time in history find their political power in literate and semiliterate masses has already set in motion the defenses of censorship and communication monopolies almost everywhere.[6] The point,

[4] Schneider, "America's Answer to Communist Propaganda Abroad," in *Department of State Bulletin*, XIX (December 19, 1948), 772–776. As an illustration of the technique, it is interesting to note that 5,000 words of American news have been radioed directly from Washington to Paris (and throughout the world). Translated into French, the news is prepared in bulletin form and distributed to 2,000 French addresses—including not only newspapers but also educators, government officials, professional men, and trade-union leaders. This service is distinct from the work of the Associated Press, the United Press, International News Service, and so forth.

[5] Within little more than a decade radio transmission has assumed a leading place in both domestic and international political life. The state-owned and controlled Soviet radio system, for example, increased its transmitters from four to fifty within two years, 1926–1928. Hitler increased the number of receiving sets within Germany from 4,307,000 in 1933 to 9,087,454 in 1938. There were only three short wave transmitters in Europe in 1930, but eight years later more than forty powerful stations were beaming their programs across the seas. For a splendid analysis of this new direction of foreign policy up to the eve of the Second World War see Grandin, *The Political Use of the Radio*, Vol. X of "Geneva Studies."

[6] *The Christian Science Monitor*, for example, printed a full-page article on December 21, 1948, entitled "Press Censorship Stretches Muzzle over Growing Areas of the Globe," in which were listed a mere handful of states—such as Uruguay and the British Dominions—still maintaining press standards comparable to the United States.

is that national cultural relations programs, however polished with the shiny catch-phrase "to promote international understanding," are guided missiles in the national interest.

From a more genuine international viewpoint, the United Nations Educational, Scientific, and Cultural Organization is endeavoring to remove the barriers to the flow of information, for it recognizes that "ignorance of each other's ways and lives has been a common cause of that suspicion and mistrust between the peoples of the world through which their differences have all too often broken into war." [7] It further insists that a wide diffusion of a culture emphasizing the education of mankind for justice and liberty is "a sacred duty which all nations must fulfill." Peace must be founded upon the intellectual and moral solidarity of mankind. The aphorisms are indisputably correct, but the very action of the organization during the past year casts an overweening shadow of doubt on its ability to further the principles of its constitution.

The former director has admitted that the clearinghouse functions of UNESCO have been progressively more emphasized than the operational activities, that stress is being laid upon technical information, advice, and the friendly publicity of national achievements throughout the world; that specific educational projects to meet regional challenges in Haiti, Peru, and China were virtually abandoned, because the technique was not equal to the task. No more scintillating clue to the real function of the organization is supplied than the large expenditure of $400,000 for "emergency equipment" for education, or, perhaps, the comment that a meeting of eighteen radio program directors in 1948 unanimously agreed that fifteen minutes *a week* should be devoted to items concerning UNESCO. Of the most pressing problem for the universe, it could honestly be stated that "a beginning has been made with the preparation of monographs" on the ways of life in different national cul-

[7] Preamble, *United Nations Educational, Scientific, and Cultural Organization Charter,* reprinted in *International Conciliation.*

tures, thus seeking to discover techniques to change psychological attitudes.[8]

Ignorance may be a source of international friction, yet it is
not really ignorance in its pure sense of not-knowing which
should be under attack, but rather misinformation, miscon-
struction of evidence, misuse of education. The prodigious rise
of literacy within both the Soviet Union and Japan has indeed
given the people new techniques of understanding which is an
undeniable boon to the development of inherent human capacities, but concomitantly the information directed at the individual was pruned and culled so closely that the magnificent
quality of imagination which all men possess and which is the
germ of freedom was stultified. Similarly, in the international
field, to envisage the unimpeded flow of information back and
forth across national boundaries as the chief mission of an international educational organization is a failure to appreciate the
dynamism of cultural-political integration and the inescapable
problem of creating a world government positively. Without
being caustic, one might say that such an approach smacks of
laissez passer in an age which has shrewdly learned to apply the
mighty lever of large-scale organization to social enterprise.
The monopoly of news agencies alone dramatizes the real character of transnational information; just prior to the Second
World War, among the big agencies only Reuter, the United
Press, and the Associated Press were not connected with governments: Deutsche Nachrichten Buro spoke for Germany;
Havas, subsidized by France, yielded to official influence; the
Italian Stefani, the Japanese Domei, and the Russian Tass agen-

[8] See the glowing report on the achievement of the United Nations Educational, Scientific, and Cultural Organization in 1948 by Julian Huxley in the
United Nations Bulletin, January 1, 1949. Mr. Huxley felt that the conference
held on the project of a cultural and scientific history of mankind, a project
dear to his heart, was eminently successful. The most poignant part of his
article is the conclusion: "I feel we are now beginning to know, in rather
general terms, what sort of projects we should undertake . . . I hope there
is general agreement that a good deal of our program is by its nature . . . long
term."

cies mouthed the blatant policies of the state.[9] In an atmosphere of lightning and thunder drowning out the individual voice, shattering the quiet contemplation of books and art and music which move across some parts of the world through the energy of UNESCO, it is difficult to perceive a democratic channel for the intellectual and moral solidarity of mankind. The argument is not whether UNESCO could fare better in the present world, organized, as it is, by states, and confronted with deep rifts in the world community,[10] but whether a different type of agency is demanded by the incontrovertible need for unison on basic tenets of government, fundamental agreement on the purposes of society, and, above all, a supreme allegiance to a body politic transcending the local interest and the nation.

The most scathing skepticism about the mission of an international cultural organization today must come from an examination of the increasing attention given to national cultural programs through larger budgetary appropriations and the establishment of new agencies within both state and education departments. There is scant doubt that state-sponsored cultural relations programs may be the very sharpest wedges for political aggression; at the very least, they are prejudiced. It may be conjectured, for example, that American Congressmen were appalled to find that not a single history of the United States in Portuguese existed in Brazil up until 1940, but it by no means impelled them to advocate a history of Russia or Germany or China in Portuguese also.[11] Indeed, the crucial challenge to UNESCO or any other cultural organization is the ability to curtail propaganda or information, whatever euphemistic term may be used, to limit, moderate, even prohibit such materials as

[9] Sir Arthur Willert, "Publicity and Propaganda in International Affairs," *International Affairs*, XVII (September–October, 1938), 809–821.
[10] The Soviet Union, of course, has never subscribed to the Organization.
[11] McMurray and Lee, *The Cultural Approach*, p. 218. The note was taken from a Report of a Subcommittee of the Committee on Appropriations, House of Representatives, 77th Congress of the United States.

contravenes the aims of the organization. The facilitation of communication is not half so much demanded, considering the remarkable mechanical devices available to any cultural promotion group, as the filtering and balancing of the information passed. Grim lessons need to be learned from the totalitarian expertness in producing mass homogeneity, but the objective must be freedom rather than order, and the end must be a democratic control over world society rather than a rigid social control over the people.

What is culture? If the search continues for a common moral foundation to support the pacific arrangement and rearrangement of all or nearly all the dynamic factors of this universe, then part of the quest is concerned with recognizing the attributes and the articulation of culture in general. "Culture," wrote Malinowski, "is an integral composed of partly autonomous, partly coordinated institutions."

It is integrated on a series of principles such as the community of blood through procreation; the contiguity in space related to cooperation; the specialization in activities; and last, but not least, the use of power in political organization.[12]

Furthermore, it is possible to distinguish in any given culture both "instrumental imperatives" which emanate from the economic, political, and related activities of a society, and "integrative imperatives" arising from magic, religion, and knowledge.

When many of the schemes and dreams for world government are stripped to the bone, their skeletal parts are found to be glued together by one or both of these major imperatives. Thus, the functional approach to world government, as presented, for instance, by David Mitrany,[13] emphasizes progressive integration through the instruments of transnational agencies in response to pressing economic needs. Other opinions,

[12] Malinowski, *A Scientific Theory of Culture*, p. 40.
[13] Mitrany, *The Progress of International Government*, chap. iii. For a later view see "The Functional Approach to World Government," *International Affairs* (London), XXIV (July, 1948), 350–360.

like those of Pitrim Sorokin,[14] chant the prophetic wail for a moral revolution of mankind. The disagreement of views, however, is a matter, not of incompatibility, but rather of stress, for it would be incongruous to find a happy superstructure of world economic agencies without an improved spiritual base for distributing the social product—or vice versa. Indeed, it is suggested that man's moral awakening is inextricable from his creativity, that his ability to conceive instrumental techniques or devices, economic or political, is the veritable reflection of his sense of honor, duty, charity, respect, altruism, in brief, his distinction between good and bad.[15]

To speak of a world culture, then, as an integral of partly autonomous and partly coordinated institutions adequate for the maintenance of a stable society is to look forward to both the development of concrete devices to mitigate the upheavals of the world and the constant reinforcement of the particular spiritual values which give birth to such agencies. Some mood of mind gives life to an organization, but unless the organization, be it UNESCO or the Comintern, positively clarifies and advances the particular sense of right which instigated its charter, its subscription, and its procedural techniques, then it can hardly be accepted as working toward one culture, but should be acknowledged as the collusion of different "cultures" in a fictitious enterprise. Is it improper to say this about the League or the United Nations?

[14] "But there must be a change in the whole mentality and attitudes in the direction of the norms prescribed in the Sermon on the Mount. When such a change occurs, to a notable degree the technical ways of remodeling the economic and political structures in this direction become easy. Without this change, no mechanical politico-economic reconstruction can give the desired results."—Sorokin, *The Crisis of Our Age*, p. 319.

[15] A simple illustration of this idea may be found in the "culture complex." The Ojibway Indians, for example, use rice for food, a distinctive cultural trait of the tribe. "Although the plant grows wild each member does not seize the food from the plant: there is cultivation of the plant, bunching of the stems to discourage birds, a gathering, hulling, storing process—all before the actual consumption . . . intimately bound up in the whole process are property rights, labor obligations, etiquette, methods of keeping time, and a number of special religious observances, prohibitions, and taboos."—Wissler, *Man and Culture*, pp. 51-52.

Apart from the instrumental and integrative imperatives which Malinowski used as criteria for distinct cultures, there is a series of observable principles upon which the integration of culture units may be based. First, of course, are the blood ties of the family, or in its more extended form, the tribe. The Chinese family units of "chia," "chih," and "tsu," each a cultural unit of increasingly large order, linked by real or imaginary blood ties, is one good illustration,[16] and the kinship bonds which dictate the customary law of a primitive tribe is another. Secondly, cultural groupings may evolve out of specialization of rank, status, or profession over the course of time. Perhaps the Hindu caste system, or the apprentice-master relationship of the medieval guild, or the Prussian-German army system of the eighteenth-nineteenth centuries,[17] will illustrate the point. But the diffusion of a particular ethos seems to be due to radiation from a dynamic core into ill-rooted or dispassionate communities, or by transplantation, superimposition, and dictation via political conquest, and this is significant for appraising the possibilities of one world community. History supplies a few clues.

Colonization of sparse areas carried Greek mores to Magna Graecia and Asia Minor; but the conquests of Alexander, quickly shattered though they were, spread a new Hellenistic civilization far and wide in the Near East. The church and Roman lawyers fanned out their dogma within the seething shell of the Western Empire. The Moslem faith came riding on war horses out of the deserts of Arabia, picking up and transmitting the high but listless Greek-Levantine-Iranian culture.[18]

[16] See Knight Biggerstaff, "The Peasant Family: the Chinese Large Family, Its Role, and Recent Trends," in *The Cultural Approach to History*, ed. by Caroline F. Ware, pp. 109 *et seq.*

[17] See Alfred Vagts, "The German Army of the Second Reich as a Cultural Institution," in Ware, ed., *The Cultural Approach to History*, pp. 182 *et seq.*

[18] "Finally, Islam endowed the Syriac Society, at last, with an indigenous universal church and thereby enabled it, after centuries of suspended animation, to give up the ghost in the assurance that it would not now pass away without leaving offspring; for the Islamic Church became the chrysalis out of which the new Arabic and Iranic civilizations were in due course to emerge."

The ethos of the Norman conquerors of England, "with their Christianity, concept of honor and personal dignity which had to be continually validated, and their competitive quest for material and non-material advantage" is what strikes history today as the island's culture pattern, yet the subjugated population seems to have been pagan, comparatively pacific, rather socially minded as indicated by their extensive communal holding of land and animals.[19] Perhaps nothing is more striking about the Western Hemisphere than the different approaches to public morality and racial tolerance north and south of the Rio Grande—largely due to the different inheritances from England and Spain. The spread of Buddhism in the fifth and sixth centuries before Christ made its way through world-weary masses in the Ganges valley: it was a clearer, stronger call to simplicity and surcease from the painful Indian wheel of life in Hindu thought as well as disgust with the rapacious, conceited Brahmins.[20] Furthermore, the preaching of Siddhartha or the Buddha was greatly abetted by its coincidence with a remarkable period of free speech and religious tolerance. Still, internal divisions and the advance of Alexander the Great into northern India might have snuffed out the flickering faith had it not been for the founding of a strong dynasty by Chandragupta in the wake of the Greek collapse. It was during the reign of Chandragupta's grandson, Asoka, in the middle of the third century before Christ that Buddhism took on a new lease of life: "Asoka had waded through blood to his throne, and then he spent the remainder of his life in spreading a religion of retirement, mercy, and peace." [21]

Arnold Toynbee, *A Study of History*, Abridgment of Vols. I–VI, by D. C. Somervell.

[19] Geoffrey Gorer, "Society as Viewed by an Anthropologist," in Ware, ed., *The Cultural Approach to History*, p. 28.

[20] See T. W. Rhys-Davids, *Lectures on the Origin and Growth of Religions*, especially pp. 17–33.

[21] Reischauer, *Studies in Japanese Buddhism*, p. 54. As Buddhism spread, of course, it fragmented into many sects, absorbing much of the local religions, and this furthered its spread. In China, for example, it incorporated parts of

The partial success of Buddhism in China, moreover, can be found in its appeal in a land where religion had been almost purely a matter of human relationships, or reversing the reason, where no spiritual depth blocked its course. Jumping down to the twentieth century, we may say that the zealots of fascism began making converts when the materialism of the nineteenth century no longer carried the convictions of progress or the heroic cries for constitutions and democracy. Then, it took black-shirted Italians and brown-shirted Germans, ready, in fact eager, to use violence, to create their gruesome new world. If militant opposition had been lacking, they would have gone on creating it.

In the high, concave mirror of history certain ways of life seem to have been dispersed over vast areas with astounding speed. For some inventions or skills this was particularly true: horse culture, for example, was adopted with great rapidity by the Indians of both North and South America after the first invasion of the New World by Cortes and De Soto—despite the lack of political integration. And there seems little doubt that our optimistic fathers of the late nineteenth century viewed the phenomenal scattering of steam engines, railroads, and electric motors to the far-away places of the earth—despite the lack of political integration—as the harbinger of a universal, pacific ethos. But the deepest stirrings of community, those which grip and root the irrational beliefs of a society, have moved at a more stubborn pace. Primitive Christianity had all the breaks; it came at a time when the old Roman civic and social virtues had lapsed, when a progressive enslavement of the Mediterranean masses had been going on for three centuries, and, like Buddhism, in a period when there was a singular toleration of religions. Thus, Christianity followed close behind a wave of other cults, such as the Anatolian worship of Cybele, the Egyptian devotions to Isis-Serapis, Mithraism, and

---

Confucianism and Taoism, while in Japan it merged with some of the Shinto doctrines and practices.

Gnosticism. Nevertheless, Christianity spread gradually rather than rapidly, and it was much slower in the Latin parts of the empire than in the Hellenistic sections. It has been reasonably estimated that more than two hundred years after the death of Jesus only one person in ten was a Christian.[22] Once having become the Roman state religion, however, Christianity made converts by the thousands.

To insure the persistence of basic social beliefs, moreover, they must be asserted again and again. Both Spain and England got hold of German tribal democracy, rough as it was, during the age of the Teutonic migrations. Indeed, Spain of the fourteenth century seems to have placed more restraints upon arbitrary government and created more legislative-constitutional devices than did contemporary England. But the very strength of the Norman kings compelled their advisors and councillors to attend them, preparing the way for habitual consultation and dropping the ladder for constitutionalism, while in Spain the weakness of the medieval monarchy led to the withering of embryonic representative organs.[23] Magna Carta assumes genuine significance only when placed in line with continuous English insistence upon rights against arbitrary authority—and the long bitter struggle from the time of the Tudor dynasty to 1689 is a reassertion of fundamental ideas. Even while those battles were being waged, Englishmen shipped out to a wild country in America, and eighty-seven years later the colonists found it necessary to draw their weapons for the same principles of liberty.

Considering, then, the incalculable progress of communication, today, and the growing monopoly of physical energy through the coal, oil, and uranium eras by larger political units, there seems to be a good argument for the possibility of diffus-

[22] For the estimate *see* Turner, *The Great Cultural Traditions*, II ("The Classical Empires") 1056. See also chap. xvii, "The Social Evolution of Christianity," for comprehensive treatment.
[23] Charles H. McIlwain, "England's Contribution to Constitutional Government," in Wace, ed., *Studies in Civilization*, p. 133.

ing a general pattern of life over a wider area in a briefer time
than has hitherto been possible, and this would also apply to
the fundamental philosophies of men, though for this there
would be somewhat less celerity. Now it is admissible that the
process of culture diffusion brings about certain changes in
the institutions, techniques, laws, manners, and so forth as they
act upon and react to different physical environments, human
temperaments, and conflicting myths through which they may
pass; it may also be that some habits are less transmissible than
are others or tend to disintegrate more rapidly. Language seems
to have fallen into that category for a long time, though the
stereotyping of tongues by the printed word, radio broadcasts,
moving pictures, and mass education is making this less true.[24]
But one general pattern of a culture, firm in its convictions,
disseminated by ardent disciples, coupled to the physical power
of giant political organizations, and, above all, given a time of
confusion, moral instability, fear, and hopelessness at its periph-
ery, could rush across space like a wind-blown brush fire. The
permanence of the sweep, finally, would depend upon the
perpetual revitalizing of the beliefs which stimulated the efflo-
rescence of the culture by means of parallel institutional
changes appropriate to such a faith.

Delving further into the need for universal cultural-psychical
integration, the investigator is suddenly confronted by at least
one baleful admonition: to grasp such unity means the throt-
tling of culture, the suffocation of all the rich diversity of
mankind, with its flights of imagination, inventions, and crafts.
Right in the middle of an expert conference on educational

[24] This does not preclude, however, the revival of such tongues as Irish and
Hebrew under ultra-nationalistic impulses, although the overwhelming number of citizens were ignorant of the languages. Nor does it preclude the
foisting of another "working language," Spanish, on the United Nations in
1949 at an approximate cost of one-quarter of a million dollars. These are
linguistic separatist tendencies largely dictated by political prestige, but, to
use only one illustration, certainly English and American would have diverged
further in recent times had it not been for the permanence of the printed
word, broadcasting, and the movies.

problems and intercultural understanding, for example, Edwin R. Embree jumped to his feet in violent protest against the trend of thinking toward one democratic world government:

Are we going to develop a world on the basis of standards of a continent at just the time that that continent . . . is in despair, if not collapse? Are we going to take a declining civilization, and, by force, spread that to the entire world in place of the values that other people might offer? [25]

Mr. Embree by no means opposed Western democracy, but, as an individual who had lived and studied outside the European orbit of thought, he earnestly appreciated the distinctive interests and achievements of other peoples. Thus, he repudiated a world under Anglo-Saxon trusteeship as sharply as he would have opposed German trusteeship.

That there is a genuine danger of rigor mortis setting into any tightly organized political organization should be recognized, for homogeneity in itself frequently demands sheeplike sulking; furthermore, the expansion of a political power over wider areas must perforce require more consistent standards of conduct throughout an area than does a conglomeration of tiny units. At this juncture, however, it is important to outline a hierarchy of cultural values available for dissemination throughout the potential world community, for it is reasonable to suppose that there is a whole gamut of culture traits between Jewish montheism and Indian basket weaving, between French equalitarianism and the music of the Balinese. To be sure, philosophical-religious doctrines often form a culture complex with an aesthetic expression, but the problem involved here is which culture traits chosen from a politically organized community need to be diffused in order to secure a modicum of world homogeneity leading to constitutional world government.

Japan always provides a convenient illustration of certain techniques of Western culture crudely grafted upon an endur-

---

[25] Bonnet, ed., *The World's Destiny and the United States*, p. 261.

ing anti-individual and anti-democratic torso. For instance, the first daily newspaper (*Yokohama Mainichi*) to appear in Japan, on December 12, 1870, was followed within a year by thirty other journals, nearly all of which were organs of the administration or sounding boards for the leading political bosses. In the late twenties, before the invasion of Manchuria, when some occidentals were foppishly lauding the superficial Western trappings of Japanese life, Harry Emerson Wildes made an exhaustive study of the contemporary journals and reported "the reading masses are being taught to look upon Westerners as heartless monsters" and "the press . . . has fallen victim to insularity, to distorted vision, and to unwarranted and contemptible prejudice" and "only slight evidence exists to justify contentions that the worst phases of censorship administration are now past, and that press liberties are advancing with rapidity." [26] As time went on it became more and more apparent that whereas Western Europe had been impelled by the desire for freedom to break the shackles of feudalism by revolutionary means, thus preparing the way for popular government, Japan had adopted new political mechanisms to catch up with those states who had forcefully violated her isolation, but that she had neither experienced a popular, liberal uprising nor discarded her feudal ideology.[27]

Central to the diffusion of a world culture is the diffusion of democratic principles of government: constitutional echelons

[26] Wildes, *Social Currents of Japan*, pp. 98, 127; also chap. vi, "Safeguards against Radicalism."

[27] See Sanson, *Japan; a Short Cultural History*, for a thorough exposition of Japanese cultural roots. "In the following pages the reader will find ample evidence to show that, throughout their history, the Japanese have been more interested in problems of government than in speculative philosophy, more concerned with the welfare of the community than with the conscience of the individual. The concept of freedom has not so far become a commonplace of their political thinking perhaps because it is compatible neither with their traditional native belief about life and society, nor with the pessimistic Buddhist doctrines which have colored their view of human existence." See also Hu Shih, "The Modernization of China and Japan," in Ware, ed., *The Cultural Approach to History*, pp. 243 *et seq.*

to a popular management of the political process, in fact, and individual respect for minority criticism. The arts and crafts are in every way subordinate to the impregnation of the world with the seed of liberalism: certainly not the economic liberalism of the callow nineteenth century, but liberalism, in the words of George Sabine,

. . . built upon the moral postulate that men have a right to be convinced, to understand and evaluate the demands that are laid upon them, and, if possible to consent to them . . . a moral judgment transcending utility, a preference for a kind of character in which action flows from conviction and conviction is reached by intelligent consideration of means and ends.[28]

The arts and crafts, to repeat, are in every way subordinate to the spread of the liberal creed for the simple reason that a vibrant democratic faith is the highest, indeed, the only guarantee for the continuous expression of man's soaring imaginative powers in art, in music, and in literature, as well as in the utilitarian sciences. A hesitant and timid democracy, isolating its political heartbeat from the warm arteries of its poetry or drama, symphony or novel, may well be the prolegomena to a more volatile social order which dragoons every breath of expression into the service of the state. The Weimar republic was launched under a sky of evil stars, yet its achievements in literature, the theater, and music during its brief, gasping life were a colorful flash of light before the ugly clouds of National Socialism in Germany. At present the government of the Soviet Union awes and frightens the world with its dictation of tastes and opinions within the state, yet it has been recently pointed out that the old Revolutionary Socialists never accepted politics as an autonomous sphere of life, for it was their religion. Russian totalitarianism, moreover, is an active religion. "Modern Christianity is in decadence because it has been relegated into a recess of the human soul and has ceased to teach a totalitarian

[28] Sabine, "The Historical Position of Liberalism," in *The American Scholar*, X (No. 1, Winter 1940–1941), 51.

attitude toward life as it should." [29] If democracy is to survive, can it do less than embrace both our daily bread and our evening songs?

The national integration of the modern state itself, which now looms as the dastard villain in many world government pamphlets, was part and parcel of the devotion of artists to a national community: in prose and lyrics the praises of the mystic fatherland, with its common tongue, soil, history, and customs, poured forth, and the brilliant sense of enlargement, spiritual by nature, contributed no little to the more rugged political process. To create a world community a similar sense of enlargement would have to be stimulated, and the arts and crafts would have to be enlisted for the purpose. Again, it is not necessary to deny the risks of standardization, but great causes cannot be divorced from great risks. Some consideration, moreover, should be given to Priestly's suggestion:

It is good that Hardy's novels should come out of Dorset soil, that Cezanne's landscapes should belong to Provence, that the symphonies and tone poems of Sibelius should give us the cold glitter of his Finnish lakes. But all this . . . is not nationalism but regionalism . . .[30]

Democratic practice is the last best hope of artistic variety. The very existence of quaint music and esoteric skills depends upon a political process which will give the most likely security against the invasion of individual habits. A failure to perceive the difference between the remote possibility of stereotyping the variegated arts and crafts of the world and the probable extermination of a social order which offers the widest range to those arts and crafts, could be utterly disastrous.

In another direction, Mr. Northrup has recently made a heroic effort to divide the thinking world into two parts by presenting the bold hypothesis that the intuitive factor in the

[29] Guins, "Soviet Culture—Old Trends and New," *The Russian Review*, August, 1947.
[30] J. B. Priestly, "Federalism and Culture," in Channing-Pearce, ed., *Federal Union*, p. 98.

aesthetic, a characteristic of the East, and the scientific, theo-retic component of understanding, a characteristic of the West, need to be blended in order to achieve a more beautiful, pros-perous, and peaceful universe.[31] Out of a wealth of brilliant material, however, it may be possible to select a mere sample to highlight the basic confusion of the problem which is germane to a constitutional world government. At one point, for example, *The Meeting of East and West* states that educa-tion aims at the empirical and rational mind, whereas religion extends to the heart and the emotions that which education has demonstrated for the intellect.[32] Apparently the West has an overabundance of education without the compassion, sensitiv-ity to the beautiful, and equanimity enjoyed by the East, while the East lacks the scientific, theoretic component of knowledge so vital to the progress of human welfare. Yet it may be objected that nothing is more characteristic of the Western liberal man, again taking liberalism in its spiritual connotation, than the sheerly intuitive perception of the equality and dignity of person and, above all, the moral freedom of the individual to declare, accept, and obey such laws as he deems "right." Mr. Northrup asserts that man is partly free, because of his ability to withdraw into the indeterminate aesthetic component of his nature (as exhibited by Eastern cultures), but he soft-pedals the moral individualism of Locke, Protestantism, and democracy while abstracting the sense-perceived, empirical, logical-theo-retic content of Western thought. However, it is to the moral individualism of man that one must turn for a genuinely affirma-tive freedom which insists upon the inherent liberty of men to judge, for right or wrong, according to the dictates of his con-

[31] Northrup, *The Meeting of East and West*, p. 375: "It appears therefore that the meaning of Eastern civilization in its relation to the meaning of Western civilization is as follows: The Orient, for the most part, has investigated things in their aesthetic component; the Occident has investigated these things in their theoretic component. Consequently each has something unique to con-tribute to an adequate philosophy and its attendant adequate cultural ideal for the contemporary world."
[32] *Ibid.*, p. 482.

science, whatever theological-scientific dogma his "practical reason" or "theoretic component of knowledge" may discover.

If our zeal to keep up with the latest thing in physics or physiology, or to mate the cultures of East and West in an epistemologically solemnized global union, leads us to a philosophy in which we can no longer even make sense of this great insight, we shall be spiritually poorer than our ancestors for all our borrowed "wisdom." [33]

Western culture, with its consequent democratic political organization, must be apprehended as a faithful insight of profound good if it is to survive, for only such conviction can stimulate the diffusion of its doctrine; only such a conviction will recruit apostles willing to preach and invent the institutions necessary to spread and strengthen that conviction universally.

The immediate challenges, then, to the promotion of a universal democratic culture are, first, the task of maintaining moral vigor and an active faith in existing constitutional practice by the encouragement and adoption of institutions furthering the concrete expression of free choice and compromise— economically, socially, and politically; secondly, the task of instilling in the peoples of the world, especially in the young, a militant zeal for self-expression and self-government; thirdly, the task of creating a nucleus of power dedicated to the two preceding principles and strong enough to overcome physically both the obstacles of reaction and anarchy.

The history of the world is a grim pageant of atrophied freedoms. Today, and with no small debt to Karl Marx, it is painfully clear that economic security is fundamental to the whole practice of liberty. The local pictures of slaveholding Athenians, Florentine merchants, English industrialists, and free-soil Vermont farmers can stand as partial illustrations of the affinity between prosperity and liberty; furthermore, by their parochialism these scenes offer a contrast to the monumental projects which the world must undertake to achieve

[33] Arthur E. Murphy, "Mr. Northrup and Mr. Locke," in Murphy and Konvitz, *Essays in Political Theory*, p. 111.

such prosperity on a large scale. Physical deprivation through-out the universe is not, in itself, the shame of mankind; the disgrace lies in the moral cynicism which deprivation breeds and the grinding animal labor which presses down upon the exhausted masses, denying to them their human qualities of self-respect and self-assertion. To propagandize for sober constitutional devices in a destitute universe would be futile: at least one reason for the success of the communist ideology in primitive labor areas is that it seems to offer an immediate respite from the blind struggle to keep alive. Democracy cannot begin to fight for world government unless it finds means to cope with the relentless gnawing of hunger.

The shocking devastation of the last war has cruelly aggravated the economic plight of the world: 30 percent of the European merchant marine tonnage was lost, while 15 percent of the railway rolling stock was either smashed or broken; the Chinese lost 80 percent of their merchant marine and more than half their motor vehicles; Malaya had her railway system bombed, and Burma found her inland waterways blocked; Indonesia's transport facilities have suffered prolonged warfare. Throughout the continents of Europe and Asia there have been shortages of equipment and machinery: mining suffered from want of tools; electric power suffered from want of coal or copper or steel; lumber production needed more sawmills. Though South America prospered during the abnormal demand for her products between 1941–45, dollars disappeared rapidly thereafter, and the basic economy remained chiefly agrarian, without tools or techniques for industrialization and with a majority of the population badly undernourished.[34] To pass on the common beliefs of democracy requires some of the contingent prosperity of the Danes and the English of a recent century, some of the contingent stability of the Swedes and

[34] For a summary see "Salient Features of the World Economic Situation, 1945–47," Economic Report, Department of Economic Affairs, United Nations and "World Economic Conditions" in *International Conciliation,*

the Swiss, some of the expanding economic opportunities of the Australians and the Americans. Indeed, the learned Secretary of State for the United States was correct in remarking that the American view of life is one which flows directly from the Renaissance, but he was even more astute in observing that "it is not that material objects in and of themselves make a better or fuller life, but they are the means by which people can obtain freedom." [35] It is difficult to see how any impoverished and miserable people can ever afford the luxury of democratic government—whether the economic plan be of the free enterprise or socialistic variety.

No operation could be more delicate than the democratic extension of minimum economic aid from the affluent to the poor, not only as a dangerous excuse for paternal-imperialism, but also for a difficult test of the economic system of the well-to-do, self-governing peoples. If democracy can be disgraced within the national mind by its failure to beget techniques and institutions for economic stability, this proposition would seem equally true for a world community and a world conscience. Therefore, unless effective trade organizations and resource development projects, for example, can be organized on a supranational level, there seems little prospect of even a fertile soil in which to plant the husbanded seeds of free fellowship. Moreover, if the techniques and institutions devised to alleviate economic disproportions within the democratic state, whether labor unions or regulatory commissions, ought to be subjected to sound public administration and feasible democratic control, so, too, the world agencies created for economic adjustments ought to meet such criteria.

No one can assert that alternative methods for advancing economic democracy on a world level are clearly traceable, yet it may be said that the more prosperous states need not only to

[35] At a press conference on January 26, 1949, Dean Acheson, commenting on President Truman's inaugural address, especially "point four"—a plan for American aid to substandard areas of the world. Reported in the *Christian Science Monitor*, January 27, 1949.

recognize their obligations to the community of men but also to be prepared to share their good fortune through relatively independent agencies. Concretely, the American Economic Cooperation Administration may serve for emergency post-war relief to Europe, and the United States Export-Import Bank may be used to tide over temporarily capital-hungry states, but these agencies are not substitutes for a strong, jointly operated and administered world bank for reconstruction and redevelopment, and it is in this general direction that all international public policy ought to be pointed. Thus, President Truman's "point four" of his 1949 inaugural address sketched out a program:

. . . we should make available our store of technical knowledge . . . in cooperation with other nations we should foster capital investment in areas needing development. . . . This should be a co-operative enterprise in which all nations work together through the United Nations and its specialized agencies wherever practicable . . . it must be a world-wide effort . . . what we envisage is a program of development based on the concepts of democratic fair-dealing.[36]

But this may not square with his other suggestions that American business, agriculture, labor, and private capital should greatly increase the industrial activity in other nations and should raise substantially their standards of living or the intimation that American guarantees to the investor might be available. The true role of the United States, it might be argued, is to make its business, labor, and so forth useful to some world economic agency and have its private investments channeled into a world capital fund. World government depends upon a concatenation of such day-by-day, week-by-week, year-by-year decisions.

The task of instilling an ardent belief in self-expression and self-government in the minds of men goes hand in hand with relief from hunger, for mere redistribution of wealth without

[36] Text of President Truman's Inaugural Address, 1949, reprinted in the New York *Herald Tribune*, January 21, 1949, p. 2.

a concomitant understanding of the social philosophy involved may simply replace one selfishness with another. Though economic needs are frankly discussed and frequently reach positive planning-execution stages, there is, especially among democratic peoples, a persistent suspicion of organized propaganda. The German Reich minister for education could decree that "all educational agencies have one common goal, the formation of the National Socialist man," which Western democrats railed against as a vicious goal of totalitarianism. But it sometimes seems as if the proud liberal retort is, "No educational agency has the formation of a democratic man as a goal." This is patently false logic. One educator, for instance, has commented that all American teachers subscribe to the principle of "purpose" as one of the first essentials to effective learning, yet the digestion of stupendous factual matter appears to have become the major purpose of learning instead of merely providing the means for a better understanding and appreciation of social democracy.[37]

Democracy now sits entrenched in a few places. It has been complacent. It has been on the defensive. It has been shaken by doubt. It has shivered with cold frustration. Such an attitude cannot be an inspiration to mankind; such a mood has never and will never rally the burning emotions of men to build a new world, which requires endless patience and the willing contribution of treasure and life. Unless democracy is capable of teaching and defending the principles of free association, consent of the governed, equality before the law, equality of economic opportunity, and the tolerance of minority criticism, then its mission on this earth may be horribly aborted for want of sustenance.

Education for constitutional world government does not consist of the pleasant interchange of books, songs, movies, even students and teachers, between states, for this is but the superficial shuttling of the bare trappings of language, beautiful

[37] Strebel, *Education, Keystone of Peace*, pp. 190–191.

landscapes, music, folkways, dances, business-industrial techniques, and curious customs. To develop a cosmopolitan democratic outlook, however, demands the mobilization of shock
troops, imbued with a confidence in their mission, positively
planning and executing a total campaign to win the minds and
hearts of all people to fundamental principles of government
and human conduct. Three years after the founding of the
United Nations a French ambassador could sincerely plead
that

despite the very laudable effort of the United Nations in the field
of public information, its work is still insufficiently known in the
European countries. . . . [and the people] often feel that they are
out of their depth in United Nations affairs and have the impression
that all these discussions taking place far away do not concern
them.[38]

The need is not simply publicity, but actual participation, an
awakening sense in many men, women, and children of belong-
ing to a larger association—and it is credible that the stimulus
for such activity can only come from a crusading organization,
not a passive one, an educating organization, not an educational
one, a preachers' union of world leaders devoted to the gospel
of democratic procedure and for whom the mass communication facilities of the modern state would be made progressively
available. The pressing need, moreover, does not seem to be
the promotion of a specific constitutional document, since the
varying forms of democracy from Sweden to the United States,
from Iceland to Uruguay, are the least danger to world cooperation, but rather is there a need for the establishment of a
vital agency dedicated to the continuous inculcation and dissemination of faith in man's rationality, in the dignity and
worth of person, in the values of compromise, concession, tolerance, and compassion. Without this creed democracy will
perish, and the ensuing anarchy or imperium will bear the

[38] Fouques-Duparc, "British and European Views of the United Nations"
International Conciliation, No. 443 (September, 1948), p. 454.

peoples of the earth upon wretched litters into purgatory.

The task of creating a nucleus of power to implement the preceding principles and to defend their assertion by force is a hurdle which needs to be met, recognized, and surmounted, for the noblest dreams of men have always remained fantasies unless someone is prepared to die for them. A democratic world order cannot demand less. Men must certainly be taken as they are, not as they ought to be: some tireless workers and practitioners of freedom; a majority of inactive souls, yet responsive to the inner conscience when stirred; some selfish, dangerous seekers of prestige and authority, defiant of human brotherhood and humility. An unarmed democracy is a contradiction of terms, for consent and free choice and equality in life are by no means "natural" to human society, but come after long perseverence and trials of strength with the ever-present egocentrism of men.

Another error about justice . . . declares: it is possible to be just without having to be brave. This is not so much an error about the nature of justice as an error about the real structure of "this" world in which justice is to be realized. For "this" world is constituted in such a manner that justice, and good generally, could not be successful of its own accord without the fighting man, ready to die for it.[39]

Translating these prescriptions into the practical requirements of a constitutional world government seems to suggest that without a willingness to organize force and to use force in the interests of a universal democratic community, the first faltering steps of any gathering of states toward this goal must end in an ignominious stumble. Unless there is a determination both to defend and to advance more liberal principles of government throughout the world as a general interest and regard-

[39] "Evil is mighty in 'this' world: this fact becomes manifest in the necessity for fortitude which means a readiness to endure injuries for the sake of the realization of the good (but) fortitude as a virtue is present only where justice is intended."—Pieper, "On the Christian Idea of Man," *The Review of Politics*, XI (January, 1949), 10.

less of individual advantage or expediency, then all grandiose plans have the weight of paper. If democracy suffers a blow anywhere, the sting will be felt everywhere, and the few remaining bastions will be cut off from another ally in a common cause.[40]

Statesmen deal with daily problems; they work for nations and rightly protect the national interest. They go to conferences, they observe, they consult, and they endeavor to make foreign policy. Considering the conditions in which they operate, they cannot possibly (nor should they be expected to) pull a world government out of their top hats. Yet statesmen are only part of a policy-making process, which includes diverse national agencies, interaction with other states, public opinion, and sometimes pure accident. In many events, however, there are alternative choices; in such choices, with the circumstances stripped to bare facts and the reasonable part of man's character at work, lies the continuous hope for a more congenial and co-operative universe. The believers in democracy make today and will continue to make tomorrow decisions about China, about Africa, about Latin America, about Europeans and Americans and Japanese. Will those decisions contribute to a reaffirmation or an erosion of free choice under economic security? Will those decisions actively promulgate the faith in equality before the law and respect for individual opinion? Will those decisions carry such convictions that armies will be mobilized to defend democracy and advance the dictum of liberty for all regardless of race, creed, or status?

The organization of constitutional world government must in the long run be founded upon a principle, not an expedient alliance: no messiah can raise his voice for a universal kingdom if he is not prepared to be a martyr for all men; no people will have justified their precious achievement of self-government unless they are resolved to defend it, teach it, and share it with

---

[40] For a penetrating and highly relevant analysis of democracy see Bryn-Jones, *Toward a Democratic New Order.*

those who would join with them in peace-loving fellowship. To do all this in an ever-changing, ever-straining world requires decision and power, the determined collaboration of all like-minded states in an organization willing to use force not only to protect incumbent democracy but also to advance the conditions for constitutional government everywhere in the world —whether by pacific or by revolutionary means. In the final analysis, the force itself must stem from the deep conviction that a universal democratic community is an absolute necessity to freedom and order in the atomic era and that the extension of fundamental principles must transcend any single national advantage.

The advancement of liberty, at home or abroad, in sovereign states or dependent colonies, is a ringing challenge to every single man enraptured by that most wondrous and sublime vision of a constitutional world government, so terribly remote, so breathlessly possible!

Part Four

DEMOCRACY AND WORLD GOVERNMENT

Chapter 10

The ancients who wished to establish illustrious virtue throughout the empire first ordered well their own states. Wishing to order well their states, they first regulated their families. Wishing to regulate their families, they first cultivated their persons. Wishing to cultivate their persons, they first rectified their hearts.

From *The Great Learning*,
based on the teachings of Confucius

Alternatives to Destiny

LIKE DEMOCRACY, world government defies a positive description, for it has clothed itself with different meanings for different people at different snatches of history. The very grandeur of the term "world government," with its explicit notion of universality and its implicit connotation of peace, has tantalized the imagination of both the sophisticate and the analphabet, of men in both the leisured and the laboring classes. Indeed, the idea of world government seems imperishable, despite the frustrations to practice, and a perennial idea in the minds of men ought never to be discounted in the annals of human society.

In religion, man strives to universalize his personal experience. To his gods or God he imputes a vague awareness of himself and others of the social circle, and he translates through his deity the causes and effects of his environment. No less does priest, pedagogue, or prince, prating about a world government, seek to bring everything and everyone within the peculiar sphere of his own observations and evaluations, for in the nature of things, the organized control and direction of society needs some purpose, and that purpose is some universalized conception of the good. Thus, each brilliant image of world government, tinctured with the rainbow splendor of a planet guided by wise and loving hands into the mists of peace, bears the imprint of the author's philosophy of life together with the crude historical situation of the moment. Those who cherished an imperial age have called for a magnanimous emperor, and those who knew the personal rule of sovereign princes have endeavored to league their kings in friendship. A world federation, therefore, could have little meaning for a people without long experience in representative government, while the acceptance of history as a battlefield of class warfare excludes all but triumphant proletarians from human brotherhood.

The historical protagonists of world government have been linked in only two respects: the suggestion of universality or aggregation and the expectation of peace. Yet, aggregation, of itself, is hardly indicative of peace; but even were it so, peace must be submitted to a thousand qualifications, for countless breeds of men have willingly chucked peace aside in order to secure what they deemed minimum rights and rewards. Should the attraction to world government stem merely out of the desire of a soul-weary world for escape from reality into a Nirvana of peace, mankind ought to be alerted, since political organization, local or hemispheric, is the use, not the abdication, of power. Those who swim toward the bait of a gleaming abstraction of peace may find themselves floundering in the capacious nets of big fishermen busily engaged in changing the stream of world society.

If universality cannot be immediately realized, there are available a host of proposals to carry the banner of world government to less sublime goals. A regional political organization encompassing several states and a functional organization of various international economic activities are put forth as beacons to the highway of world government. In the first instance, with larger geographic divisions of the globe there is faint promise of mitigating the basic causes of world friction; on the contrary, such greater monolithic spheres of influence might well intensify the rivalry of world powers. In the second instance, there is an intimation that common techniques of production, transportation, and communication will breed similar social values, leading to a more comprehensive political community, yet this remains dubious insofar as the final distribution of the product, the complex key to civilized cooperation, rests upon a moral consensus. Seizing upon this last objection, the ideological blocs call for either cores of communism or democratic unions as primary organizations of world government. The immediate likelihood of cohesion, however, within the broad ideological framework, is questionable, because of the persistence of nationalism. Even having shrugged off this fleeting tremor of disbelief, one can levy against such plans the same charges that embarrass regionalism.

True world government would be not only universal but also total. Given the inordinate resources of the world, the unparalleled disparities in wealth and education, the enormous expanse of territory and swarms of peoples to be governed, it would be fatuous to conceive of anything but a gigantic, sprawling bureaucracy. The most severe military dictator would require a multitude of armies—and their appropriate economic supports—while the social-service world state, if the twentieth-century nation is any clue, would enlist and enmesh every occupation and pursuit of the planet. Because of the totalitarian nature of world government, nothing could be more threatening to the liberties men have consciously won within their nation-states than premature unification of the globe under single political domination, that is, before a long habit of mutual respect and tolerance has been established. The omnicompetence of military control and the ubiquity of government regulation, unless firmly based upon public responsibility, could more easily lead to a world oppression than the rivalries of a few great powers whose ambitions check one another.

Presuming, however, that all conditions are ripe for the plucking of the rare fruit of world government, a successful political integration could never rest upon its past achievement, but must, like any other government, continue to find ways and means of easing the natural tensions which develop in dynamic societies. The lure of power, prestige, and wealth and the attractions of respect, leisure, and security will continue to bedevil men, generating heat from passions and requiring political solutions. A universal organization no less than a town meeting has the ceaseless challenge of *re*-integrating its citizenry. Merely because it is bigger, it cannot guarantee peace. It does suggest more pervasive solutions of certain difficulties, but the solutions themselves depend upon the governing ideals of the society; the inability on the part of world government to harmonize tugging wills within the universal corporation may lead to violent planetary explosions of civil war at least as devastating as the contemporary cataclysmic world wars.

Sometimes world government is regarded as an advanced mold of society, a form which is destined to evolve out of the raucous contradictions of modern industrial patterns thereby bringing to mankind the ultimate achievement of the good society through the beneficence of divine ingenuity. Such a new view of society, as progressing toward real wealth and greatness in a miracle of ingenious inventions designed to cope with every human challenge, stoutly bears the imprint of Western rationalism and eighteenth-century optimism. Bolstered by scientific theories of evolution, with their charm of greater competence, greater adaptability, and greater adequacy for the trials of life, the discovery of remarkable physical coincidences or laws imperceptibly got hitched to the predictability and confident expectation of improved psychic and moral standards. Thus, it seemed reasonable for mankind to look forward inevitably not merely to an epoch of universal government but also to the coming of a better world for all.

Certainly the experience of Europe in the nineteenth century was blissfully married to the idea of progress, for the economic revolution of the century nourished amazing increases of population, disruption and realignment of the social structure on a more popular foundation, and proliferation of intergovernmental agencies to meet the accelerating world business as invention begat invention. In the Western world, at least, there was a genuine release from physical suffering and slavery, as well as a breathtaking pause in wholesale warfare. The consolidation of the nation-state, moreover, at such close hand appeared to be a vindication of larger forms of political organization and the democratic process, but serious qualifications of progress toward world government have had to be introduced in the twentieth century, largely because many of the splendid comparisons of that unique creature man and that unique creation human society with other phenomena of organized life on this globe were inadequate and remain inadequate to this day.

Society is in some degree formed as a result of a selection of alternatives by individual human beings, and to this extent analogies with mechanisms or organisms are partly defective. Aside from the broader consideration that the spread of democracy and humanitarianism and prosperity was less universal and less pervasive than supposed at the opening of the twentieth century, the mere aggrandizement or extension of the political unit has no intrinsic value except as it serves the individual, who remains the common denominator of all the many patterns social organization has taken in the past and may take in the future. To put the idea of progress toward world government on any other plane save the increasing satisfaction of both the economic and spiritual wants of the individual runs into the specious comparison of human society with precision machines or biological specimens. Sheer growth or complexity in government may indicate either tyranny or freedom—as the large bureaucratized nation-state is by no means necessarily happier or more prosperous than the small—but the intelligent organization of society for agreed-upon satisfactions of the individual can make many useful techniques available. World government is but a technique of doing something on a large scale, not a guarantee of a better life for all.

In the face of overwhelming odds, a world government would have the primary task of braking any violent shifts of wealth from area to area, while aiming at a general improvement of economic life throughout the polity, for the world passes through one economic ordeal after another as the scant wealth of society trickles into various unexpected channels. Indeed, the wonders of inventive genius and mass production during the past two hundred years have been carried to the far corners of the earth, and the simple realization of millions of people that an escape from drudgery is possible and that a more comfortable way of life is actually within the grasp of all human beings who stretch out for it, shakes the roots of ancient cultures and scatters the dust into a whirlwind of ambition. Simultaneously, a Europe which once raced ahead in its technical improvements and thereby throttled the world, a Europe which purged the earth of its cheap resources and transformed them into gold and steel power, now lies sick and dislocated, but determined to resist the disease of ill-fortune.

Thus far international economic cooperation has given inadequate adjustments to the vibration of the world economy and insufficient rewards to the teeming masses of the world. Unified political planning and management has been lacking. Altruism in the nation-state cannot be depended upon in the long run to rectify the disparities of wealth and the fluctuating resources of a world economy. But the very disproportions of wealth between the nation-states which most seriously need adjustment indicate paradoxically that the paramount share in the control of any contemporary organization would be parceled out to a few great and rich states. At a moment in history in which the number of equally strong powers has declined to so few as at present, an oligarchical form of world government would be a real though undesirable possibility. On the other hand, the presumption that any one state could impose a single economically beneficial order upon the rest of the world is open to serious question. Not only does such an idea anticipate a lofty benevolence within the successful imperial state to share its good fortune with its subdued dependents, but it fails to realize that any wholesale devastation and employment of force over industrialized economies would result in a net loss in modern wealth—the basis of which is voluntary, organized production.

When it is suggested that instead of a radical political change economic unions may be the prelude to more pacific political integration and consequently genuine economic progress, then caution is also necessary, for economic unions are themselves political devices, and it is important that the partners of a union be as nearly equal as possible lest economic dependence lead into political slavery. The present array of abysmally poor and weak states laboring in the shadows of a few powerful empires hardly leads to a reasonable expectation of a sound economic partnership, but rather an oligarchy in any widespread unification movement with perhaps the hope of gradually enriching the majority. To realize this hope, however, would require public control of world monopoly in much the same fashion as the public got the upper hand on free enterprise within the democratic state. But the present array of power does not preclude either regional or universal unification by force and the subsequent retrogression of the individual's welfare.

In addition to increasing the satisfaction of man's economic needs, world government would have to answer to the sentimental spiritual character of human beings in order to be deemed a progressive form of universal organization. The modern nation-state is the object of the deep-rooted, nonrational attachment of its citizens, an attachment which is stubborn and enduring. To expect that the citizens' allegiance will be transferred to a more comprehensive polity is to anticipate the stir of emotions and a heartfelt appreciation of world government beyond the logical persuasions of economic efficiency. Unless a world patriotism comparable to the irrational devotion to the nation-state could be awakened in the peoples of the world, an essential element of cohesiveness would be absent and instead the nations of the universe might be chained together like snapping dogs.

Sentiment, however, can be both slave to and master of the establishment of world government in the same fashion as the nation-state has aroused mass emotion sometimes for individual liberty, sometimes for ruthless imperialistic crusades. Intolerant world patriotism would be no more desirable than intolerant nationalism. Achieving unity at the price of all experimentation and cultural diversity would produce an unspeakably dull world, and the dreamy march of stereotypes would promise little satisfaction for the capricious imagination of men. The sentiment which should bind men together, curiously enough, ought to be the toleration of diversity if world unity in this respect is to be considered an advance from the particular emotional satisfactions of the nation-state.

The toleration of cultural diversity may come about in two ways: either through the grant of an imperial power or through a juxtaposition of forces which work toward a reciprocal recognition of rights, duties, and privileges. The first course relies upon the will of the imperial government and has the drawback of not being translated into political responsibility, for separate languages, churches, arts, and literatures are permitted only as long as is convenient, not as an intrinsic duty or right, and certainly not as the rationale of the government. The second course depends upon a configuration of power within an organization which provides checks and counterchecks to each of the various political units adhering to it, for the possibility of resistance of all to any one element of power may lead to respite from aggression and a recognition of the mutual privileges which ought to be respected and defended by all.

The monopolization of international power in the twentieth century does not indicate a fortuitous arrangement of countervailing forces able to check each other collectively, but even should such an equilibrium be attained temporarily, it needs to be accompanied, within the units of power themselves, by an ethical climate which nurtures tolerance. This is another prerequisite for the establishment of a "progressive" world government, again progressive in the sense of further liberating and developing the individual's nonrational, imaginative, and aesthetic sensibilities. If statesmen can bear only rancor and blind rivalry from the bosom of their states to world councils, then the angry cries for the dictator will mount to an unbearable crescendo and imperium may be the ultimate, hollow answer. The big government would not in that case be the better government for the individual's soul.

At least one hopeful sign is on the horizon: the monopolization of power in the recent history of the world has also brought a clearer realization of the necessity for fostering nonmaterial needs of a community within a military-economic power context. Thus, new empires have a conception of positively promoting the folkways and unique personalities of peoples within a larger utilitarian unity, and such a tentative grasp upon the nature of the good society is a tiny insight to the total problem. Clearly, however, the blocs of political power throughout the world do not promise at the moment a universal stability which offers collective restraint upon all, nor is there a genuine propagation within each state of the universal tolerance essential to a world government which aims to give the widest development to the creativity of all individuals. The total plan will never be formulated in one flash of genius, but each individual can take a responsibility for the dissemination of tolerance within his own circle, and this practice is essential to progress through world government.

In his own way each man seeks justice, a conception of right interwoven with experience and intuition. Since good government ought to embody justice for its community, an approach to this problem in world government, with its claim to universality, is vital. Now, unless certain ideas of what is right can be translated into the effective law of a world society and thereby guide or temper the hard striation of ingrained custom, the radiant hope of working toward planetary justice will be quickly eclipsed. But before such a translation can take place, there must be, first, some parallel or coincidental ideas on what is right for men in general in this world, and, secondly, there needs to be the political balance of force which may permit the circulation and adoption of such thought by means of universally effective laws.

In one by-gone epoch the church tried to postulate the nature of justice and teach a universal code of conduct in harmony with its definition; however, the dogma not only was contradicted by the practice of the institutionalized church but also was jarred loose from its moral position by the dynamic convictions of the new "science." In another epoch, then, with empiricism as a guide to truth, the modern world has sometimes caricatured the face of justice by drawing it upon the pebbled pages of history; that is, by using history as the laboratory of truth and justice. But this approach disregards the moral evaluation which must be applied to any selection of past events for future reference, for history without human interpretation is absolutely meaningless. Does not the interpretative ability of man originate with that unique faculty of choosing alternative values and does not the whole idea of right rest upon some ability to select one course of action rather than another?

The perpetuation and extension of free choice in every sphere of human activity should top the hierarchy of human needs for a more just world insofar as the primary condition for describing right as against wrong is the presence of alternatives and the opportunity of the individual to make a selection whose consequences will be known. And where the law of the community tends to widen the conditions for free choice, the law tends to an approximation of justice. An unbounded free choice for everyone might be ideal justice, but its terms are patently impossible; thus, men introduce the concept of compromise, of achieving a conciliation of wills, of giving free expression and some choice to all participants whose desires clash, but who would not subvert the principle of compromise itself, for this is the bedrock upon which the possibility of choice and the possibility of approximate justice stands.

The compromise of contention is a slow process—and the temper of the rival parties must be mollified at times by the lurking threat of armed retaliation as well as good nature and intelligence. Without a roughly balanced disposition of power, the opportunities for working out a compromise are considerably circumscribed. To secure justice in the crude world community men have not turned to world tribunals, but to the executive powers, the states, who can at least offer some security against anarchy, some alignment of force capable of restraining an overbearing enemy. Men have turned to these executives until such time as negotiation between peoples is conducted by compromise and concession as well as with supreme loyalty to the principle of endless arbitration. Thereafter, international tribunals would find their services called for and used.

Thus, it is on the level of international negotiation that "justice" for world government may be engendered, for if the mechanism of peaceful change, so essential to the dynamic pace of world society, can be equated with continuous compromise among nations, then, in due time, a lasting principle may catch hold upon the hearts of men. Justice, therefore, becomes identified with a formula to moderate the conflicts of life and, while not promising any absolute solution, it always offers the possibility of reassessing and rejudging the old decisions.

But the most sanguine observer could scarcely claim that he perceives either a wholesome mood of compromise on the contemporary international horizon or a flexible alignment of power units to deter anyone from resorting to force. It is not that the Christian community of the past broke down, but that it singularly failed to transfuse its tenets into the practical business of living under government on this earth. The shift of the center of power, moreover, from the king to the sovereign people within the nation-state scarcely improved the selfish temper of international life, but rather intensified it. Economic interdependence and pristine Marxism have made their pleas for a world community against the running tide of nationalism, but somehow state governments have managed to channel these concepts into a rigid, narrow interpretation of justice. If free choice and compromise ought to be encouraged as both universally just and the mechanisms for universal justice, the fixed mold of the nation-state will first have to be filled with this conviction. If such "justice" be nationally asserted and defended, there may be some hope that its principles will coincide with similar convictions abroad. Then, given some restraint upon the impetuous use of force, a universal acknowledgment of right procedures for government might be the foundation for a world government of justice in the terms defined.

The legally minded, in their reflections upon the problem of world government, have had an intricate pattern of international relations to observe, criticize, and build upon, namely, international law. To a large extent the development of international organizations to maintain peace has been stimulated by those who sought better legal definitions for the controversies between nation-states and the immediate canalization of difficulties or disputes to judicial procedures. Once upon a time it was felt that the increasing number of adjudications between states were actually leading the way to a world community, but today it is perhaps better to say that a world community must lead the way to more adjudications.

Traditional international law was a network of custom and court decisions and conventions which touched especially upon the multiplying political-economic contacts of the Western nation-states after the Renaissance. Underlying the framework of the law of nations were commonly acknowledged precepts of Christianity and a highly developed Roman jurisprudence, so that in fact European international law was the outgrowth of a unique religious-cultural inheritance. The Industrial

Revolution and the burst of prosperous humanitarianism which accompanied the nineteenth century contributed further to the proliferation of international pacts which were subsumed under the grand euphemism "law."

As Europe spread its magnificent power abroad to societies untutored in Western notions of sovereignty, property rights, legal procedure, or social good, it impressed upon peoples outside the orbit of Roman-Christian civilization the matrix of its international law. But since the forms were not indigenous to the character of the alien societies and, moreover, merely clothed the economic exploitation of African and Asian peoples in legal symbolism, many of the high hopes for an earth-spanning rule of law requisite to world government were bound to be dashed onto the rocks of miscalculation. Furthermore, the European citadel of traditional international law rested upon rotting foundations, for the scruples of Christianity, never very effective in world politics, were themselves challenged and vigorously repudiated by totalitarian cults; meanwhile, the brief honeymoon of international economic interdependence and free commerce, another aspect of Western international law, quickly came to an end as the inequities generated by the nineteenth-century system galvanized governments into defensive action and political retaliation which made international harmony increasingly more difficult.

While the participation of states today in world agencies of a very limited economic or social character ought not to be taken as *prima facie* evidence of a growing competency of international law, and while it seems clear that much of the traditional intercourse between states would be more properly labeled "etiquette" rather than "law," nevertheless, such expedients of ceremony and ritual and reciprocal courtesies as the states of the world do observe at least attempt to bridge the dangerous incompatibilities of national societies. If the "laws" now seem inadequate for the trials of world politics, it is because they were adjusted to another century and another community; no new homogeneous community has risen to reformulate their provisions. World law, which must accompany world government, by definition would be both comprehensive and pervasive; such law cannot be anything but the product of the common aspirations, fears, and needs of a world community, so that the paramount problem is to create a feeling of togetherness extending throughout the major portions of the earth.

Yet the problem is not simply to extend *any* social cohesiveness, but rather the kind of cooperative action and feeling of the togetherness which would endow world government with attributes of progress for the individual in his economic and spiritual character. The efforts of the nation-states during the past century to spread information and international understanding, presumably leading towards a greater unity, have been highly colored by national rivalries. Thus, propaganda has become a separate interest of separate states lacking collaboration, a powerful instrument of national politics in both domestic and foreign affairs. The United Nations, on the other hand, proclaimed an international organization which would endeavor to break down ignorance and mistrust, while formulating such education as would lead to justice and liberty for mankind. But the project has made negligible headway at a snail's pace, partly because several states are not reconciled to its purposes, partly because it has failed to enlist the imagination of the world because of its emphasis upon a neutral function of exchanging informational and educational apparatus.

To bring on the kind of world culture good for the kind of world government which would further emancipate the spiritual expression of man, while offering him the possibility of greater economic opportunity, requires a more positive program than a mere interchange of national educational achievements. Separate cultures have found their coherence on a number of traits such as kinship ties or occupational distinction, but the actual diffusion of a single culture involving deep-rooted values of life would depend upon a singular combination of force and dynamic faith. With moral and physical confusion at its circumference, a strong, impassioned nuclear society could under modern conditions spread its way of life, spiritual and economic, throughout a large portion of the world, and though no one could delineate the ultimate universal culture—since the superstructure would be somewhat modified as it encountered other traditions—there remains the long-term possibility of establishing roughly equivalent social values everywhere.

In this connection the threat of a dead world still hovers over the head of any single culture mobilized for mass propagation; but this dilemma may be escaped by advocating the stamp of democracy at every turn of the engine driving for single-mindedness. A unifying culture not based upon the idea that men have a right to opinions and a right to make judgments in important areas of their communal life will most certainly create a sterile society; however, the insistence upon toleration, minority criticism, and compromise ought not emasculate a democratic culture, ought not entangle it in a pitiful weighing of opinion against opinion until all recognition of the revolutionary faith in the character of man is lost and the procedures of the democratic system prostituted to anti-democratic purposes.

To associate Western culture with sheer scientific method and, implicitly, material values is fabulously untrue, for where the political organization has given some explicit recognition to the tenets of equalitarianism and fraternity emanating from the Mediterranean basin and transfused by Christianity to Europe, there is a profound moral insight and faith of which no one should be ashamed. To clarify and articulate this belief, however, requires institutions appropriate to their environment; they have not always been forthcoming; they will not be the same institutions in Europe, Africa, Asia, and America. But if a democratic culture is to survive and flourish and offer itself as a rationale for world society and world government, then the belief in democracy must be dynamic, and institutions to spell out its hopes will have to be improvised.

To reinvigorate democracy where it now flags under the challenge of internal contradictions of an economic, social, or political nature is a major undertaking in itself, and highly essential to promoting the world cause. Beyond this, however, the democratically minded states must seek to apply their faith to the aspirations of people everywhere, probing the problem not from the viewpoint of rich merchants and farmers of the nineteenth century, but recognizing economic prosperity as the indispensable overture to democratic practice. Unless radical methods for alleviating widespread physical misery can be found and wholeheartedly applied, the exponents of democracy will win few converts—either nationally or internationally.

Economic planning for the world, however, should be locked to a fervent educational campaign to inspire knowledge of and respect for the democratic way of life in its social and political virtues if a democratic culture is to be diffused. Here missionaries are required; here men of vision and persuasion, deeply devoted to a brotherhood of mankind, affirming the broad principles of individual integrity and rationality, must go forth and teach all nations with concerted efforts and systematic organization. This is a game for Titans unmistakably, but the stakes are cosmic. The appeal must be to the mind and heart as well as to the body.

Finally, there can be no naïve assumption that the heavens will be moved and the kingdom of darkness rolled away without the use of force. Every democracy has had to be forged out of the molten steel of war, revolution, or rebellion; and each new generation must be prepared to fight for what its fathers have so perilously won or else admit that the ideals are worthless. Clearly the coming of constitutional world government would demand as much. Economic planning and the propagation of a culture can be important parts of a universal political process, but hardly a match for the immediate armies of those states opposed to world organization on any terms but their own. Without a determination to add combat soldiers to the economic attacks upon poverty and the intellectual attacks upon intolerant provincialism, any primary organization looking toward one democratic world will fail. Alliances bring states together against transient military threats—and this historical occurrence has not been without value to international cooperation. But unless a principle of unity deeper than incipient attack holds peoples together, a principle of jointly maintaining and fostering common values of life and standards of action, then alliances disintegrate. The test for a nuclear organization looking toward constitutional world government would be the individual conviction of all members that democracy ought to be encouraged everywhere by joint action and the willingness to supply resources, intelligence, and armed forces toward this end. In the world today there is no such organization, yet each man can contribute to the brilliant possibility of such a time-shattering event by first working for such principles in the domestic and foreign policies of his own state; and if tyrannous world government or anarchy should descend upon the universe in some distant black ages to come, the screeching wails of the dying shall not damn his humble efforts.

Bibliography

LITERATURE REFERRED TO SPECIFICALLY IN FOOTNOTES

Acton, Lord, The History of Freedom and Other Essays. London, Macmillan & Co., 1922.

Allen, Carleton Kemp, Law in the Making. London, Oxford University Press, 1939.

American Bar Association Committee, Postwar International Judicial Organization, March 29, 1943.

Angell, Norman, The Great Illusion. New York, G. P. Putnam's Sons, 1911.

—— The Unseen Assassin. London, Hamish and Hamilton, 1932.

—— The Steep Places. New York, Harper and Bros., 1947.

Aristotle, Basic Works, New York, Random House, 1941.

Ault, W. D., Europe in the Middle Ages. Boston, D. C. Heath, 1932.

Bagehot, Walter, Physics and Politics, reprinted in Mrs. Russell Barrington, ed., The Works and Life of Walter Bagehot, London, Longmans, Green and Co., 1915.

Bakounine, Michel, Œuvres. Paris, P. V. Stock, 1912.

Baldwin, Marshall W., The Mediaeval Papacy in Action. New York, The Macmillan Co., 1940.

Beals, Carleton and others, What the South Americans Think of Us. New York, R. M. McBride, 1945.

Becker, Carl L., How New Will the Better World Be? New York, Alfred A. Knopf, 1944.

Bemont, C., and G. Monod, Mediaeval Europe, from 395 A.D. to 1270 A.D.; tr. by Mary Swan. New York, Henry Holt and Co., 1902.

Bentwich, Norman, and others, Justice and Equity in the International Sphere. London, Constable and Co., 1936.

Beveridge, Sir William, The Price of Peace. London, Pilot Press, 1945.

Birkett, Justice, "International Legal Theories Evolved at Nuremberg," *International Affairs* (London), July 1947, pp. 317-325.

Blood-Ryan, H. W., The Political Testament of Hermann Göring. London, John Long, 1939.

Bonnet, Henri, ed., The World's Destiny and the United States. Chicago, World Citizens Association, 1941.

Born, Lester K., The Political Theories of Erasmus. New York, Columbia University Press, 1936.

Bowden, W., M. Karpovich, and A. P. Usher, Economic History of Europe since 1750. New York, American Book Co., 1937.

Brewer, W. C., Permanent Peace. Philadelphia, Dorrance and Co., 1940.

Brierly, J. L., "International Law: Some Conditions of Its Progress," *International Affairs* (London), XXII (July, 1946), 352-360.

Brinton, Crane, From Many One. Cambridge, Harvard University Press, 1948.

Bryce, James, Modern Democracies. New York, The Macmillan Co., 1921.

Bryn-Jones, David, Toward a New Democratic Order. Minneapolis, University of Minnesota Press, 1945.

Bryson, Lyman, and others, eds., Approaches to National Unity. New York, Harper and Bros., 1945.

Bukharin, Nicholas, A Program of Communists. Communist Labor Party, 1918.

Burnham, James, The Struggle for the World. New York, John Day Co., 1947.

Burns, Emile, Handbook of Marxism. New York, Random House, 1935.

Burton, John Hill, Benthamania. Philadelphia, Lea and Blanchard, 1844.

Burtt, E. A., The English Philosophers. New York, Random House, 1939.

Bury, J. B., The Idea of Progress. London, The Macmillan Co., 1924.

Carr, Edward H., The Twenty Years Crisis, 1919-1939. London, The Macmillan Co., 1939.

—— Conditions of Peace. London, The Macmillan Co., 1942.

—— Nationalism and After. New York, The Macmillan Co., 1945.

—— The Soviet Impact on the Western World. New York, The Macmillan Co., 1948.

Case, C. M., Social Process and Human Progress. New York, Harcourt, Brace and Co., 1931.

Chafee, Zechariah, Government and Mass Communication. Chicago, University of Chicago Press, 1947.

Channing-Pearce, M., Federal Union. London, Jonathan Cape, 1940.

Cobban, Alfred, National Self-Determination. Chicago, University of Chicago Press, 1947.

Cole G. D. H., Social Theory. New York, Frederick A. Stokes, 1920.

Commager, Henry Steele, ed., Documents of American History. New York, F. S. Crofts, 1945.

Commins, S., and R. N. Linscott, The Philosophers of Science. New York, Random House, 1947.

Comte, August, The Positive Philosophy; tr. by Harriet Martineau. London, Trubner and Co., 1875.

Condenhove-Kalergi, R. N., Crusade for Pan-Europe. New York, G. P. Putnam's Sons, 1943.

Condillac, E. B. de, Treatise on the Sensations, tr. by G. Carr. London, The Favil Press, 1930.

Condorcet, Jean de, Outlines of an Historical View of the Progress of the Human Mind. New York, Columbia University Press, 1941.

Corbett, Percy E., Post-War Worlds. New York, Farrar & Rinehart, 1942.

Cornell, Julien, New World Primer. New York, New Directions Books, 1947.

Crankshaw, Edward, Russia and the Russians. New York, The Viking Press, 1948.

Creasy, Sir Edward, Turkey. Philadelphia, John D. Morris, 1906.

Croce, Benedetto, History of Italy, 1870–1914; tr. by Cecilia M. Ady. London, Oxford University Press, 1929.

Crutwell, C. R. M. F., A History of Peaceful Change in the Modern World. London, Oxford University Press, 1937.

Culbertson, Ely, Total Peace. New York, Doubleday Doran, 1943.

Curtis, Lionel, Commonwealth of God. London, The Macmillan Co., 1938.

—— Faith and Works. London, Oxford University Press, 1943.

—— War or Peace. London, Oxford University Press, 1946.

Dallin, David, The Big Three. New Haven, Yale University Press, 1945.

Dante, Alighieri, Latin Works. London, J. M. Dent, 1904.

Darwin, Charles, The Origin of the Species. London, John Murray, 1873.

Dawson, William H., The German Empire and Unity Movement. New York, The Macmillan Co., 1919.

Day, Clive, A History of Commerce. London, Longmans, Green and Co., 1919.

Dean, Vera Micheles, "Economic Trends in Eastern Europe," *Foreign Policy Reports* (New York), XXIV (April 1 and April 15, 1948), 14–27, 30–39.

De Huszar, G. B., ed., New Perspectives on Peace. Chicago, University of Chicago Press, 1944.

—— Persistent International Issues. New York, Harper & Brothers, 1947.

Delaisi, Francis, Political Myths and Economic Realities. New York, The Viking Press, 1927.

De Maeztu, Ramiro, Authority, Liberty and Function in the Light of War. New York, The Macmillan Co., 1916.

De Maistre, Joseph, Essay on the Generative Principles of Political Constitutions. Boston, Little, Brown & Co., 1847.

Deroque, Gilbert, Le Projet de paix perpetuelle de l'Abbé de Saint-Pierre. Paris, Rousseau et Cie, 1929.

Dewey, John, Freedom and Culture. New York, G. P. Putnam's Sons, 1939.

Doman, Nicholas, The Coming Age of World Control. New York, Harper and Bros., 1942.

Dulles, John Foster, War, Peace and Change. New York, Harper and Bros., 1939.

Earle, Edward Mead, The Federalist. New York, Random House, 1937.

Ebenstein, W., The Nazi State. New York, Farrar & Rinehart, 1943.

Einstein, Albert, "Atomic War or Peace," *The Atlantic Monthly* (Boston), CLXXX (November, 1947), 29–32.

Eliot, Charles W., The Road toward Peace. Boston, Houghton Mifflin Co., 1915.

Elliot, William Yandell, The Need for Constitutional Reform. New York, McGraw-Hill Book Co., 1935.

Emerson, Rupert, State and Sovereignty in Modern Germany. New Haven, Yale University Press, 1928.

Fay, Sidney, Origins of the First World War. New York, The Macmillan Co., 1928.

Finch, G. A., The Sources of Modern International Law. Washington, Carnegie Endowment for International Peace, 1937.

Finer, Herman, The United Nations Economic and Social Council. Boston, World Peace Foundation, 1946.

Firsoff, V., The Unity of Europe. London, Lindsay Drummond, 1947.

Focques-Duparc, Jacques, "British and European Views of the United Nations," *International Conciliation*, New York, September, 1948.

Friedmann, W., "The Growth of State Control over the Individual, and Its Effect upon the Rules of International State Responsibility," in British Yearbook of International Law, 1938.

Friedrich, Carl J., Inevitable Peace. Cambridge, Harvard University Press, 1948.

Fromm, Erich, Escape from Freedom. New York, Farrar & Rinehart, 1941.

Geneva Institute of International Relations, Problems of Peace. Fifth Series. London, Oxford University Press, 1931.

—— Problems of Peace, Tenth Series. London, Oxford University Press, 1936.

Gentilis, Alberico, De iure belli, tr. by J. C. Rolfe, ed. by James B. Scott. London, Oxford University Press, 1933.

Ginsberg, Morris, Reason and Unreason in Society. Cambridge, Harvard University Press, 1948.

Gonner, E. C. K., Germany in the Nineteenth Century. Manchester, University of Manchester Press, 1912.

Goodrich, Leland M., and Marie J. Carroll, Documents on American Foreign Relations. Boston, World Peace Foundation, 1945.

Gott, Virginia L., "The National Socialist Theory of International Law," *The American Journal of International Law*, XXXII (October, 1938), 704–718.

Grandin, Thomas, The Political Use of the Radio. Geneva Research Center, 1939.

Grant, Madison, The Passing of the Great Race. New York, Charles Scribner's Sons, 1916.

Green, M. S., The Making of the Union of South Africa. London, Longmans, Green and Co., 1946.

Green, T. H., Works. New York, Longmans, Green and Co., 1891.

Grotius, Hugo, De jure belli ac pacis, tr. by F. W. Kelsey and others; ed. by J. B. Scott, Classics of International Law Series. London, Oxford University Press, 1925.

Guins, George, "Soviet Culture—Old Trends and New," *The Russian Review*, August, 1947.

Haily, Lord, Future of Colonial Peoples. Princeton, Princeton University Press, 1944.

Hall, W. E., A Treatise of International Law. London, Oxford University Press, 1895.

Hassall, Arthur, The Balance of Power, London, Rivington's, 1941.

Hayes, Carlton J. H., Essays on Notionalism. New York, The Macmillan Co., 1926.

—— The Historical Evolution of Modern Nationalism. New York, Richard E. Smith, 1931.

Hazen, C. D., Europe since 1815. New York, Henry Holt, 1929.

Hegel, Georg, The Philosophy of History. New York, Willey Book Co., 1944.

Heimann, Eduard, Freedom and Order. New York, Charles Scribner's Sons, 1947.

Hemleben, Sylvester John, Plans for World Peace through Six Centuries. Chicago, University of Chicago Press, 1943.

Hentze, Margot, Pre-Fascist Italy. London, George Allen and Unwin, 1939.

Hertslet, Edward, Map of Europe by Treaty. 4 vols., London, Butterworth, 1875.

Hertz, Frederick, Nationality and Politics. New York, Oxford University Press, 1944.

Hicks, John D., A Short History of the American Democracy. Boston, Houghton Mifflin Co., 1943.

Hobhouse, Leonard, Social Evolution and Political Theory. New York, Columbia University Press, 1922.

Hobson, J. A., Imperialism; A Study. London, Archibald Constable, 1905.

Holmes, Olive, "Latin-America and the United States," *Foreign Policy Reports* (New York), January 15, 1948, Vol. XXIII, No. 21, p. 262–71.

Hosack, John, Rise and Growth of the Law of Nations. London, John Murray, 1882.

Hudson, Manley O., International Legislation. Washington, D.C., Carnegie Endowment for International Peace, 1941.

—— International Tribunals. Washington, D.C., Carnegie Endowment for International Peace and the Brookings Institute, 1944.

—— "The 26th Year of the World Court," *The American Journal of International Law*, January, 1948, pp. 1–19.

Hutcheson, H. H., "The European Recovery Program," *Foreign Policy Reports* (New York), December 15, 1947.

Hutchins, Robert, "Preliminary Draft of a World Constitution," in *Common Sense*, Vol. I (No. 9, March 1948).

James, William, A Pluralistic Universe. New York, Longmans, Green and Co., 1925.

Jenks, Edward, Law and Politics in the Middle Ages. New York, Henry Holt, 1898.

Jennings, W. Ivor, Federation for Western Europe. London, Cambridge University Press, 1940.

Jessup, Philip, A Modern Law of Nation. New York, The Macmillan Co., 1948.

Johnson, A. H., Europe in the Sixteenth Century. London, Rivington's, 1941.

Johnson, F. Ernst, ed., Religion and the World Order. New York, Harper and Bros., 1944.

Keeton, G. W., The Development of Extraterritoriality in China. London, Longmans, Green and Co., 1928.

Keynes, John Maynard, Economic Consequences of the Peace. New York, Harcourt, Brace, and Howe, 1920.

Kohn, Hans, Nationalism in the Soviet Union. London, G. Routledge and Sons, 1933.

—— Force or Reason. Cambridge, Harvard University Press, 1937.

—— The Idea of Nationalism. New York, The Macmillan Co., 1944.

—— World Order in Historical Perspective. Cambridge, Harvard University Press, 1941.

Koo, Wellington, Jr., Voting Procedures in International Political Organizations. New York, Columbia University Press, 1941.

Korovin, Eugene A., "The Second World War and International Law," *The American Journal of International Law*, XL (October, 1946), 742–755.

Krabbe, Hugo, The Modern Idea of the State. New York, D. Appleton, 1927.

Kuhn, Arthur K., "The Extension of Sovereign Immunity to Government Owned Commercial Corporations," *The American Journal of International Law*, Vol. XXXIX (October, 1945).

Ladd, William, Prize Essay on a Congress of Nations. Boston, Whipple and Damrell, 1840.

Larson, Laurence M., The Earliest Norwegian Laws. New York, Columbia University Press, 1935.

Laski, Harold J., The Dangers of Obedience. New York, Harper & Brothers, 1930.

—— State in Theory and Practice. New York, The Viking Press, 1935.

—— "Crisis of Our Civilization," *Foreign Affairs*, October, 1947.

Latourette, K. S., The Chinese; Their History and Culture. New York, The Macmillan Co., 1946.

Lauterpacht, H., The Function of Law in the International Community. Oxford, Clarendon Press, 1933.

Laves, W. H. C., The Foundations of a More Stable World Order. Chicago, University of Chicago Press, 1941.

Lawrence, T. J., The Principles of International Law. 4th ed., Boston, D. C. Heath & Co., 1910.

League of Nations, Legal Section of the Secretariat, Arbitration and Security (pursuant to the Council's Resolution of December 12, 1925).

—— Records of the First Assembly. Geneva, 1920.

Leonard, Paul, "Atomic Union Now," *The Christian Science Monitor* (Boston), March 27, 1948.

Levy-Bruhl, Lucian, Primitive Mentality; tr. by Lilian A. Clare. New York, The Macmillan Co., 1923.

Lippmann, Walter, U.S. Foreign Policy. Boston, Little, Brown & Co., 1943.

—— U.S. War Aims. Boston, Little, Brown & Co., 1944.

—— Public Opinion. New York, Penguin Books, 1946.

Lucas, Henry S., Renaissance and Reformation. New York, Harper & Brothers, 1934.

Luke, Sir Henry, Making of Modern Turkey. London, The Macmillan Co., 1936.

—— The Web of Government. New York, The Macmillan Co., 1947.

McCartney, C. A., National States and National Minorities. London, Oxford University Press, 1934.

McGuire, Paul, Experiment in World Order. New York, William Morrow, 1948.

MacIver, Robert M., Towards an Abiding Peace. New York, The Macmillan Co., 1943.

McKay, Vernon, "Nationalism in British West Africa," *Foreign Policy Reports*, XXIV, (March 15, 1948), 2–11.

McMurray, Ruth Emily, and Muna Lee, The Cultural Approach—Another Way in International Relations. Chapel Hill, University of North Carolina Press, 1947.

Magid, Henry M., "Freedom and Political Unity," *Ethics*, (Chicago), January, 1941.

Maine, Sir Henry Sumner, International Law with introduction and notes by Sir Frederick Pollock. New York, Henry Holt and Co., 1888.

—— Ancient Law. 10th ed., London, John Murray, 1930.

Malinowski, Bronislaw, A Scientific Theory of Culture. Chapel Hill, University of North Carolina Press, 1944.

Mantoux, Paul, The World Crisis. London, Longmans, Green, 1938.

Marvin, F. S., Unity of Western Civilization. London, Oxford University Press, 1915.

Mazzini, Joseph, Essays; tr. by T. Okey, London, J. M. Dent, 1894.

Meyer, Cord, Jr., Peace or Anarchy? Boston, Little, Brown & Co., 1947.

Mill, James, Law of Nations. New York, Doubleday Doran and Co., 1935.

Mill, John Stuart, On Representative Government. London, J. M. Dent, 1920.

Mitrany, David, The Progress of International Government. New Haven, Yale University Press, 1933.

—— A Working Peace System. London, Royal Institute of International Affairs, 1943.

—— "The Functional Approach to World Government," *International Affairs*, (London), XXIV, (July, 1948), 350–360.

Morgenthau, Hans, Peace, Security, and the U.N. Chicago, University of Chicago Press, 1946.

Mousley, Edward, The Democratic Advance. London, Andrew Dakers, 1942.

Murphy, Arthur E., and M. R. Konvitz, Essays in Political Theory. Ithaca, Cornell University Press, 1948.

Murphy, Gardner, ed., Human Nature and Enduring Peace. Boston, Houghton Mifflin Co., 1945.

Newfang, Oscar, World Federation. New York, Barnes and Noble, 1939.

—— World Government. New York, Barnes and Noble, 1942.

Newton, Arthur P., Federal and Unified Constitutions. New York, Longmans, Green and Co., 1923.

Nicolson, Harold, Diplomacy. New York, Harcourt, Brace and
    Co., 1939.
Niebuhr, Reinhold, The Nature and Destiny of Man. New York,
    Charles Scribner's Sons, 1943.
Northrup, F. S. C., The Meeting of East and West. New York,
    The Macmillan Co., 1946.
Nussbaum, Arthur, A Concise History of the Law of Nations. New
    York, The Macmillan Co., 1947.
Oakes, Sir Augustus, and R. B. Mowat, The Great European
    Treaties of the Nineteenth Century. London, Oxford Univer-
    sity Press, 1918.
Ogg, David, Europe in the Seventeenth Century. London, Adams
    and Charles Black, 1946.
Oppenheim, Lassa, International Law. 2d ed., London, Longmans,
    Green and Co., 1912.
——— International Law. 3d ed., London, Longmans, Green and
    Co., 1920.
——— International Law. 5th ed., London, Longmans, Green and
    Co., 1935.
——— The Future of International Law. Oxford, Clarendon Press,
    1921.
Ortega y Gasset, José, Revolt of the Masses. New York, W. W.
    Norton, 1932.
——— Toward a Philosophy of History. New York, W. W. Norton,
    1941.
Owen, Robert, A New View of Society. New York, E. P. Dutton,
    1927.
Paine, Thomas, The Rights of Man. London, Watts and Co., 1937.
Pares, Bernard, History of Russia. New York, Alfred A. Knopf,
    1937.
Peaslee, Amos J., A Permanent United Nations. New York, G. P.
    Putnam's Sons, 1942.
Perry, Ralph Barton, One World in the Making. New York, Cur-
    rent Books, 1945.
Phillipson, Coleman, The International Law and Custom of Ancient
    Greece and Rome. London, The Macmillan Co., 1911.
Pieper, Josef, "On the Christian Idea of Man," *The Review of Poli-
    tics*, XI (January, 1949), 3–16.
Popper, K. R., The Open Society and Its Enemies. London, George
    Routledge & Sons, 1945.
Potter, Pitman B., "Universalism versus Regionalism in Interna-

tional Organization," *American Political Science Review*, XXXVII (October, 1943), 856–858.

Pound, Roscoe, Introduction to the Philosophy of Law. New Haven, Yale University Press, 1922.

—— Federalism as a Democratic Process. New Brunswick, N.J., Rutgers University Press, 1942.

Price, Charles, "The USSR and International Organization," *The American Journal of International Law*, XXXVI (July, 1942), 425.

Public Affairs Press, International Agencies in Which the United States Participates. Washington, D. C., 1946.

Rand, Benjamin, Modern Classical Philosophers. Boston, Houghton Mifflin Co., 1936.

Randall, J. H., A World Community. New York, Frederick A. Stokes Co., 1930.

Ranshofen-Wertheimer, Egon, "International Administration; Lessons from the Experience of the League of Nations, *The American Political Science Review*, October, 1943.

Ransome, Patrick, Studies in Federal Planning. London, The Macmillan Co., 1943.

Rappard, William E., "The Beginnings of World Government," in *Problems of Peace*, 5th Series, Geneva Institute of International Relations. London, Oxford University Press, 1931.

—— The Quest for Peace. Cambridge, Harvard University Press, 1940.

Reinach, Salomon, Orpheus—A History of Religions. New York, Horace Liveright, 1930.

Reinsch, Paul, Public International Unions. Boston, Ginn and Co., 1911.

Reischauer, A. K., Studies in Japanese Buddhism. New York, The Macmillan Co., 1917.

Reves, Emery, The Anatomy of Peace. New York, Harper and Bros., 1945.

Rhys-Davids, T. W., Lectures on the Origin and Growth of Religions. London, Williams and Norgate, 1881.

Rider, Fremont, The Great Dilemma of World Organization. New York, Hadham Press, 1946.

Ripka, Hubert, Small and Great Nations. London, Czechoslovak Ministry of Foreign Affairs Information Service, 1944.

Robinson, Cyril E., History of Greece. New York, Thomas Y. Crowell Co., 1929.

Robinson, Howard and others, Toward International Organization. New York, Harper and Bros., 1942.

Rousseau, Jean Jacques, The Social Contract. London, J. M. Dent, 1947.

Royal Institute of International Affairs, International Sanctions, London, Oxford University Press, 1938.

—— Nationalism. London, Oxford University Press, 1939.

Russell, Betrand, Which Way to Peace? London, Michael Joseph, 1936.

——Philosophy and Politics. London, Cambridge University Press, 1947.

Sabine, George, "The Historical Position of Liberalism," *The American Scholar*, Winter, 1940–41.

Sadler, William S., Prescription for Permanent Peace. Chicago, Wilcox and Follett, 1944.

Saint-Pierre, Abbé de, Ouvrages de politique. Rotterdam, Jean-Daniel Beman, 1738.

Sanson, G. B., Japan; a Short Cultural History. New York, D. Appleton-Century Co., 1943.

Sayre, Francis B., Experiments in International Administration. New York, Harper & Brothers, 1919.

Schneider, Douglas, "America's Answer to Communist Propaganda Abroad," in Department of State Bulletin (Washington, D.C.) XIX (December 19, 1948), 772–776.

Schuman, Frederick L., "Regionalism and Spheres of Influence," in Hans J. Morgenthau, Peace, Security, and the United Nations, Chicago, University of Chicago Press, 1946.

Schwarzenberger, George, Power Politics. London, Jonathan Cape, 1944.

Scott, James B., An International Court of Justice. New York, Oxford University Press, Carnegie Endowment for International Peace, 1916.

—— The International Conferences of the American States, 1889–1928. New York, Oxford University Press, 1931.

—— The Spanish Conception of International Law and of Sanctions. Washington, D.C., Carnegie Endowment for International Peace, 1934.

Scott, J. F., and Alexander Baltzly, Readings in European History since 1814. New York, F. S. Crofts, 1934. .

Seagle, William, The Quest for Law. New York, Alfred A. Knopf, 1941.

—— The History of Law. New York, Tudor Publishing Co., 1946.

Sereni, Angelo P., The Italian Conception of International Law. New York, Columbia University Press, 1943.

Sharp, Walter R., and Grayson Kirk, Contemporary International Politics. New York, Farrar and Rinehart, 1940.

Short, William H., Program and Policies of the League to Enforce Peace. New York, League to Enforce Peace, 1916.

Shotwell, James T., ed., Governments of Continental Europe. New York, The Macmillan Co., 1940.

—— The Great Decision. New York, The Macmillan Co., 1944.

Simon, Yves R., Community of the Free. New York, Henry Holt, 1947.

Sorokin, Pitrim A., The Crisis of Our Age. New York, E. P. Dutton & Co., 1941.

Sousa, Nasim, The Capitulatory Regime of Turkey. Baltimore, Johns Hopkins Press, 1933.

Spahr, Margaret, Readings in Recent Political Philosophy. New York, The Macmillan Co., 1935.

Spengler, Oswald, The Decline of the West; tr. by C. F. Atkinson. New York, Alfred A. Knopf, 1928.

Staley, Eugene, World Economy in Transition. New York, Council on Foreign Relations, 1939.

Stammler, Rudolph, Theory of Justice. New York, The Macmillan Co., 1925.

Stapleton, Laurence, Justice and World Society. Chapel Hill, University of North Carolina Press, 1944.

Stassen, Harold E., "We Need a World Government," *The Saturday Evening Post*, CCXV (May 22, 1943), 11 f.

Stephens, Waldo E., Revisions of the Treaty of Versailles. New York, Columbia University Press, 1939.

Strebel, Ralph F., Education, Keystone of Peace. Syracuse, Syracuse University Press, 1947.

Streit, Clarence, Union Now. New York, Harper & Brothers, 1940.

—— Union Now with Britain. New York, Harper & Brothers, 1941.

Sturzo, Luigi, International Community and the Right of War. London, George Allen and Unwin, 1929.

—— Nationalism and Internationalism. New York, Roy Publishers, 1946.

Suarez, Francisco, On Laws and God the Lawgiver; tr. by Gladys

L. Williams and others; ed. by James B. Scott. New York, Oxford University Press, 1944.

Sulzbach, Walter, National Consciousness. Washington, D.C., American Council on Pacific Affairs, 1943.

Swing, Raymond, In the Name of Sanity. New York, Harper & Brothers, 1946.

Taft, William H., The United States and Peace. New York, Charles Scribner's Sons, 1914.

Taracouzio, T. A., The Soviet Union and International Law. New York, The Macmillan Co., 1935.

Thomas, Norman, Appeal to the Nations. New York, Henry Holt and Co., 1947.

Toynbee, Arnold, A Study of History; abridgment of Vols. I–VI, by D. C. Somervell. New York, Oxford University Press, 1947.

—— "The International Outlook," *International Affairs* (London), XXIII (October, 1947), 463–476.

Tryon, James, "Proposals for an International Court," in American Society for the Judicial Settlement of Disputes, December 4–6, 1913, Proceedings of the 4th National Conference.

Turner, Ralph, The Great Cultural Traditions. 2 Vols., New York, McGraw-Hill Book Co., 1941.

United Nations, Salient Features of the World Economic Situation, 1945–47. Lake Success, Department of Economic Affairs, January, 1948.

United States, Department of State, State Papers and Publick Documents of the United States, 1789–1796. Boston, T. B. Witt and Sons, 1845.

—— Commission on Extraterritoriality in China. Report. 1926.

—— Declaration of Principles Known as the Atlantic Charter. August 14, 1941.

—— Declaration of United Nations. Washington, D.C., January 1, 1942.

—— Report on Cultural Cooperation Program, 1938–43, prepared by Haldore Hanson.

—— "Act of Chapultepec," *Bulletin*, March 4, 1945.

—— Report to the President on the Results of the San Francisco Conference. June, 1945, No. 2349.

—— Aspects of Current American Foreign Policy, November, 1947, No. 2961.

—— International Trade Organization Charter, April, 1948, No. 3117.

—— *Bulletin*, December 19, 1948.

United States, Department of Commerce, Foreign Commerce Yearbook. Washington, D.C., U.S. Government Printing Office, 1939.

Vestal, S. C., The Maintenance of Peace. New York, G. P. Putnam's Sons, 1920.

Victoria, Francisco de, Lecture concerning Civil Power; tr. by G. L. Williams and ed. by J. B. Scott. London, Oxford University Press, 1934.

Voltaire, Letters of Voltaire and Frederick the Great; tr. by R. Aldington. New York, Brentano's, 1927.

Wace, Alan J. B., ed., Studies in Civilization. Philadelphia, University of Pennsylvania Press, 1941.

Wallace, A. R., and others, The Progress of the Century. New York, Harper & Brothers, 1901.

Wallas, Graham, Human Nature in Politics. London, Archibald Constable, 1908.

Ware, Caroline F., ed., The Cultural Approach to History. New York, Columbia University Press, 1940.

Weber, Max, Essays in Sociology; tr. and ed. by H. C. Gerth and C. Wright Mills. New York, Oxford University Press, 1946.

—— Theory of Social and Economic Organization; tr. by A. M. Henderson and T. Parsons. New York, Oxford University Press, 1947.

Weldon, T. D., States and Morals. New York, McGraw-Hill Book Co., 1947.

Welles, Sumner, The Time for Decision. New York, Harper & Brothers, 1944.

Wells, H. G., The New World Order. London, Secker and Warburg, 1940.

Westlake, John, The Collected Papers of John Westlake; ed. by L. Oppenheim. London, Cambridge University Press, 1914.

Wheare, K. C., Federal Government. New York, Oxford University Press, 1946.

Whitehead, Alfred North, Science and the Modern World. New York, The Macmillan Co., 1926.

Wild, Payson S., "What Is the Trouble with International Law?" *The American Political Science Review*, June, 1938.

Wildes, Harry Emerson, Social Currents of Japan. Chicago, University of Chicago Press, 1927.

Willert, Sir Arthur, "Publicity and Propaganda in International

Affairs, *International Affairs* (London), September–October, 1938.

Williams, J. H., The Task of Economic Recovery," *Foreign Affairs*, XXVI (July, 1948), 616–631.

Williams, M. W., The People and Politics of Latin America. Boston, Ginn and Co., 1938.

Willkie, Wendell, One World. Reprinted in Prefaces to Peace, New York, Simon and Schuster, Doubleday, Doran, Reynal and Hitchcock, Columbia University Press, 1943.

Wissler, Clark, Man and Culture. New York, Thomas Y. Crowell, 1923.

Woolf, Leonard, International Government. London, George Allen and Unwin, 1916.

Wright, Martin, Power Politics. London, Royal Institute of International Affairs, 1946.

Wright, Quincy, A Study of War. 2 vols. Chicago, University of Chicago Press, 1942.

Wynner, Edith, and Georgia Lloyd, Searchlight on Peace Plans. New York, E. P. Dutton & Co., 1944.

Yesipov, B. P., and N. K. Goncharov, I Want to Be Like Stalin; tr. by George S. Counts and Nucia P. Lodge. New York, The John Day Co., 1947.

York, Elizabeth, Leagues of Nations—Ancient, Mediaeval, Modern. London, Swarthmore Press, 1919.

Young, Sir George, Federalism and Freedom. London and New York, Oxford University Press, 1941.

Zimmern, Sir Alfred, The League of Nations and the Rule of Law. New York, The Macmillan Co., 1936.

—— Spiritual Values and World Affairs. Oxford, Clarendon Press, 1939.

—— "World Peace Authority," *The Saturday Review of Literature*, XXXI (July 10, 1948), 6–8.

GENERAL REFERENCES

Ascoli, Max, The Power of Freedom. New York, Farrar, Straus, 1949.

Barker, Ernest, Reflections on Government. London, Oxford University Press, 1942.

Bingham, Alfred M., The United States of Europe. New York, Duell, Sloan and Pearce, 1940.

Brailsford, Henry Noel, A League of Nations. New York, The Macmillan Co., 1917.

Briggs, Herbert, The Law of Nations. New York, F. S. Crofts, 1946.

Brooks, Robert C., Government and Politics of Switzerland. New York, World Book Co., 1920.

Carnegie Endowment for International Peace, The International Law of the Future. Washington, D.C., Carnegie Endowment, 1944.

Carr, E. H., International Relations since the Peace Treaties. London, The Macmillan Co., 1937.

Cohen, Morris R., The Faith of a Liberal. New York, Henry Holt, 1946.

Curry, W. B., The Case for Federal Union. Hammondsworth, Penguin Books, 1939.

Curtis, Lionel, World War, Its Cause and Cure. New York, G. P. Putnam's Sons, 1946.

Davis, Harriet Eager, Pioneers in World Order. New York, Columbia University Press, 1944.

Dickerson, Oliver Morton, American Colonial Government. Cleveland, The Arthur H. Clark Co., 1912.

Dopsch, Alfons, The Economic and Social Foundations of European Civilization. New York, Harcourt, Brace and Co., 1937.

Drucker, Peter F., The End of Economic Man. New York, John Day Co., 1939.

Durbin, E. M. F., War and Democracy. London, Kegan Paul, Trench, Trubner and Co., 1938.

Ferrerro, Guglielmo, The Unity of the World. London, Jonathan Cape, 1931.

Foreman, Clark, The New Internationalism. New York, W. W. Norton & Co., 1934.

Fox, W. T. R., The Super-Powers. New York, Harcourt, Brace and Co., 1944.

Glover, T. R., Democracy in the Ancient World. New York, The Macmillan Co., 1927.

Gonella, Guido, A World to Reconstruct. Milwaukee, Bruce Publishing Co., 1944.

Greaves, H. R. G., Federal Union in Practice. London, George Allen and Unwin, 1940.

Hackworth, Green D., Digest of International Law. Washington, D.C., U.S. Government Printing Office, 1940.

Harris, Norman Dwight, Europe and the East. Boston, Houghton Mifflin Co., 1926.

Heymann, Hans, Plan for Permanent Peace. New York, Harper and Bros., 1941.

Howard, Burt Estes, The German Empire. New York, The Macmillan Co., 1906.

Hyde, Charles Cheney, International Law Chiefly as Interpreted by the United States. Boston, Little, Brown & Co., 1947.

Kelsen, Hans, Law and Peace in International Relations. Cambridge, Harvard University Press, 1942.

Kingsley, J. Donald, and David W. Petegorsky, Strategy for Democracy. New York, Longmans, Green and Co., 1942.

Lasker, Bruno, Asia on the Move. New York, Henry Holt, 1945.

Lasswell, Harold D., and Dorothy Blumenstock, World Revolutionary Propaganda. New York, Alfred A. Knopf, 1939.

Leighton, Joseph A., Social Philosophies in Conflict. New York, D. Appleton–Century Co., 1937.

Lindley, M. F., The Acquisition and Government of Backward Territory in International Law. New York, Longmans, Green and Co., 1926.

Malinowski, Bronislaw, The Dynamics of Cultural Change. New Haven, Yale University Press, 1945.

Marriott, John A. R., Commonwealth or Anarchy? London, Philip Allan and Co., 1937.

Moore, John Bassett, International Law and Some Current Illusions. New York, The Macmillan Co., 1924.

Orton, William Aylott, The Liberal Tradition. New Haven, Yale University Press, 1945.

Rappard, W. F., Uniting Europe. New Haven, Yale University Press, 1930.

Reves, Emery, A Democratic Manifesto. New York, Random House, 1942.

Riches, Crowell A., Majority Rule in International Organizations. Baltimore, Johns Hopkins Press, 1940.

Rocker, Rudolf, Nationalism and Culture. New York, Covici-Friede, 1940.

Ross, Alf, A Textbook of International Law. London, Longmans, Green and Co., 1947.

Russell, Bertrand, Prospects of Industrial Civilization. London, Allen and Unwin, 1923.

Russell, Frank M., Theories of International Relations. New York, D. Appleton–Century Co., 1936.

Schlesinger, Rudolph, Federalism in Central and Eastern Europe. New York, Oxford University Press, 1945.

Shenton, H. N., Cosmopolitan Conversation. New York, Columbia University Press, 1933.

Sloane, William M., The Powers and Aims of Western Democracy. New York, Charles Scribner's Sons, 1919.

Smith, H. A., The Crisis in the Law of Nations. London, Stevens and Sons, 1947.

Souleyman, Elizabeth V., The Vision of World Peace in 17th and 18th Century France. New York, G. P. Putnam's Sons, 1941.

Spalding, H. N., Civilization in East and West. London, Oxford University Press, 1939.

Stace, W. T., The Destiny of Western Man. New York, Reynal and Hitchcock, 1942.

Stalin, Joseph, Marxism and the National and Colonial Question. New York, International Publishers, n.d.

Strausz-Hupé, Robert, The Balance of Tomorrow. New York, G. P. Putnam's Sons, 1945.

Tawney, R. H., Equality. New York, Harcourt, Brace and Co., 1929.

Trueblood, Benjamin F., The Federation of the World. Boston, Houghton Mifflin Co., 1899.

Uyehara, George Etsujiro, The Political Development of Japan. London, Constable Co., 1910.

Van Vollenhoven, Cornelius, The Law of Peace. London, The Macmillan Co., 1936.

Veblen, Thorsten, The Nature of Peace. New York, B. W. Huebsch, 1919.

Waller, Willard, War in the 20th Century. New York, Random House, 1940.

Ward, Barbara, The West at Bay. New York, W. W. Norton & Co., 1948.

Wolfers, Arnold, Britain and France between Two Wars. New York, Harcourt, Brace and Co., 1940.

Wood, F. L. W., The Constitutional Development of Australia. London, George G. Harrap & Co., 1933.

Zurcher, Arnold J., Experiment with Democracy in Central Europe. New York, Oxford University Press, 1933.

Index